LAST CHANCE
TO GET IT RIGHT!

LAST CHANCE
TO GET IT RIGHT!

How to Avoid Eight Deadly
Mistakes Made with Money

J. Thomas Moore, CFP®

WILEY

John Wiley & Sons, Inc.

For general information on our other products and services, or technical support,
please contact our Customer Care Department within the United States at
800-762-2974, outside the United States at 317-572-3993 or fax 317-572-4002.

Wiley also publishes its books in a variety of electronic formats. Some content that
appears in print may not be available in electronic books.

For more information about Wiley products, visit our web site at *www.wiley.com*.

ISBN 0-471-47962-4

Printed in the United States of America

10 9 8 7 6 5 4 3 2 1

I t gives me great pleasure to dedicate this book to Paul Shatz, who hired me in 1978. Paul was more than a boss; he inspired me to be the best I could be. He is a gentleman of great integrity. Paul retired several years ago, but he continues to be an enthusiastic supporter of the investment industry. Before he retired, the leaders in the mutual fund industry honored Paul with the title "Mr. Mutual Funds."

This dedication provides me the opportunity to again thank Paul Shatz for the positive influence he has had on my life.

ACKNOWLEDGMENTS

Several people have played important roles in creating *Last Chance to Get It Right*. Because of their support, this book became a reality.

This book began over 25 years ago, before my son, Peter, was born. Peter was my original inspiration for writing this book. I wrote a few chapters in the late 1970s, but other priorities forced me to put the book aside, to be finished at some later date. When Peter graduated from college a few years ago, I realized it was time to focus once again on my dream of writing this book. In many ways, I'm glad I waited so long to complete this book, because I have been able to gain invaluable experience to provide you the best advice I can.

I want to thank A.G. Edwards & Sons, and especially Paul Shatz, who hired me in 1978. The next 23 years provided me the opportunity to expand both my knowledge of and love for the securities business. I truly enjoyed going to work every day at A.G. Edwards & Sons.

Three close friends, Barbara Fullenkamp, Raymond Stevison, and Carole Nail, were kind enough to read this book and offer suggestions to make it reader friendly. Their advice has been most helpful.

An enormous thank you goes to my daughter, Dana Jacobs. Dana is a whiz on the computer. I, unfortunately, can barely type. She made the book presentable before I sent it to John Wiley & Sons, Inc.

I also want to give special thanks to my editor, Debra Englander, who supported my efforts and made it possible to bring the book to market.

And last, but not least, I thank my wife, Sharon. I am not a fast writer. Writing *Last Chance to Get It Right* was a two-year process. She backed my commitment to the book and prodded me when I needed it.

I am most grateful to all of you for your help.

CONTENTS

PART ONE

THE KEYS TO BUILDING WEALTH

A Lifetime of Risk Management

Most families spend more time planning next summer's two-week vacation than they devote to planning their long-term financial futures! Have you ever wondered why that is? Planning a vacation is always fun. Making critically important financial decisions is often emotionally difficult. It's not fun, because it usually involves making difficult choices. We all know we should be saving more for our children's education and our retirement, but we also enjoy driving a brand-new car on our exotic vacation. Impulse buying has led the average family to credit card debt exceeding $8,000, the highest level in history. We also see personal bankruptcies at an all-time high.

For more than 30 years I have helped investors clarify and achieve their financial goals. I wrote this book because I have a mission to help you create a minimum of $100,000 of additional financial benefits for you and your family. Many of you can achieve additional benefits of $250,000, $500,000, or even more by following the strategies in this book.

The first thing we need to consider is how emotions affect our decisions. Having feelings, opinions, and attitudes is natural. It's part of the way we make most, if not all, of life's decisions. For example, consider the role emotions played in important decisions you have made, such as getting married (or getting divorced). Let's assume you are married. How did you approach that important decision? Did you conduct an in-depth review of your partner's financial history? Did you examine the health history of your partner and his or her family? Did you and your partner take psychological compatibility tests? Or, as for most of us, were other factors involved in your decision-making process?

Buying a car can also evoke all kinds of emotions. Do you enjoy haggling with the car salesman? Did the color of the car affect your decision? It did for me. My oldest grandchild picked the color for grandpa's new car.

Now let's look at how our feelings and emotions affect our investment decisions. When you think about investing and the word *risk*, what comes to mind? Most people think of the stock market. In the early to mid-1990s, I would hear statements like, "Investing is easy! Just buy a few good mutual funds and let nature take its course. I'll be rich in no time!" History prior to 2000 would certainly make you think investing is easy. In July of 1932, the Dow Jones Industrial Average was at a low of 40.56. In early January 2001, the Dow was over 11,000. This incredible long-term history would make you think everyone would feel comfortable being invested in the stock market today, but emotions—not just past performance—affect our decisions.

What investment decisions have you been making lately? Are your decisions being swayed by emotions? Consider the high-flying Nasdaq Composite Index, which closely reflects the performance of technology stocks. In March of 2000, the Nasdaq peaked at an incredible 5,048. On June 11 of 2002, it was down to 1,497, a drop of 70 percent in a little over two years. The news was depressing on June 12, 2002. The headline in the *St. Louis Post-Dispatch* shouted, "Market Plunge Wipes Out Tech-Stock Index." If you had inherited $10,000 that day, would you have bought into that depressing market or would you hold back, waiting for good news?

I'd like to share with you the results of four studies that address this important issue of investor behavior. Important studies like these are generally found in industry trade publications available only to investment professionals, but this is exactly the type of information that you, the investor, should be aware of.

The first study analyzed the investment return of active stock traders. Many investors prefer to buy and sell individual stocks rather than invest in mutual funds. Perhaps you are a successful day trader. In recent years, traders have owned Cisco and Microsoft stock for an average of only eight days before selling and moving on to something else. There are a few day traders who are successful, but not very many, according to this study by Terrance Odean published in the April 1998 issue of *Journal of Finance*. Odean found that frequent traders earned only 11 percent during the six years prior to his study, compared to the stock market average of 18 percent during that period. Taxes and trading costs might be part of the problem, but the biggest obstacle is emotional buying and selling.

Rather than day trading individual stocks, let's assume your serious money is in mutual funds, the investment of choice for busy baby boomers. The second study, "Quantitative Analysis of Investor Behavior," was completed in 1999 by DALBAR, a company dedicated to analyzing mutual fund investor behavior. That study revealed important facts. During the 15-year period prior to the study, the stock mutual funds returned, on average, 17.9 percent per year—not bad at all. But only a small percentage of fund investors experienced this investment rate of return. Why? During this 15-year period, the average investor moved from one fund to another every 2.8 years, hoping to improve the rate of return. Did it work? No! This behavior of jumping from one fund to another caused the average mutual fund investor to experience only a 7.25 percent average rate of return over this 15-year period. This behavior cut potential investment return by more than 50 percent.

These statistics are for years prior to 2000–2002! Can you imagine how recent market volatility is affecting investor behavior? Forget the general public for a moment. How about you? How long have you held the mutual funds you currently own? Have you made drastic changes in the last few years? Do you have the urge to substantially alter your portfolio in the near future? Why do you change from one fund to another? Are your decisions based on emotion or on portfolio changes necessary to adhere to a specific investment strategy? Do you have a well-defined investment strategy, or are you making decisions based on what feels good at the moment?

Consider the results of a third study completed by the Phoenix Investment Partners and reported in the April 2001 issue of *Journal of Financial Planning*. This study covered a different time frame, from January 1990 through March 2000, and focused on a different investor behavior. Most mutual fund companies advertise their previous year's best fund. Unfortunately, many investors are attracted to these funds because of the heavily advertised recent past performance. This study pointed out that purchasing last year's best-performing fund is not the answer. The mutual fund investor using this strategy experienced a 20 percent lower return than the mutual fund industry average. Most of us are familiar with the investment rule, "Buy low, sell high." Chasing last year's winner breaks this rule. Buying last year's heavily advertised winner usually results in below-average future performance. In disgust, we sell that disappointing fund and seek out another.

And how do you feel about taxes? Taxes will play a major role in your financial success over time. Are you paying as much as 35 percent in taxes on short-term gains triggered by active trading? Or are you paying the more favorable long-term capital gains tax of 15 percent on gains taken after one year? Do you sell your winners or your losers when you sell? The fourth study is another report by Terrance Odean, published in the October 1998 issue of *Journal of Finance*. This study found that most sellers tend to sell their winning stocks, triggering taxes. From a tax standpoint, they would be better off selling their losers and using the tax loss to offset capital gains and ordinary income.

These four studies should convince you that you may need to rein in your emotions when making future financial decisions.

As you're probably aware, income taxes will have a major impact on the future benefits you and your family enjoy. If a major portion of your portfolio is designated for your children's education or your future retirement, is it compounding without current taxes? Are you doing all you can to compound these investments without current taxation?

Most of us are building sizable accounts in our employer-sponsored retirement plans. How do you allocate your investments in the company's retirement plan? Let's assume your employer has a 401(k) plan that allows you to choose between 10 accounts—nine stock mutual funds and one bond mutual fund. You might put equal amounts in each of the 10 funds. The result? You end up with 90 percent in stocks and 10 percent in bonds, which may or may not be the best mixture. What if your 401(k) plan offers only four accounts—three stock funds and one bond fund? Again, if you invest in each account equally, you have an entirely different allocation—75 percent stocks and 25 percent bonds.

Real wealth, lasting wealth, requires even more decisions. For example, most investors don't want to experience even a temporary market decline of 20 to 40 percent in their portfolio. How would you react to a permanent loss of as much as 67 percent? Many of us are building our wealth in employer-sponsored retirement plans such as 401(k) plans, 403(b) plans, 457 plans, profit-sharing plans, and/or pension plans. Most of us also have IRAs. In most cases, we have little or no cost basis in these accounts, which means these assets will be subject to income tax when they're used for retirement income. These assets will also be taxed when they are liquidated by our beneficiaries. They might also be subject to estate taxes. Wealthy families might have to pay estate taxes, which can be as high as 49 percent in 2003, as well as ordinary income taxes on inherited qualified plan and IRA assets. Without careful planning, estate taxes and income taxes could confiscate up to 67 percent of this portion of your estate, leaving as little as 33 cents of every dollar for your children and grandchildren.

Many baby boomers feel there is little need to save for retirement. Therefore, the savings rate of this generation is lower than that of any previous generation in history. The younger generation X is saving more for the future than the baby boomer generation. Perhaps boomers expect to receive a large inheritance from their parents, but this may not happen. We have just seen that taxes can drastically affect this picture, but there are other issues as well. For example, many parents do not intend to distribute their estates evenly between all of their children. I see more trust planning being done by today's concerned parents and grandparents than by previous generations. They want to make sure their estates are carefully distributed according to rules established in their trust document. In addition, today's retirees are also spending more of their assets as they are living longer, more active lives. Interest rates have dropped drastically since the early 1980s. Many retirees have seen their CD rates drop from 18 percent to less than 3 percent. Many retirees are being forced to spend their principal or purchase immediate annuities to create adequate income. Your parents (and you) will also have to deal with long-term health care needs, which can drastically reduce assets over time. And, some parents just don't care about leaving a large inheritance to their children. Many are planning to leave some (or all) of their estate to charities. In short, you need to build your own assets rather than hope for a large inheritance.

These are just some of the financial concerns you should have. Dealing with these issues is not always fun, but it is critically important. I'll make the process as painless as possible. I promise it will be financially and emotionally rewarding.

First, recognize there are several risks that must be addressed to be financially successful:

- *Market risk:* Market volatility is a fact of life, not just for this year but for the rest of your life.

- *Inflation risk:* Prices can easily double, if not triple, during your years in retirement. (If inflation averages 3.75 percent, you will see prices triple during your retirement. At 5 percent inflation, prices will more than quadruple.)

- *Tax risk:* Income taxes and estate taxes can be more destructive to building and keeping your wealth in your family than market risk.

- *The risk of outliving your income:* Baby boomers are living longer than their parents and grandparents. The average life expectancy increased by more than three decades in the last century, and this trend continues today. Your sources of retirement income will be substantially different than the sources that provided your parents and grandparents with a comfortable retirement. Social Security will play a smaller role in creating your retirement income. Your parents and grandparents retired with lifetime income provided by their employer's defined benefit pension plan. Few baby boomers will enjoy a monthly pension check for life. Why? Today's employers provide mostly 401(k) plans, profit-sharing plans, or 403(b) plans. These plans place the investment responsibility on the employee. Because of these changes, many boomers run a major risk of outliving their retirement income.

- *Long-term health care risk:* We are living longer, healthier lives. But the day may come when there are additional demands on your savings and investments. Long-term health care costs can drain a family's resources. We have all heard horror stories about the costs of nursing homes. You need to make some decisions on how you will create the cash needed to meet these expenses.

All of these lifetime risks will be dealt with in the coming chapters. I will help you understand these risks and provide practical solutions to allay your fears. Learn about each risk; get to know each risk intimately, so there will be no surprises down the road. According to the Employee Benefit Research Institute, 80 percent of current retirees have household incomes of less than $23,000, including Social Security. I don't believe this is the retirement plan you have in mind for yourself.

Eleanor Roosevelt pointed out, "You gain strength, courage, and confidence by every experience in which you stop to look fear in the face." This book will help you recognize and deal with the biggest mistakes investors make with their money. Please read the following list carefully. It is time to meet the enemy!

The Eight Deadly Mistakes Investors Make with Money

They Make Investment Decisions Based on Emotion Rather than Logic

They tend to get excited about one type of investment, which leads them to take too much risk. It's easy to fall into the emotional trap, experiencing greed, impatience, concern, fear, panic, and so on. Investors need to follow time-tested investment strategies that work, such as establishing a diversified long-term investment portfolio.

They Fail to Plan for the Devastating Effects of Inflation

Planning for long term needs, such as a child's college education or your retirement, must be adjusted for inflation. Remember, inflation never retires!

They Don't Take Advantage of Opportunities to Control Taxes on Their Savings and Investments

Taxes can often be avoided or deferred by using IRAs, 529 college savings plans, annuities, trusts, and employer-sponsored retirement plans. You may not be able to control inflation, but you certainly can control your taxes.

They Have Not Decided What They Want to Accomplish with Their Money

How important is your children's education? With advanced planning, the cost of your children's education can be dramatically discounted. How about your retirement? Will you be prepared for a secure retirement that will last 20 to 40 years? Without careful planning, you will not meet your goals.

They Don't Protect Themselves, Their Families, and Their Assets with Adequate Insurance

Younger breadwinners need to protect their families by purchasing adequate life insurance and disability income insurance. Older investors need to preserve their investments by insuring against loss with adequate long-term care insurance. Wealthy individuals need to protect their assets from estate taxes, which can reduce their estate by as much as 49 percent.

They Fail to Establish a Written Plan for the Orderly Distribution of Their Wealth

Do you have the necessary legal documents, such as a will, a durable power of attorney, and possibly a trust, to carry out your wishes? An effective plan needs to be designed for the distribution of your wealth.

They Procrastinate, Finding It Much Easier to do Nothing than to Address Difficult Decisions

We say we are too busy, but in reality we don't want to deal with difficult, emotional issues. But we are responsible for those we love and therefore we must make important decisions and then take necessary action. Dealing with procrastination is the only way to create financial peace of mind.

They Don't Seek Professional Advice

Creating and implementing a plan can be difficult. Mistakes and procrastination can be very costly. Seek professional guidance. Lawyers, CPAs, and qualified financial consultants have the expertise to make sure you avoid serious mistakes in your planning. They have the resources, tools, experience, and expertise to help you create, implement, and adjust the plan that will bring financial peace to you and your family.

Many of my comments throughout this book are focused on baby boomers for several reasons:

- There are so many of you! You are the largest generation in American history. There are 76 million of you raising kids and preparing for retirement.

- Every seven seconds, one of you turns 50. Most of you want to retire in far less than 15 years.

- Your generation is spending too much and not saving enough for the future.

- Time is no longer your friend. You must act now to create a secure retirement for you and your spouse.

However, this book is not just for baby boomers. Many of you are part of a younger generation. If so, take advantage of your youth. Time is your number one asset. Use it to your advantage and you can accumulate tremendous wealth. You need to learn how to avoid the mistakes made by older generations. Most of you understand that Social Security will change drastically before you retire.

If you are older than the baby boomers, there is much you need to do to get your financial affairs in order. As of April 17, 2002, new IRS regulations make it possible for you to leverage the value of your IRA in ways never before feasible. With proper planning, your IRA can be worth 6 to 10 times more when passed down to your heirs. For example, a $100,000 IRA left to your children can now be worth up to $1 million in income for your heirs. And there are several new tax laws that make it possible to create additional benefits for you and your family. For example, many of us are grandparents and we would like to offer financial help in the funding of our grandchildren's future college expenses. There are new programs with special tax incentives that will have a tremendous impact on your ability to build savings for these future expenses. If you take full advantage of these new programs, it is possible to reduce future college out-of-pocket costs by up to 75 percent, and possibly even more.

I have spent more than 30 years learning what I will share with you in this book. Let me give you some highlights of my background. My investment career began in 1968, when I joined the St. Louis office of an investment firm. I was honored that year as Rookie of the Year. The national recognition was rewarding, but it was a painful year. I made many mistakes and relied on trial and error. I had little confidence in myself and in the recommendations I was making. I was fortunate to get practical advice from two men who helped me survive my first few years without hurting my clients or myself. For 10 years, I helped individuals like you clarify their goals and take the steps to make it all happen. Using financial tools such as stocks, bonds, mutual funds, annuities, and life insurance, we established plans to meet their financial goals:

- Reduce their income taxes year in and year out
- Create the capital necessary for a long, enjoyable retirement
- Provide the funds for higher education for their children and grandchildren
- Reduce their estate taxes to preserve the assets they have spent a lifetime building
- Leave a legacy to those charitable organizations that are important to them

Financial goals have not changed for most families since the 1970s, but the tools available to meet these goals have changed dramatically.

The firm was growing rapidly, and new employees were faced with the same problem I had experienced: little or no training. I made a decision to help others beginning their careers. By the mid-seventies, I was wearing two hats—helping my own clients and teaching new investment brokers in the firm to be successful. By the early seventies, the office had grown to over 60 investment professionals. Unfortunately, I was stretching myself too thin. I had to make a difficult decision: Either focus on my personal clients or devote my energies to training other investment professionals to do a better job with their clients. I chose training.

In 1978, I joined a top-10 New York Stock Exchange firm at their national headquarters in St. Louis. I joined this exceptional investment firm because of their commitment to initial and ongoing training of their financial professionals. Few firms are as dedicated to helping their representatives be the best they can be. I truly enjoyed this opportunity to teach and advise so many professional financial consultants. When I joined the firm, there were 970 consultants. By the time I retired in 2002, the firm had grown to over 7,300 professionals throughout the country. I like to feel that I played a significant part in this incredible sevenfold growth. Many of my days were spent teaching in the classroom. I've also had the opportunity to meet and address 7,000 to 10,000 investors per year at seminars conducted throughout the country. Much of my time was spent helping these professionals create personalized solutions for their clients with unique situations. These professional men and women were my clients for over 23 years. My goal was to prepare them to help you. In short, for over 23 years, I advised the advisors.

Now my career is coming full circle. I began by working with individual investors. This evolved into training and advising investment professionals, which led to talking and listening to thousands of investors by way of public seminars. And now, through this book, I hope to provide vital information to all individual investors looking for answers.

I do not want to be your personal advisor—I want to be your pre-advisor. When it comes to selecting an advisor, you will be better served if you select a qualified individual living in your community who can provide you and your family with the personal attention you deserve. We will discuss this in Chapter 13.

Today, there is more financial noise (not news) than ever before. Much of my time is spent sorting through this noise to clarify those things that are important to you, the investor. I will provide you with the education and tools necessary to get you started. Many of you will choose to make your own decisions. Many will prefer to work with a qualified financial advisor. In either case, as your pre-advisor, I'll help you get prepared.

Many years ago, a wise financial professional taught me a very important lesson that has become my motto: "I am not in the business of making people rich. I'm in the business of making sure they will never be poor." Financial peace is an attainable goal for you and your family. It is my goal to help you develop a solid plan based on fact and reason rather than the emotional noise of the day. You will learn practical tips designed to reduce your risks and make it possible to fulfill your dreams for you and your family. Your life will be far less hectic if you avoid the eight deadly mistakes investors make with their money. Small mistakes are OK. It is the big mistakes that can really hurt you!

Before you start the next chapter, I want you to slow down. Take a big breath and relax for a moment. Let me share with you my wife's advice: Don't speed read this book! Slow down and read carefully. You paid good money for the advice you are about to receive. Take notes and underline as you read. Get your money's worth. Financial peace is within your reach, so let's get started.

LESSONS AND STRATEGIES

The Eight Deadly Mistakes Investors Make with Money

1. They make investment decisions based on emotion rather than logic.
2. They fail to plan for the devastating effects of inflation.
3. They don't take advantage of opportunities to control taxes on their savings and investments.
4. They have not decided what they want to accomplish with their money.
5. They don't protect themselves, their families, and their assets with adequate insurance.
6. They fail to establish a written plan for the orderly distribution of their wealth.
7. They procrastinate, finding it much easier to do nothing than to address difficult decisions.
8. They don't seek professional advice.

Investment Risk

Mistake 1: Making Investment Decisions Based on Emotion Rather than Logic

E motion plays a major role in all of our important long-term decisions. The tendency is not to buy what we need, but to buy what we want. Our wants are based on feelings.

To fully understand this concept, let's look again at a specific example mentioned in the previous chapter regarding marriage. Again, let's assume you are married. Getting married was one of the most important long-term decisions of your life. What process did you use in making this long-term commitment? Did you and your spouse exchange detailed financial records? Did each of you fully disclose your health history and that of your family? Did each of you submit to in-depth psychological testing to see if you would be would be compatible for life? Or were there other, less logical considerations involved in the decision to get married?

You cannot prevent emotions from having a role in your decisions. This chapter is devoted to helping you recognize how history (both recent and in the last 75 years) has played a major role in creating your feeling and attitude about investing. Once we better understand the emotional aspects of investing, we can explore strategies to create and maintain a successful investment plan. These proven investment strategies, which are based on facts, long-term trends, and your personal needs, are the subject of Chapter 3.

But, before we look at investment strategies, we need to consider how emotions can affect your attitude about investment risk. What is your reaction to the phrase *investment risk?* There is a good chance you are thinking, "No one wants to take risk! Investing can hurt you!" Unfortunately, you can't avoid risk. You need to know what the financial risks are, so you can prepare yourself accordingly.

The main financial risks are:

- Investment risk
- Inflation risk
- Risk of outliving your income

Let's see how emotional we can be about investment risk.

Stock Market Risk

Before the bull market of the 1990s, many investors would cry, "I could lose all of my money in the stock market! I remember the crash in 1929!" (Or, "My parents/grandparents told me all about the crash in 1929.") "You can't fool me! I'll keep my money in the bank where it will be safe."

There is no question about it; emotions and attitudes are involved in making financial decisions. From the 1930s through the 1980s, most investors wanted little market risk because their memories of the horrors of the stock market crash in 1929 were so vivid. In fact, most investors were so market risk averse that they lost out on tremendous opportunities. How much? In July of 1932, the Dow Jones Industrial Average hit a low of 40.56. But on January 1, 2002, the Dow stood at 10,595. I'd say there was a trend there! But many older people missed most, if not all, of this 70-year opportunity. Why? They feared another market crash like the one in 1929.

In the early 1980s, baby boomers began making their investment decisions. By the end of the 1990s, baby boomers were on the carefree end of the mood pendulum. I consider 1995 through 1999 "The Giddy Years." I heard investors gleefully comment, "Investing is easy! The S&P 500 has gone up over 20 percent every year for five years in a row. Who needs help? I certainly don't need a broker. I can pick Internet stocks by myself. In fact, I don't even need to buy professionally managed mutual funds. I'll just buy a mutual fund indexed to the S&P 500 and round out my portfolio with my Internet stock picks."

In early 2003, I again heard the cry, "What is happening? The S&P 500 was down 11.6 percent in 2000, down over 13 percent in 2001, and down another 23.4 percent in 2002! Three down years in a row for the stock market! I can't believe this is happening. I have to look all the way back to the Depression to see a market this bad. Just like my parents/grandparents did back in the 1930s, I could lose all my money in the stock market!"

The emotional pendulum has quickly moved from one extreme to another as panic has set in for many investors. Frightened investors, both young and old, openly admitted their fears, making statements such as, "I'm selling every stock I own. I'm sick and tired of this market."

Maybe you aren't that depressed, but you may be lamenting, "I guess I'll have to put off any thought of early retirement. I'm not in the mood to invest any more right now. I think I'll sit on the sidelines and wait until things settle down."

Emotional swings like these create havoc in long-term investment decisions. One of my major concerns is that the emotional doubts of frightened investors will cause them to miss the great investment opportunities that will occur over the next several years. My biggest challenge will be to convince you that the future is much brighter than the recent past.

In order to prepare for the future, we need to understand the past. We need to examine the market in a logical way if we are to avoid emotional mistakes in the future. To better understand market history, let's consider several parts of the puzzle:

- *Indices:* what they measure and what information they provide
- *Time frames:* from the market crash in the early 1930s to the Giddy Years of the 1990s to the Gruesome Years of the early 2000s
- *Portions of the market:* from stocks to bonds to international investing
- *Sectors:* from technology stocks to pharmaceutical stocks
- *Sizes of companies:* from small cap (capitalization) to mid-cap to large cap

The Major Stock Indices

Let's begin by looking at the three most widely known stock indices:

1. The Dow Jones Industrial Average
2. The S&P 500
3. The Nasdaq

We need to have a general understanding of these indices for two reasons:

1. These indices are quoted in the financial news every day. If the news is to have any benefit, we need to understand what these indices represent.

2. Several mutual funds are designed to invest like a specific index. For example, the Vanguard S&P 500 indexed fund is not a managed fund. It is a mutual fund that is designed to duplicate the S&P 500 index. If you are investing in one or more of these indexed mutual funds, you need to know what you are buying and the risks you are taking.

THE DOW JONES INDUSTRIAL AVERAGE   Let's begin with the Dow Jones averages. Charles Dow, the first editor of *The Wall Street Journal*, created two indices back in 1896:

1. The Dow Jones Industrial Average

2. The Dow Jones Railroad Average (now called the Dow Jones Transportation Index)

The Wall Street Journal used these two indexes to describe what was happening in the market and explain trends as they developed. In the early 1900s, our economy was still developing as an industrial nation. These two Dow Jones indexes tracked each step of the manufacturing process, providing information to savvy investors. Using the Railroad Average, it was possible to estimate the amount of raw materials shipped by railroads to industrial plants. The Industrial Average indicated trends in production of major industrial companies, such as American Cotton Oil, American Tobacco, General Electric, National Lead, Tennessee Coal, U.S. Leather, and U.S. Rubber. The Railroad Average could then be used to track the movement of finished goods on their way to market.

In 1929, a third index was created, the Dow Jones Utility Index, which tracks 15 various utility stocks. The editors of *The Wall Street Journal* continue to select the stocks represented in these indexes.

Today, the Dow Jones Industrial Average is by far the most quoted index, both in *The Wall Street Journal* and other media. The index was set at 100 when it began back in 1896. In late 1982, the index broke 1,000. In late 1995, it passed 3,500. In early 2000, it reached its high of 11,722.98. From time to time, stocks are removed from this list of 30 companies and new companies are added to reflect changes in the economy. General Electric is the only surviving company from the original list.

There are several criticisms about the Dow Jones Industrial Average, such as:

- The index only measures 30 stocks.

- Only New York Stock Exchange stocks are considered. The New York Stock Exchange is the oldest and largest of the exchanges. It opened in 1792 and today trades stocks of roughly 2,300 companies, valued at roughly $5 trillion. The NYSE is sometimes called the Big Board. (For many years, Intel and Microsoft were not listed on the NYSE and therefore could not be part of the Dow Jones. They were finally added to the index in 1999.)

- The 30 stocks that make up the index are changed infrequently. For example, in 1997, Westinghouse, Texaco, Bethlehem Steel, and Woolworth were removed. Hewlett-Packard, Johnson & Johnson, Travelers Group, and Wal-Mart Stores replaced them.

- The index is price weighted in favor of the higher-priced stocks included in the index. The index is computed by summing the prices of the 30 stocks in the average and then dividing that number by a constant number, called the *divisor*. The divisor is published in *The Wall Street Journal* and is currently about 0.14. This formula favors those stocks with the higher prices. For example, the price to buy a share of IBM was recently $85, while the price to buy a share of Sears was only $28. Let's assume both stocks appreciate by 10 percent. A share of IBM would go up by $8.50, while a share of Sears would increase by only $2.80. In this example, IBM's greater price movement has a bigger effect on the calculation of the Dow Industrial Average than Sears. This price-weighted index does not take into consideration how many shares are outstanding.

THE S&P 500 INDEX   The Standard and Poor Corporation (a division of the McGraw-Hill Companies, Inc.) began creating various indices in the 1920s. In 1957, they created the S&P 500 Index, which tracks 500 leading companies in various industries. Many consider this index a better gauge of the overall stock market because it is based on more stocks. It is a more accurate index because this index is calculated by multiplying the price of each stock by the number of shares held by the public. Companies with the most outstanding shares have the greatest impact on the S&P 500 Index. This index is known as a market-weighted index, whereas the Dow Jones Industrial Average is a price-weighted index.

The S&P 500 represents roughly 70 percent of the value of the U.S. stock market, but it does have some drawbacks:

- It does not include foreign stocks.

- It excludes some large companies because their stock is not actively traded.

- It gives more weight to large companies, which have issued more shares of stock than smaller companies. Because of this market weighting, the performance of a small number of large companies creates most of the movement of the index. For example, in 1999, this index showed a gain of more than 20 percent. Fifty percent of that gain came from the performance of just eight stocks. But not all of the stocks in this unmanaged index were enjoying a profit that year. In fact, 230 of these 500 stocks were selling at prices below where they had been two years earlier.

- The composition of the index has changed dramatically since 1964. In 1964, only one technology stock was in the top 10 stocks in the index.

- In 1964, the top stocks were more conservative, well-established companies, including names like AT&T, GM, Exxon, Texaco, Dupont, GE, and Eastman Kodak. By 2000, 6 of the top 10 stocks were technology stocks, including newer, faster-growing companies, such as Microsoft, Cisco Systems, Intel, Lucent, and Citigroup.

- In June of 2000, the stocks of just four companies (GE, Intel, Cisco, and Microsoft) accounted for over 25 percent of the entire value of the index.

- Currently, over 30 percent of the S&P 500 consists of fast-growing tech stocks.

Remember, this is a market-weighted index. As a result, the performance is driven higher (or lower) by a handful of the largest stocks that post the greatest gains or losses. This concentration in a small selection of aggressive stocks has changed the nature of the S&P 500 index, creating a greater risk for investors who own S&P-indexed mutual funds.

THE NASDAQ The Nasdaq was originally called the National Association of Security Dealers Automated Quotation. The Nasdaq is a computer network that allows brokers to trade stocks among themselves. The Nasdaq is sometimes referred to as the *over-the-counter market* because there is no centralized exchange. It is an electronic stock market that is run by the National Association of Securities Dealers (NASD). Brokers get their price quotes using the computer network and then buy or sell stocks by way of telephone or computer orders. This index of technology-driven companies was created in 1971 to focus on the stock market's new companies. The companies traded on the Nasdaq tend to be smaller and younger than those sold on the floors of the major exchanges such as the New York Stock Exchange. However, there are some exceptions. For example, both Microsoft and Intel are traded on the electronic Nasdaq market as well as the floor of the New York Stock Exchange.

Like the S&P 500, the Nasdaq composite index is a market-weighted index. This index tracks a far greater number of stocks than the Dow Jones's 30 stocks or the S&P's 500 stocks. The Nasdaq composite index measures all the stocks listed on the Nasdaq market, which totals more than 5,000 companies. Many investors and money managers follow this index because it is so broadly based. But there are some limitations to keep in mind.

- Many of the companies trading on the Nasdaq are quite small. The shares of companies with a capitalization under $1 billion are called *small-cap stocks*. The future of small-cap companies tends to be either much better or much worse than that of larger companies. Therefore, these stocks tend to be more volatile.

- These stocks are also very sensitive to the company's profits. In a bull market (a rising stock market) these stocks can appreciate rapidly, because there is a small supply of stock available to meet the demand for these rapidly moving stocks.

- In a bear market (a falling stock market), these stocks drop rapidly. If a company fails to meet investor expectations (or the entire market is falling), there are no buyers to be found.

As we go forward, you will see how these three indices have responded in different historical time frames.

The 1929 Market Crash

This is the crash everyone has heard about. Our parents or grandparents have told all of us horror stories of the Depression. The Dow Jones Industrial Average had reached a high of 386 in

September 1929. It would hit a low of 40.56 in July 1932. This was a drop of 89 percent over three painful years.

This crash, like all major corrections, followed a spectacular bull market that began in 1914 and lasted for 15 years. The Dow was just 80 at the beginning of the bull market. The Roaring 1920s was a decade of great prosperity. World War I was over and the economy was prospering. It was the beginning of installment purchase plans. Consumers jumped at the chance to create consumer loans. They went on a major spending spree, buying refrigerators, washing machines, radios, and automobiles on the new "easy payment" plans.

The Dow reached a high of 386 in September 1929, up over 480% in this 15-year bull market. Investors were so confident in the economy that they were borrowing large sums of money to buy stock. The most aggressive investors were borrowing up to 90 percent of what they were investing. These large loans caused part of the panic that would occur later that year. For example, let's assume an aggressive investor bought a $10 stock, paying $1 in cash and borrowing the other $9. If the stock dropped more than 10 percent, the investor lost his or her entire investment, and the lender would also be losing money.

Let's take a brief look at what happened in November of 1929. The day everyone talks about was November 29, often called Black Tuesday. The stock market's problems actually began weeks earlier. Small speculators began suffering losses they could ill afford when the market began its decline in early September. On Thursday, November 24, 1929, the Dow was down 20 percent. This was the day that most small investors gave up, selling close to 13 million shares on the New York Stock Exchange. Their brokers and bankers forced them to sell their stocks to cover the loans. On the following Friday and Saturday, things calmed down as big investors and bankers stepped in to buy stocks, thinking the market had bottomed out.

On Sunday, November 27, both investors and traders on the Exchange had time to consider their options. Many were concerned their remaining profits would evaporate. Others were concerned with their outstanding margin loans. (Investors had been reminded about their outstanding loans over that weekend.)

On Monday, the 28th, the markets opened nervously. Both traders and investors hoped it would be a calm day, but that was not to happen. The Dow closed down 13.5 percent for the day.

On Black Tuesday, November 29, 1929, the stock market crashed, dropping another 11.5 percent. At the opening bell, huge blocks of stock were put up for sale at whatever price the market would bring. Before noon, it seemed like everyone was selling, including any remaining small investors and the large investors as well. Over 16 million shares would be sold on the New York Stock Exchange that day. The number of shares sold on Black Tuesday was only slightly more than the number sold on Thursday of the previous week, but the amount of dollars lost was much larger.

Over this six-day period, from Thursday, November 24 through Black Tuesday, November 29, the market lost $25 billion, roughly one-third of its value.

It is difficult to pinpoint the cause of the crash, but here is a partial list of events leading to the historic event on November 29:

- Consumers were no longer buying consumer goods to the degree they were in the Roaring Twenties, leading to a slowdown in business profits and the economy.

- Investors had become overconfident and aggressive in the way they were investing (borrowing).

- Europeans were selling their U.S. stocks.

- Banks failed to play a major role in slowing down the market's decline.

- Large institutional buyers experienced a general loss of confidence in the market.

- There was a total lack of buying by the general public. Many had been forced to sell out on the previous Thursday because of margin calls on their stock loans.

- Mob psychology had set in as investors in all markets in every part of the country panicked.

The market had peaked in September of 1929. In less than two months, the Dow had lost 39.6 percent. But that is not the full picture. The market would continue to fall until July of 1932, when the Dow bottomed out at 40.56. Investors watched in disbelief as the market lost almost 89 percent of its value over this three-year period.

The federal government was determined to rein in the borrowing binge that led into the crash. To slow down borrowing, the government increased interest rates. As interest rates rose, both consumers and businesses stopped borrowing and the economy went into a long decline. The country was heading into the Depression, which would last for many years. It would be decades before the economy fully recovered and the Dow Jones returned to the levels it had achieved before the crash.

The Crash of 1929 was not the first bear market, and it would not be the last. It is important to realize that a bull market has followed every bear market, and each new bull market has set new market highs. The Dow Jones Industrial Average went from a low of 40 in 1932 to a high of roughly 1,000 in the early 1970s.

The 1973-1974 Bear Market

It would be roughly four decades before we would experience another major bear market. Let's review the events and concerns that led to this major stock market correction in the years 1973 to 1974:

- There was a strong stock market prior to 1973, referred to as a two-tier bull market. One tier comprised small, aggressive stocks. In the late 1960s, investors had been loading up on aggressive "go-go" mutual funds that featured these stocks. (The stocks of these smaller companies would run out of steam by 1973.) The second tier was made up of blue chip stocks of large companies that investors had come to believe were infallible. These stocks were known as the *nifty-fifty*.

- Richard Nixon had just won a second term in November 1972, easily defeating George McGovern. The market celebrated a week later as the Dow Jones Industrial Average closed above 1,000 for the first time in history.

- In January of 1973, the Dow hit a high of 1,051. Remember, the Dow was as low as 40.56 in July of 1932. That's a 2,600 percent increase in 41 years!

- Five months later, in April of 1973, the news reported that President Richard Nixon's top aides had broken into the Democratic National Committee Headquarters in the Watergate complex. The break-in had occurred in June of 1972, during the presidential campaign. The Watergate scandal would be in the headlines on a daily basis.

- In October, Vice President Spiro Agnew resigned under pressure. He had been fined for income tax evasion tied to bribes and kickbacks he received when he was governor of Maryland.

- That same month, the Organization of Petroleum Exporting Countries (OPEC) began the first oil embargo as a way to control both the production and the price of oil. Overnight, oil prices increased over 60 percent from $3 to $5 a barrel.

- By November of 1973, high interest rates were beginning to take their toll on the economy. The country was falling into a deep recession.

- Inflation had risen to 8½ percent in the United States and was even higher in other parts of the world.

- The nifty-fifty blue chip stocks fell 20 percent in the first five weeks of the recession. These stocks could no longer maintain their high values while the rest of the market was suffering.

- The Dow Jones Industrial Average bottomed out at 788 in December of 1973, down 25 percent from its high of 1,051 in January of that year.

- The moral scandals in Washington were the major cause for the market woes of 1973. The stock market had no idea how to react to the misdeeds of both a president and a vice president all in one year. There was deep concern about the long-lasting effects this moral collapse in government would have on the nation.

- In 1974, the economy continued to slide due to the oil embargo. Oil prices jumped to $11.65 a barrel in January, an increase of 228 percent from just three months earlier.

- President Nixon sought voluntary rationing to cut demand for oil. He asked both households and businesses to turn down their thermostats to reduce oil consumption. Businesses were asked to reduce work hours to save energy. Gas stations were asked to sell no more than 10 gallons of gas to a customer.

- OPEC's stranglehold on oil production created panic buying and short tempers at gas stations throughout the country. Cars would be lined up for blocks to purchase gas. Wives would feed the children at home and then walk to the gas line to relieve their husbands. The husbands would then walk home to eat and have time with the children. All too often, the gas pumps ran dry, creating more frustration. Gas station owners were accused of hoarding gasoline for their personal use. Angry customers attacked more than one station owner. Newspapers featured stories and photos of these gasoline shortages. There were also stories of new businesses being created to serve customers while they waited for hours in gas station lines. For example, kids were selling sandwiches, soda, and lemonade to people as they sat in their cars. Most family cars were gas guzzlers, getting only 5 to 15 miles to the gallon. The price of a gallon of gas went from 30 cents to $1.20 during this period, an increase of 400 percent.

- In August of 1974, President Richard Nixon resigned from office.

- The Dow Jones Industrial Average began another terrible decline, dropping to 577 in early December of 1974, off 45 percent from its peak.

Let's look at some of the destruction in the nifty-fifty category. Table 2.1 shows the total value of the 10 largest stocks during the 1973–1974 bear market. It illustrates the value of the outstanding shares in billions in December of 1972, the percentage drop in two years, and the values in December of 1979, five years after the bear market ended.

You can see that many of the nifty-fifty companies had not recovered their losses by 1979, five years after the bear market ended. It was a slow struggle for the nifty-fifty to regain momentum. This painfully slow recovery took its toll on the emotions of the average investor.

Those investors who had loaded up on the nifty-fifty were in shock and angry about their investment portfolios. These stocks

TABLE 2.1

Stock	Value in December 1972	Percent Change by December 1974	Value in December 1979
IBM	$47	−48%	$38
AT&T	$29	−14%	$37
Eastman Kodak	$24	−58%	$8
General Motors	$23	−62%	$15
Exxon	$20	−26%	$24
Sears	$18	−58%	$6
General Electric	$13	−54%	$12
Xerox	$12	−65%	$5
Texaco	$10	−44%	$8
3M	$10	−46%	$6

represented companies that were the leaders in their industries. Investors bought them in the late 1960s and early 1970s with the belief that they could buy these stocks and forget about them. The demand for these fifty stocks pushed their prices to new highs.

Unfortunately, the pricey nifty-fifty provided no protection for investors when the market plunged during the 1973–1974 bear market. Many would sell all of their stocks, either at the market bottom in 1974 or during the five years that followed. Like investors after the Crash of 1929, they vowed never to invest in the stock market again. These negative emotions would cause them to miss the incredible bull market that was to follow.

1975 through 2000

By March of 1975, portions of the stock market were on their way to recovery. The Federal Reserve was easing interest rates and the economy was coming out of the recession that had bottomed out the year before. The broader S&P 500 was recovering better than the much narrower nifty-fifty, up a total of 24 percent for the five years after the market bottom. The S&P 500 earned a modest return of less than 5 percent per year for five years.

The 1970s were known for stagflation. It was a period of very high unemployment (stagnation) coupled with rising prices (inflation) due to rising oil prices. The best-performing stocks during this period were energy, defense, and gold stocks. Bonds lost money in the late 1970s as a direct response to rising inflation rates, which in turn caused interest rates to rise. As interest rates rose, bond prices dropped.

The 1980s were known as the decade of consumerism. It was the longest peacetime period of expansion in our history. The stocks of companies in the food, tobacco, and alcohol industries performed well. All of this consumption also helped the waste management industry. Bonds performed well as interest rates and inflation began to decline in the early 1980s.

The 1990s were famous for the tech revolution. Stocks of companies in the telecommunications and software industries did exceedingly well. The economy continued the steady expansion that had begun in the previous decade. Inflation was subdued. Bonds continued to reward investors as interest rates continued the decline that began in the early 1980s.

Let's take a look at the highlights of this extraordinary bull market that lasted for 24 years. From 1975 to 2000, the S&P 500 enjoyed:

- Seven years with market performance over 30 percent
- Thirteen years with market performance over 20 percent
- Sixteen years with market performance over 15 percent
- An average return that exceeded 18.75 percent

As we have seen throughout history, bull markets are followed by corrections called bear markets. Some bear markets have lasted for many years, while others have been relatively short. But all bear markets are painful! A short but painful crash happened in the middle of this 24-year bull market. This abrupt market correction would become known as the Crash of 1987.

The Crash of 1987

Just prior to the 1990s, investors survived the Crash of 1987. On "Black Monday," October 19, 1987, the Dow Jones Industrial Average plunged over 500 points, losing almost 23 percent of its value in one day. That far surpassed the one-day loss of 13 percent that began the Crash of 1929.

The Crash of 1987 had some similarities to the Crash of 1929. Let's look at some of the events leading up to October 19, 1987:

- In early September, investors were becoming worried as interest rates had begun to rise.
- On September 24, stocks tumbled because of increases in interest rates. The Dow dropped over 75 points that day, a record at that time.
- On October 6, the Dow lost over 91 points (3½ percent of its value). It was a new record for a market drop in one day. (It would be followed by more record days.)
- On October 8, the market again suffered a major decline as a result of rising short-term interest rates.
- On October 14, the market set another new record for a market drop.
- On the 16th, the market dropped again in heavy trading, losing over 108 points (4.6 percent of its value). A record volume of 338 million shares was traded that day.

- On October 19, 1987, the market crashed. Over 604 million shares were traded that day, while the Dow Jones Industrial Average fell 22.6 percent.

Table 2.2 shows the damage done in the stock market in one day— October 19, 1987.

The Wilshire 5000 Stock Index is another index often quoted in the press. This market capitalization–weighted index now includes over 7,000 U.S.-based equities. It includes stocks listed on the New York Stock Exchange, the American Stock Exchange, and the Nasdaq. Many consider this the best measure of the overall stock market in this country, because it covers so many companies and includes all types of companies, from the blue chips found on the NYSE to the small new companies traded on the Nasdaq.

Table 2.2 doesn't fully reflect the pain investors were feeling, because it only illustrates what happened on one day. The stock market had already suffered several major drops prior to this day. In fact, the Dow was now down almost 37 percent from its high, set less than two months before the crash.

Do you remember the headlines in the news at that time? People were panicking. The phone lines at Fidelity Mutual Funds in Boston were overloaded with incoming concerned phone calls. No one was buying. Every phone call was either to sell stock mutual funds or to confirm that the account still existed. Fidelity's phone lines were tied up for two solid weeks. Many customers, unable to get through by phone, drove to Fidelity's headquarters in Boston to make sure their funds were safe. Newspaper articles included photos of investors standing in lines on the streets in Boston, waiting to get into Fidelity's building. Other mutual fund groups were having similar problems, but Fidelity caught most of the bad press because it was the largest fund group with these problems. E*Trade, the online investing company, also had trouble handling

TABLE 2.2

Index	Closing Value	Net Change	Percent Change
Dow Jones Industrial Average	1,738.74	−508.00	−22.6%
S&P 500	224.84	−57.86	−20.5%
Nasdaq	360.21	−46.12	−11.4%
Wilshire 5000	2,310.29	−503.18	−17.9%

the volume. Clients were unable to pull up their accounts for as long as 2½ hours.

Fortunately, within a matter of weeks, the investor panic had eased. Unlike the Crash of 1929, the 1987 market quickly rebounded. On October 20, 1987, the Dow was up over 102 points. The following day it was up over 186 points. By September of 1989, the Dow had regained all of its losses.

This crash was blamed on program trading by computers designed to automatically sell or buy large blocks of stock when certain trends prevailed. The New York Stock Exchange and the Chicago Mercantile Exchange have since put restrictions on these computer trades in hopes of preventing this problem from happening again. But there were other events leading to this correction, including:

- Rapidly increasing interest rates
- Low dividends on stocks
- Very high price-earnings ratios on stocks
- Too much optimism in the years leading to the crash
- Too much pessimism in the months just before the crash
- Pure panic leading to irrational selling

The negative emotional impact of the Crash of 1987 didn't last long. Although investors suffered the largest dollar loss ever recorded, the economy was strong enough to avoid a recession or a depression. In fact, the S&P 500 returned 5.25 percent that year. Unfortunately, this relatively short-term crash led investors to the false assumption that all future down markets would be short and all up markets would be long and prosperous. This assumption was given credibility by the incredible bull market decade of the 1990s that followed.

The 1990s

What a fine decade it was! Let's look at the S&P 500 in Figure 2.1.

During the 1990s, the S&P 500 averaged an increase of almost 19 percent per year. (The previous 50 years experienced an average increase of only 11.6 percent per year.) We enjoyed an incredible nine years in a row of positive returns. The one negative year was barely noticeable: down 3 percent in 1990.

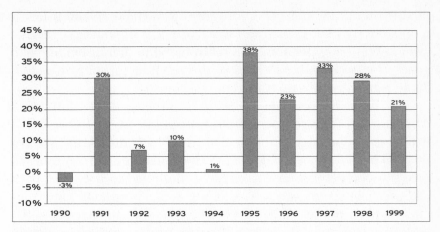

FIGURE 2.1 **S&P 500—1900 to 1999. (Courtesy of Wiesenberger, a Thomson Financial Company)**

THE NASDAQ MARKET: 1971 THROUGH 1999 We have seen how well large-company stocks (S&P 500) performed from the mid-1970s through the 1990s. Let's now look at the exciting, volatile Nasdaq Composite Index, first published in 1971. Two-thirds of the stocks in the Nasdaq are computer-related or telecommunications companies. The index began at 100. The Nasdaq was pretty boring for its first 20 years of its existence. It wasn't until 1991 that it crossed 500. Then things started getting exciting.

The Nasdaq topped 1000 in 1995. In 1996, a record 70 Silicon Valley companies went public. The Valley was flush with cash, dreams, and hope for a bright future. In 1997, for the first time in history, there were more e-mails sent than letters. Both consumers and businesses were going online. Young upstart companies included Amazon.com, Yahoo!, and eBay. In 1998, the Nasdaq zoomed past 2000. That was also the same year we saw WorldCom complete its $40 billion buyout of MCI, making it the second-largest long-distance telephone provider. (It was also the year President Bill Clinton was impeached, an indication of how lax morals had become.)

On November 3, 1999, the Nasdaq passed 3,000. It went from 500 to 5,000 in just nine years. It took only four months to go from 3,000 to 5,000. Originally, there were approximately 2,500 stocks listed on the Nasdaq. Today, there are roughly 5,000 new companies traded on this exchange.

Part of the excitement came as a result of the rapid acceptance of the Internet. It took 38 years for radio to reach 50 million users. It required only 13 years before TV reached 50 million users. Internet growth was truly phenomenal, reaching 50 million users in just 5 years. The stocks of the technology-driven Internet companies that made it all happen were traded on the Nasdaq.

Let's look at just one of these Internet-driven companies, Amazon.com. This company first went public in May 1997. What happened to the price of the stock during the Giddy Years? It went up 3800 percent since going public. The general public continues to love this company, whose sales have continued to rise. In May of 2003, Amazon.com's stock was selling at $28 per share. Eight million shares a day were being bought and sold. At that price, the stock was selling at 2.79 times the company's sales (the price to sales ratio). But Amazon.com has yet to make a consistent profit. (They recently made headlines because they had a quarter of a year in which they made a profit.) The earnings per share in May of 2003 were a negative 40 cents per share. This is a company whose sales have exploded, but they have yet to figure out how to earn a steady profit. Amazon.com continues to sell books and related merchandise at or below cost. At $28 per share, investors are betting the company will figure out how to make a consistent profit at some time in the near future.

Let's return to the Nasdaq market as a whole. During the 1990s, the Nasdaq exploded from less than 500 to over 4000. But during this incredible period, it experienced two bear markets. (A bear market is defined as a market drop of 20 percent or more; a correction is a drop of 10 to 19 percent.) In both 1990 and 1998, the Nasdaq had losses of over 30 percent. These two years of substantial losses show how volatile the stocks listed on the Nasdaq can be, even in a bull market.

The price investors were willing to pay for these aggressive stocks increased 10-fold over this decade. There is a way to measure how pricey a stock has become, referred to as the P/E ratio. This ratio divides the market price of the stock by the earnings of the company for one year. For example, if a stock is selling at $20 per share and the company is currently earning $1 per share, the P/E ratio is 20. In 1991, the P/E ratio for the Nasdaq was 20. By 1999, it had exploded to 200! Investors were willing to pay 200 times what these companies were earning, hoping they would show a dramatic increase in profits.

Unfortunately, the prices for these high-flying stocks were increasing faster than the earnings of the companies were growing. From the beginning of 1999 through its peak in March of 2000 (a 15-month period), the Nasdaq soared 130 percent. Investors had become completely unrealistic in their expectations for the future earnings of these stocks. They were no longer investing. They were now gambling.

HIGHLIGHTS OF THE 1990s Prior to the 1990s, the Dow Jones had never experienced more than five years in a row with positive returns. But in the 1990s, the Dow set an incredible nine-year record of positive performance from 1991 to 1999.
There were several events that created this success:

- The mutual fund industry was exploding. In 1990, there were 3,081 mutual funds. By the end of 2000, there were 8,171 funds.

- Interest rates had dropped dramatically since the early 1980s, turning savers into investors as they looked for higher returns than were possible in the bond market.

- Inflation was extremely low, measuring less than 2 percent in 1997 and 1998 and only 2.7 percent in 1999.

- Computer usage in the workplace produced a major increase in productivity. Corporate profits surged as a direct result of this investment in technology. Think back a few years. How many employees had a computer or e-mail or voice mail in 1990? How many salesmen had cell phones or pagers? Compare that to today!

- In March 2000, the economic expansion had entered its 108th month, making it the longest in history.

- The technology-laden Nasdaq Composite Index was up a record 86 percent in 1999. No broad index of American stocks has ever appreciated so much in any previous calendar year.

- By the end of the decade, investors were buying and selling stocks at a feverish pace. Many were day trading at a frantic pace. The average holding period of the publicly held shares of Amazon.com and Yahoo! was only eight days. People were no longer investing. They were now gambling.

- Over 30 mutual funds returned in excess of 150 percent in 1999. That kind of performance was unheard of. (The mutual funds with these super track records were in the right place at the right time. The portfolios of most of that year's top-performing mutual funds were concentrated in high-tech stocks.) The 1999 track records of these high-flying funds were touted in the financial press, attracting many new investors to these very aggressive portfolios.

- In 1999, there were 177 mutual funds that delivered a total return in excess of 100 percent. Remember, those top-performing fund managers took the largest amount of risk in the process of creating those returns.

- Even the average mutual fund returned 15.4 percent over the 10 years of the 1990s.

1995-1999 Consider the last five years of the 1990s. The markets had performed incredibly well for 20 years (since 1974). And things were just getting started! Take a close look at Figure 2.2, which illustrates the last five years of the 1990s.

During the last five years of the 1990s, the S&P 500 averaged a whopping 28.7 percent increase per year. I doubt you will ever see a five-year period in the S&P 500 like this again.

It wasn't just the S&P 500 that was enjoying record returns for the last five years of the 1990s. For example, look at Table 2.3.

I've just introduced three more indices for comparison. The Frank Russell Company is a recognized authority in several areas of the financial industry. For decades, they have been consulting to

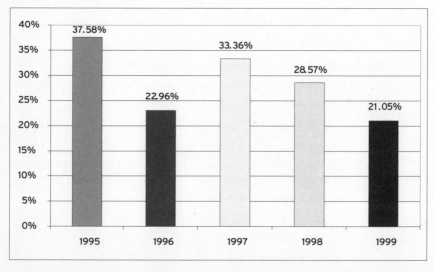

FIGURE 2.2   S&P 500—1995 to 1999. (Courtesy of Wiesenberger, a Thomson Financial Company)

TABLE 2.3

Index	Average Return, 1995–1999
Dow Jones Industrial Average	27.2%
S&P 500	28.7%
Nasdaq	41.9%
Wilshire 5000 Total Market Index	27.2%
Russell 1000	28.2%
Russell 2000	17.2%
Russell 3000	27.1%

Courtesy of Wiesenberger, a Thomson Financial Company

major corporations around the world, advising them on the management of more than $3.5 trillion in pension assets. Russell created several indices that are used to evaluate pension money managers. The three most recognized indices are:

1. The Russell 1000 Index, which measures the stock performance of the 1,000 largest U.S. companies

2. The Russell 2000 Index, which measures the performance of the next 2,000 companies in size (half of these companies are listed on the Nasdaq)

3. The Russell 3000 Index, which measures the performance of the 3,000 largest companies in the U.S. stock market

Table 2.4 compares the seven leading U.S. equity indices.

TABLE 2.4

Index	Dow Jones Industrial Average	S&P 500	Nasdaq Composite	Wilshire 5000	Russell 1000	Russell 2000	Russell 3000
Size of Companies	Large cap	Broad market	Nasdaq exchange	Broad market	Large cap	Small cap	Broad cap
Number of Stocks	30	500	4,000	7,000	1,000	2,000	3,000
Weighting	Price	Market cap	Market cap	Market cap	Market cap	Market cap	Market cap

Courtesy of Frank Russell Company

There is some overlap in these indices, but together they tell the story of the U.S. stock market. On any given day (or other period of time) these indices can move at different speeds and even in different directions.

During the Giddy Years of the 1990s, practically all portions of the U.S. stock market had tremendous returns.

INCREASING RISK   Making fortunes in the stock market looked like a slam dunk. Just buy stocks; whether you chose stocks in the S&P 500, the Dow or the Nasdaq, it didn't seem to matter. Just buy something, sit back, and you'd be rich in no time. Right? Maybe not. Let's look closer at how investment risk was increasing.

As mentioned earlier, the Nasdaq was up 86 percent in 1999. There were days when the trading volume on the Nasdaq exceeded 2 million shares. It would hit its peak a few months later in March of 2000, soaring 130 percent over this 15-month period. Even the more conservative Dow Jones Industrial Average was exploding in value, passing 10,000 for the first time in history.

By the end of the decade, the P/E ratio of the S&P 500 had risen to 28.8 times current earnings. This means investors were willing to pay 28.8 times what the average large-company stock was earning in 1999. Earlier, in 1990, the average P/E ratio was only 15.2. In short, the risk in owning the 500 largest companies in America had almost doubled during the Giddy Years of the 1990s. It is unfortunate that the stock market reported such fantastic numbers during this period, because the average investor began taking more market risk than I have seen since 1929. If these companies failed to meet these lofty expectations of earnings, the stock prices would plummet.

Bond investors also enjoyed this period of time. An extended bull market in bonds began in 1981 and continued into the early 2000s.

Both stocks and bonds did well over this historical period. The incredible performance and longevity of this period relieved the pain of the 1973–1974 bear market, which was becoming a distant memory. Unfortunately, future expectations had become very unrealistic. Investors were expecting future returns of 15 to 30 percent year in and year out.

Years ago, I heard the phrase, "When a pig becomes a hog, it gets slaughtered." Unfortunately, aggressive investors were about to be slaughtered.

PROBLEMS ON THE HORIZON In the late 1990s, problems began to surface. One company was very much in the news in 1999: WorldCom. At its peak, WorldCom was selling for more than $60 per share. At that time, the total value of the outstanding stock was more than $120 billion. Here is a brief history of WorldCom:

- It was founded in 1983 with the name of Long Distance Discount Service (LDDS).

- The company purchased MCI Group in 1998. At that time, it was the largest corporate merger in history.

- That year, it also bought CompuServe, a major e-mail provider.

- In 1999, it purchased SkyTel, a messaging service company. It was then operating in over 65 countries.

- The company employed over 85,000 people.

- In the United States, it had over 20 million long distance clients and 2 million local telephone customers.

Unfortunately, this company was a house of cards built on deceit and fraud that would fall apart in the years to come.

The Gruesome Years: 2000, 2001, and 2002

YEAR 2000 In January of 2000, we watched Super Bowl XXXIV. It was a great game for those of us living in St. Louis, as we watched the Rams and Kurt Warner beat the Tennessee Titans. One of the highlights of watching the Super Bowl each year is the opportunity to see new and entertaining TV commercials. Do you remember how bizarre the commercials were that year? Many of the commercials were for new start-up dot-com companies, such as Monster.com and Pets.com. Many of these commercials made little if any sense. The start-up companies wasted millions of dollars on these ads. Many of those companies are no longer in business. Monday Night Football also had its share of dot-com ads. One such company, Rythyms Net-Connections, went public in 1999 at $21 a share. It screamed up to $75 that day. This new high-speed Internet connecting company raised over $1.8 billion dollars during its short lifetime. It would be in bankruptcy by August of 2001.

By the year 2000, almost 79 million individuals were investing in the stock market. During the first three months of the year, investors poured $140 billion into stock mutual funds. This flow of new investment dollars into the market created the best quarter in mutual fund history. The pendulum had moved to the very end of the swing toward greed.

On January 14, 2000, the Dow Jones Industrial Average peaked at over 11,500. This index of large blue chip stocks could not maintain this lofty performance. Let's look at Table 2.5 to see how far these 30 stocks dropped by March 7, 2000 compared to their peaks that occurred during the previous 12 months.

Many high-tech stocks were selling at incredibly high prices. It was difficult to justify P/E ratios over 40 for large companies. Table 2.6 shows how pricey the market had become.

Investors were frantic to buy Yahoo!, even though the stock's P/E ratio was extremely high at 1,714. Even Cisco's P/E ratio was far above average. Investors willing to buy Cisco were paying 209 times what the company was earning. The only rationale for these high prices was anticipation of tremendous future growth in profits. If any stock sporting a high P/E ratio failed to grow at its expected rate, the stock price would plunge. By comparison, the

TABLE 2.5

Stock	Percent Change from 52-Week High	Stock	Percent Change from 52-Week High
Phillip Morris (Altria Group, Inc.)	−55%	JP Morgan	−28%
Procter & Gamble	−45%	IBM	−26%
Caterpiller	−49%	Alcoa	−26%
International Paper	−44%	American Express	−25%
McDonald's	−40%	Home Depot	−25%
Honeywell	−39%	Microsoft	−23%
DuPont	−38%	General Motors	−21%
Merck	−38%	3M	−20%
Johnson & Johnson	−37%	General Electric	−21%
Coca-Cola	−34%	AT&T	−17%
United Technologies	−34%	Citigroup	−16%
Wal-Mart Stores	−32%	Walt Disney	−7%
Eastman Kodak	−30%	Exxon Mobil	−7%
SBC Communications	−30%	Hewlett-Packard	−6%
Boeing	−29%	Intel	−3%

TABLE 2.6

Large Company Stock	P/E Ratio on March 31, 2000
Yahoo!	1,714.0
Cisco Systems	209.0
Intel	62.5
Microsoft	66.8
Sun Microsystems	121.7
Qualcomm	81.1
Dow Jones Industrial Average	22.9

S&P 500 was priced at 31.1 times earnings. The more conservative Dow Jones Industrial Average stocks had a P/E ratio of 22.9.

Let's see how these indices suffered over the next three years. Figure 2.3 shows the performance of the Dow Jones Industrial Average, the S&P 500, and the Nasdaq from 2000 through 2002.

The severity of this three-year decline in all three major indices reflects how overpriced the markets had become in the late 1990s.

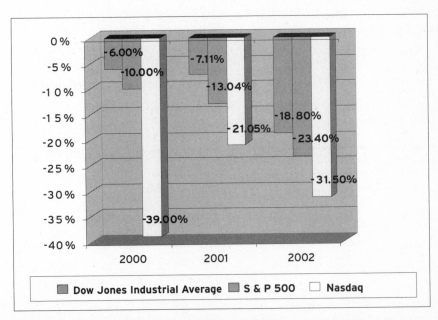

FIGURE 2.3   Declines in major indexes from 2000 through 2002. (Courtesy of Wiesenberger, a Thomson Financial Company)

The Nasdaq peaked on March 10, 2000 at 5,048. Three years after hitting this high, the Nasdaq would be at only 1,305, down 74 percent from its peak. The only down market that compares was the 89 percent plunge the Dow Jones Industrial Average suffered from September 1929 to July 1932.

Table 2.7 shows what happened to some of the leading technology stocks during this three-year plunge in the market.

In July of 2000, another major company was in the news, and the news was not good. Rite Aid, the nation's third-largest drugstore chain, filed for bankruptcy. Criminal charges were brought against top management for their role in accounting schemes intended to make the company appear attractive to investors. The accounting fraud masked losses of $1.6 billion. Their schemes worked for a while: The stock got as high as $50 per share before it plummeted.

By the end of 2000, the Internet bubble had burst. Here are a few of the lowlights of the year 2000:

- The Nasdaq was down 39 percent for the year. (It had been up 86 percent the year before.)

- The S&P 500 was down 10 percent for the year, its first losing year since 1990.

- The Dow Jones Industrial Average ended its incredible nine-year streak of gains, losing 6 percent for the year.

- More than 20,000 employees of Internet companies lost their jobs.

- Two hundred twenty-five Internet companies went out of business.

TABLE 2.7

Stock	3-Year Plunge
Cisco Systems	−75%
Intel	−63%
Microsoft	−55%
Qualcomm	−79%
Rambus	−59%
Yahoo!	−93%
Amazon.com	−79%
AOL	−84%

■ A record number of IPOs were shelved because there was almost no demand for initial public offerings (IPOs). Investors no longer wanted any part of buying into new start-up companies, especially Internet companies.

The bad news was not over. There was more to come in the following year.

YEAR 2001 2001 would be another rough year for the major markets. Table 2.8 shows what happened in 2001.

The 7.11 percent loss for the Dow doesn't reflect the volatility this index of blue chip stocks suffered. During the year, the Dow plunged 3,287 points from its peak to its low point before recovering some of this loss before the end of the calendar year. The Nasdaq also experienced a more volatile year than the annual numbers in Table 2.8 indicate. At its high point on March 10, 2000, the Nasdaq was over 5,000. One year later, on March 31, 2001, it would be at 1,840, down 64 percent from the previous year's high.

September 11, 2001 is, of course, a day like no other. On that day, terrorists attacked the World Trade Center in New York and the Pentagon in Washington. The stock market was closed for four business days. Trading resumed on September 17. This was the longest suspension of the stock market since the Depression. The Dow dropped more than 14 percent in that first week of trading after the attacks. It was the fourth-worst week for these blue chip stocks in over 100 years. But the financial markets had been in trouble for many months before this tragic event. In March of 2001, the economy had already entered a recession. Here are some of the lowlights of the year resulting from the recession and the tragic events of 9/11/01:

TABLE 2.8

Index	Percentage Drop in 2001
Dow Jones Industrials	−7.11%
S&P 500	−13.04%
Nasdaq	−21.05%

Courtesy of Wiesenberger, a Thomson Financial Company

- Enron filed for bankruptcy. It would be the second-largest bankruptcy in history.
- Two hundred fifty-two major companies filed for bankruptcy.
- Five hundred thirty Internet companies closed.
- Thirty-four public telecom companies filed for bankruptcy.

Here is a partial list of companies that declared bankruptcy in 2001:

- Enron
- Burlington Industries
- Aladdin Casino
- Planet Hollywood
- Midway Airlines
- Bethlehem Steel
- Loews Cineplex Entertainment Corporation
- Wehrenberg, Inc.
- Pacific Gas & Electric Company

There would also be several Internet and telecommunications companies seeking bankruptcy protection:

- 360networks
- Covad Communications
- NorthPoint Communications
- Tiligent
- Winstar Communications
- Net2000

Net2000 first went public in March of 2000 and traded as high as $40 per share. It was bankrupt just one year later.

It wasn't just small start-up companies that were having trouble in 2001. We would see many household name products disappear that year:

- AMF bowling balls
- Polaroid cameras
- Converse sneakers

- Schwinn bicycles
- Sunbeam appliances

Enron was in the headlines for much of the year. Enron was the seventh-largest U.S. company by sales when it filed for bankruptcy on December 2, 2001. It went from a respected energy trader and pipeline concern to bankruptcy in a matter of months. A year earlier, the company's stock was valued at $77 billion. By the end of 2001, it was worth only $500 million. The biggest losers were the Enron employees, who were forced to hold more than 60 percent of their retirement plan assets in Enron stock. They watched in horror as the stock dropped from $90 per share in late 2000 to just 25 cents per share in less than a year. Enron's employees would lose $800 million in their retirement accounts.

Several events led to these bankruptcies and the recession:

- The booming 1990s created overconfidence and aggressive investing.

- Telecom companies, such as telecommunication equipment companies, were overstocked as the demand for cable plummeted. This hurt companies like Lucent and Nortel.

- Y2K created a huge demand for new computer equipment and software before the year 2000. That demand was over by 2001. Cisco Systems was hurt when large customers deferred future technology upgrades.

- Business owners expanded too rapidly in the late 1990s. They borrowed heavily from banks and borrowed too much from investors through bond issues. Their debt was too large when sales began to drop.

- Banks were cutting back on business loans, making it difficult for many companies to survive the tough business climate they were experiencing.

- Many business owners no longer considered bankruptcy a dirty word. They saw it as a way to escape costly leases, large bank loans, and expensive union contracts.

- The terrorist attacks on September 11 severely damaged the travel industry and related businesses, such as airlines and hotels.

Pause for a moment and remember your feelings on 9/11. We had been attacked on our own soil. No one felt safe. We began to question the long-term effects the attacks would have on our country.

The Federal Reserve Board reduced short-term interest rates a record 11 times during the year. In January, the rate was 6 percent. By the end of the year, it was reduced to 1.75 percent. It would drop even further in future years.

THE 2000 AND 2001 BOND MARKET The one bright investment area over this two-year period was the bond markets, as highlighted in Table 2.9.

Only corporate high-yield bonds suffered a loss in 2000. Investors were selling their stocks and buying bonds as they sought safety and a better return.

YEAR 2002

Bad news continued in 2002. Enron had filed for bankruptcy in December of 2001. The string of record-setting bankruptcies continued in 2002, as shown in Table 2.10.

Much of the news for the year would involve corporate fraud. WorldCom, the nation's second-largest long-distance telephone company, was guilty of accounting fraud that would total more than $11 billion. Here is some of the pessimistic news we heard:

- May 15: WorldCom's stock dropped 14 percent. More than 670 million shares were traded, making it the most actively traded stock in a single day. Back in June of 1999, the stock was as high as $62 a share. It closed this day at $1.24 per share.

TABLE 2.9

Bond Market	Total Return, Year 2000	Total Return, Year 2001
Investment-grade corporate bonds	+9.1%	+10.7%
Intermediate-term U.S. treasury bonds	+10.2%	+8.1%
30-year treasury bonds	+20.1%	+3.5%
Municipal bonds	+17.1%	+4.5%
Emerging markets bonds	+14.7%	+5.2%
Corporate high-yield bonds	−5.1%	+4.5%

TABLE 2.10

All-Time Rank*	Company Name	Company Assets
1	WorldCom	$103.9 billion
3	Conseco	61.1 billion
6	Global Crossing	25.5 billion
7	UAL	25.2 billion
8	Adelphia	24.4 billion
11	Kmart	17 billion

*Enron was number two on this all-time list, but it filed the previous year.
Courtesy of The Wall Street Journal

- July 2: The stock closed at 6 cents a share in very active trading. Almost 1.5 billion shares were sold, breaking the one-day record for trading in a single stock, set back in May.

- In July, the company filed for Chapter 11 protection. It was the largest bankruptcy in U.S. history.

The Securities and Exchange Commission (SEC) launched a record number of investigations that year into companies including WorldCom, Global Crossing, Xerox, Tyco International, Adelphia Communications, and so on.

Investors wondered if they could trust the financial records of any corporation. They also doubted the advice they were getting from their stockbrokers. Large brokerage firms work closely with major corporations to help them find capital though stock offerings and the sale of corporate bonds. At the same time, these brokerage houses are recommending the stock of those companies to the investing public. This can lead to a major conflict of interest. Several major brokerage firms were fined over $1.4 billion for issuing biased stock research reports. Citigroup (Solomon's parent) was fined $350 million. Merrill Lynch was fined $100 million.

In August, we read how the airline industry continued to be in terrible financial shape. US Airways was in bankruptcy. American Airlines stock was 35 percent lower than it had been 15 years earlier. United Airlines was down 90 percent during the same 15 years. Even the stock of Southwest Airlines was down 50 percent.

BAD NEWS IN 2002 2002 was the worst year for the stock market in a quarter century. To understand investors' concerns, consider what they saw by the end of the year:

- Seventy percent of stocks listed on the major exchanges lost value in 2002.

- The average stock mutual fund was down 20 percent for the year.

- Utility mutual funds (considered a conservative type of fund by many investors) were down 23 percent on average. The losses were due to deregulation in the energy and telecommunications industries. These changes led to fierce competition and substantial losses for many companies in these industries.

- Telecom, science, and technology funds were down over 40 percent.

- The Dow was down 16.8 percent, its worst year since 1977.

- The S&P 500 lost 23.4 percent, its worst year since 1974.

- The Nasdaq fell 31.5 percent and was down a total of 74 percent from its peak in 2000.

Many investors were so depressed they didn't even open their investment statements. They just wanted all the bad news to go away. How were you reacting to this third year in a row of bad financial news?

WORST NEWS IN 2002 In my opinion, the worst news of 2002 was the way many investors reacted to all of this negative news. Investors pulled more than $100 billion out of stock mutual funds, the largest withdrawal in history. July was the worst month, with $53 billion withdrawn. In July, the Nasdaq was down to almost 1,400. Investors who had bought high were now selling low. That is the exact opposite of how to make money in the market!

For the first time in nearly 20 years, employees reduced their participation in company-sponsored 401(k) retirement plans. They were missing out on the opportunity to purchase great businesses (stock) at the lowest prices seen in years. They were making major investment decisions based on emotions rather than logic.

GOOD NEWS IN 2002 Let's look at the good news in 2002:

- Inflation was low.

- Short-term interest rates continued to decline, to 1.25 percent.

- Homeowners were able to refinance their long-term mortgage debt and reduce their payments.

- Interest charges on credit cards and car loans decreased.

- Real estate mutual funds were up 4 percent for the year.

- The average P/E ratio of S&P 500 stocks dropped to 15 times the forward-looking 12-month earnings. This was the lowest level in five years.

- Near the end of July, the Dow scored sharp gains in four days of trading, up more than 1,000 points (13.1 percent). This four-day gain was the biggest since 1933.

- October was another good month, as the Dow was up 11 percent.

After this runup, some investors carefully, slowly added $3 billion back into stock mutual funds. (Remember, they had pulled over $53 billion out of the market back in July, missing most if not all of this July and October recovery.)

YEAR 2003 Corporate fraud continued to be in the news. Health-South Corporation, the largest operator of rehabilitation hospitals in the United States, was found guilty of inflating earnings and overstating the value of its assets. It is estimated that executives inflated earnings by $2.5 billion since 1997.

Adelphia Communications Corp., the fifth-largest cable operator, pleaded guilty to $2.5 billion in accounting fraud.

Tyco International continued to fire top executives. A year earlier, the CEO and two executives were fired for looting more than $600 million from the company.

WorldCom, in bankruptcy since 2002, removed an additional $80 billion from its balance sheet to reflect the dropping value of the company. The assets were now worth $10 billion. That seems like a lot, but at its peak, the company was valued at $180 billion.

In February, our attention turned to international problems including Iraq, North Korea, and the War on Terrorism. The February 24, 2003 edition of *Newsweek* featured stories that added to our fears. One of their stories told us how to prepare for chemical, biological, and radiological terrorist attacks. The story included a picture of worried New Yorkers buying up all the available supplies of plastic sheeting and duct tape to cover windows and doors as part of their plan. Once again, fear was the major emotion gripping the economy.

On March 20, 2003, our attention was focused on the war in Iraq as we began bombing Baghdad. The daily news highlighted the demonstrations against the war. Several countries, including France and

Russia, were opposed to our involvement in the war. Everyone was glued to the TV, watching round-the-clock news about the war. Every day, the news media featured long in-depth discussions on how long the war would last. Baghdad would fall just three weeks later.

Our economy has begun the long road to recovery. Investors feel more confident in the strength of both our armed forces and our economy. But more important, investors are returning to more logical decisions rather than emotional decisions. They are once again focusing on corporate earnings.

One last time, remember what history tells us: A bull market follows every bear market.

Today's Risks: Bonds

The stock market is no longer the towering risk it was back at the end of the Giddy Years in 1999. Today's major investment risk is in bonds. Bond prices drop when interest rates go up. A recent study by Vanguard Mutual Funds showed that 70 percent of investors do not understand the relationship between bond prices and interest rate movements. It's worth repeating: Bond prices drop when interest rates go up. For example, let's assume you bought a $1,000 Treasury note that matures in 10 years. If you bought this note in early 2003, it would pay you about 3.8 percent ($380 in interest) each year for 10 years. But what happens if interest rates go up in the near future by 2 percent to a total of 5.8 percent? The value of your investment would drop to about $900. Why? If you were to sell your Treasury note in the bond market before it matures, you would have to compete with new bonds paying more interest. To make your low-interest Treasury note attractive to buyers, you would have to offer to sell it at a discount.

Interest rates can only move in one of three directions:

1. They can stay exactly where they are.

2. They can move down.

3. They can increase.

New issue bonds are sold at a price of $1,000. If interest rates stay the same, bond prices will not change. If rates go down, existing bonds appreciate in value (as we saw happen from the early 1980s through the early 2000s). But if interest rates increase, bond prices will drop. Table 2.11 shows how the value of bonds with different maturities can react to changes in interest rates.

TABLE 2.11

Interest Rate Change	5-Year Bond	20-Year Bond	30-Year Bond
+1.5%	$946	$897	$816
+1.0%	$964	$930	$871
+0.5%	$982	$964	$932
0	$1,000	$1,000	$1,000
−0.5%	$1,019	$1,038	$1,075
−1.0%	$1,038	$1,077	$1,159
−1.5%	$1,057	$1,118	$1,252

Based on duration calculations

Let's look at how changes in interest rates can affect the price of 30-year long-term bonds. Consider interest rate movements of 1.5 percent both up and down. At first glance, you would expect the interest rate movement to have the same dollar effect on your principal, but Table 2.11 shows that is not the case. If interest rates drop 1.5 percent, these 30-year bonds are projected to appreciate from $1,000 to $1,252 (a gain of $252). But what happens if interest rates go up by 1.5 percent? This same bond will drop in value to $816 (a loss of $184). Remember, bonds pay interest. Even if interest rates increase, the bond owner continues to enjoy the yield the bond pays every year until it matures. This yield acts to soften losses when interest rates are going up. Conversely, if interest rates drop, the value of existing bonds will appreciate. The appreciation is greater than you might expect, because the higher-yielding bonds will pay more income for many years.

Let's look at the shorter-maturity five-year bonds. These bonds typically pay less interest, but they are much less volatile.

How low could interest rates go? Rates on 10-year Treasury notes are currently 3.8 percent. Mathematically, future rates could drop to zero, but that is highly unlikely. What is the probability we will see interest rates drop significantly? Not much at all. Interest rates are at the lowest point they have been in 41 years.

Today's risk is increasing interest rates, which would hurt bond prices. As recently as the year 2000, the rate on 10-year Treasuries was 6.8 percent. We could see rates move back to this level, or even higher, in the future. Several economic events suggest interest rates will be going up, including the following:

- Budget surpluses have disappeared. In 2001, there was a surplus of $184 billion. A budget deficit of $383 billion is projected for 2003.

- Tax revenues have been decreasing while government spending has been increasing as a result of the costs of the War on Terrorism and the war in Iraq.

- Inflation could rise as the economy continues to improve.

- Foreign investors have been major buyers of U.S. government bonds for several years. But recently, the dollar has dropped in value compared to foreign currencies, such as the euro. If this trend continues, foreign investors will look for alternative investments. Interest rates on U.S. government bonds would have to increase to continue to attract foreign buyers.

- Many investors who sold their stocks in the early 2000s loaded up on bonds. As the stock market comes back into favor, many bondholders will sell their low-yielding bonds to get back into the stock market, hoping for better returns.

- Interest rates are at 41-year lows. Historically, the bond market has moved in 40- to 50-year cycles. Should history repeat itself, interest rates will begin climbing over the next several years.

How high could interest rates go? Let's consider 30-year government bonds. In early 2003, the rate was only 4.8 percent. Back in 1981, these bonds paid 14 percent interest. Could we see 14 percent rates again? Yes, it is possible. Could rates go higher than 14 percent? Yes! And that is why there is more risk in owning bonds than stocks.

Should you sell all your bonds today? Should you jump back into the stock market? Should you just sell everything and go to cash and wait until things calm down? Many of us are paralyzed with indecision. Once again, we need to recognize the role emotion can play in our decisions. We will look at what you need to do going forward in the next chapter.

LESSONS AND STRATEGIES

1. Emotions affect our attitudes about investing. It is important to guard against making investment decisions based on feelings and attitudes we have at the moment.
2. Financial news headlines are not necessarily your friend. Too often, their message is noise, not news. Their objective is to sell

newspapers and magazines. To do that, they focus on your emotions.

3. Emotional decisions will cause many frightened investors to miss the great investment opportunities that should occur over the years to come.

4. In the short run, the market moves according to emotions.

5. In the long run, the market direction is based on corporate earnings.

6. We are fortunate to live in the number one capitalistic country in the world. We not only live here, but we have the opportunity to own the great companies in our society.

7. Reviewing history will help you develop long-term projections and a disciplined investment process to help you going forward.

8. You can't avoid risk. If you attempt to avoid all investment risk, you are subjecting yourself to greater losses. You will expose yourself to a greater risk—the risk of outliving your income.

9. Indices, such as the S&P 500, will help you learn the history of the stock market. Follow those indices that best represent the types of stocks or stock mutual funds you own. Remember that some indices and investments can be very volatile. When you read mutual fund literature, see how the fund's performance compares to benchmark indices that hold similar stocks.

10. Today's largest investment risks are in the bond market, not the stock market. If a large portion of your portfolio is in bonds, it is important to examine your investment risks going forward.

An Investment Plan You Can Live With

A successful investment plan is one you can live with for a long period. Your plan will be successful if it:

- Controls volatility
- Incorporates strategies that make sense on a historical basis
- Is easy to implement and adjust
- Provides peace of mind

Volatility

Controlling volatility is important for emotional reasons, because it keeps us from making foolish decisions. For example, let's assume you can retire with dignity in four years, as long as your assets grow at 10 percent on average for the next few years. Let's assume your nest egg is currently $100,000. Let's further assume you meet your 10 percent growth rate for two years in a row. Now your account is worth $121,000. But what if your return in year three were minus 15 percent? Your account would drop to $102,850. How much must you earn in year four to get back on track for a 10 percent average growth rate? A whopping 42 percent! Can it be done? Maybe. But it's risky to try to get 42 percent in year four to catch up;

you could make a foolish decision, gambling for a 42 percent return. How will a loss of 15 percent affect you emotionally? Would you be inclined to sell, seeking a safer investment? Would you stay fully invested, hoping to get back on track within a year or so? Would you panic? Would you become depressed at the thought that you'll have to delay your planned retirement for several years? No one enjoys investing if they are experiencing these negative emotions.

The second important reason to control volatility is to improve your long-term investment performance. Let's compare two port-folios of $100,000 to see the impact volatility can have on your capi-tal. Portfolio 1 is exciting, with lots of market action. Portfolio 2 is quite boring, plodding along at 8½ percent for 5 years. (See Table 3.1.)

If you look only at the average rate of return percentage, it seems like portfolio 1 is the winner, with 8.8 percent. But look at the dollar value of these two portfolios in five years. Portfolio 1 would be worth $147,141, while the boring portfolio 2 would be worth $150,365. Boring can be beautiful if your objective is to build wealth over a period of time!

"But wait," you say. "Wouldn't it come out differently if the bad year's performance happened in year 1? I could recoup my loss over the next four years and be way ahead of the game." Table 3.1 shows the loss in year 4. Table 3.2 shows the loss occurring in the first year.

As you can see, the results are the same! It is volatility, not timing, that makes a difference over time.

Historically, the stock market has suffered losses in one out of

TABLE 3.1

Year	Exciting Portfolio 1	Boring Portfolio 2
1	12%	8½%
2	15%	8½%
3	20%	8½%
4	−15%	8½%
5	12%	8½%
Yearly average	8.8%	8½%
Value in 5 years	$147,141	$150,365

TABLE 3.2

Year	Exciting Portfolio 1 With Loss in Initial Year	Boring Portfolio 2
1	−15%	8½%
2	12%	8½%
3	15%	8½%
4	20%	8½%
5	12%	8½%
Yearly average	8.8%	8½%
Value in 5 years	$147,141	$150,365

four years. There is no way of knowing exactly when those down years will occur. We have to accept the very real possibility this long-term trend will continue, so we need to incorporate ways to control volatility, or at least use it to our own advantage.

How do you reduce the risk in an investment portfolio?

- Diversify your portfolio.
- Implement asset allocation for your existing investments.
- Use dollar-cost averaging for future investments.

Diversification

Will Rogers once suggested, "Put all your eggs in one basket. Then, *watch that basket*." That comment makes for a great comedy routine, but it is not sound investment advice. Diversification is a more reliable approach.

The overwhelming choice for today's investors is mutual funds. Mutual funds offer an easy, safe way to automatically create and maintain a diversified portfolio. Money managers typically build and maintain a diversified portfolio of 20 to 200 securities in a mutual fund. Diversification is only part of the answer, but it is an important part.

Remember the employees of Enron who were forced to hold most of their retirement plan assets in Enron stock? This lack of diversification made them the biggest losers in the collapse of Enron. Make sure you don't make the same mistake. If you have choices in your company retirement plan, choose mutual funds or whatever else is available other than your employer's stock. Keep no more than 10 percent of your retirement plan assets in your employer's stock. You don't want to be at the mercy of your employer. You already depend on him for your paycheck and your health insurance. Diversify! Too often, we get emotionally attached to just one or two stocks.

It's also a great idea to own more than one mutual fund. I've never met a mutual fund owner who was emotionally attached to the 20 to 200 securities in each mutual fund he or she owned. That's the beauty of owning mutual funds: The daily business decisions of managing the portfolios are in the hands of professionals. If you have chosen your mutual funds carefully, the diversification (and emotional detachment) will improve the probability that you will meet your long-range goals.

Asset Allocation

Diversification is only part of the answer. We can accomplish much more by incorporating an investment technique called *asset allocation*.

Your investment goals should include:

- Reduction of investment risk (volatility)
- Greater predictability of performance

In Chapter 2, you saw how stocks and bonds performed from 2000 to 2003. Many investors owned only stocks during that difficult three-year period. Had these investors owned a simple blend of stocks, bonds, and cash, they would have reduced the volatility of their portfolios and improved their overall rate of return. For example, if they owned only stock mutual funds during this three-year period, their portfolios would have lost roughly 8 percent. But, if their portfolios were composed of 65 percent stock funds, 25 percent bond funds, and 10 percent in cash, their losses would have been only 3 percent.

What is currently in your portfolio? Do you own more than one mutual fund? Do you own both stock and bond funds? If so, that is a great start, but you can still do more to properly allocate your portfolio.

Investment Asset Classes

There are six major investment asset classes you can use to build your long-term investment plan:

1. Large-cap equities

2. Small-/mid-cap equities

3. Developed foreign equities

4. Emerging markets

5. Bonds

6. Real estate

There are also subclasses for each of the major investment asset classes. Let's look first at the equity classes and subclasses.

LARGE-CAP EQUITIES These are the stocks of the companies that have the most capital, a value of $10.5 billion or greater. These are recognized companies such as IBM, General Motors, Westinghouse, GE, Coca-Cola, and so on. Let's look at one of these giants—General Electric (GE). GE is one of the largest companies in the world, manufacturing everything from light bulbs to locomotives. It is also a major player in the credit card industry. The GE Capital unit alone has assets in excess of $345 billion. GE has more than 340,000 employees and offices in more than 100 countries. Now that is a large-cap stock!

SMALL-/MID-CAP EQUITIES Companies are considered small if their market capitalization is under $1.5 billion. Mid-cap stocks are those of companies valued between $1.5 billion and $10.5 billion. These might be relatively new companies or well-established mature companies. We have seen many periods in history when the stocks of these small- and mid-cap companies have greatly outperformed the stocks of larger companies.

DEVELOPED FOREIGN EQUITIES Approximately 60 percent of available equities are domiciled outside the United States. Many of these are stocks of well-run companies in countries such as England, Germany, France, and Japan. Companies such as Burger King, Nestlé, Honda, and Mercedes are just a few examples of foreign-based companies you are familiar with. The Europe, Asia, and Far East (EAFE) index, prepared by Morgan Stanley, tracks the performance of leading stocks in 20 developed foreign countries. The return for 1999 for the EAFE Index was 25.27 percent. At times, foreign equities have outperformed U.S. stocks.

Over the 30-year period ending in 2002, a portfolio made up of the large-cap stocks would have returned 12.2 percent. At the same time, a different portfolio consisting of 50 percent large-cap stocks with 25 percent in small-/mid-cap stocks and 25 percent in developed foreign stocks would have returned 13.2 percent. This blended approach not only improves performance, but also reduces the year-to-year volatility of the portfolio.

EMERGING MARKETS The fourth asset class provides the opportunity to invest in less developed equity markets, referred to as *emerging markets*. Many of the world's economies are still in the early stages of their development. Keep in mind that, once upon a time, the U.S. economy was an emerging market. In 1865, less than 150 years ago, we were an economy in reconstruction. Our economy was in a shambles! Buying ownership in a start-up/rebuilding United States business at that time would have been considered very risky. But careful selection would have been very rewarding. Those same opportunities are still available today in countries such as Argentina, Brazil, the Czech Republic, Greece, Hong Kong, Hungary, Indonesia, Israel, Mexico, the Philippines, Poland, Singapore, South Africa, Thailand, and Turkey.

Unfortunately, some foreign countries are very risky and unstable today. One example of an unstable economy today is Russia. The Russian work ethic is very low. For generations, the Russian people have depended on the government for their existence. That government dependency created an economy with incredibly low productivity. Many Russian citizens are morally corrupt. Part of that can be explained by the fact that religious worship was not tolerated for generations. Today, we see the Russian Mafia as an example of the moral corruption in their system. We also see alcoholism as a major threat to their economic growth. For these reasons, investing heavily in Russia is very risky and may remain so for many years to come.

But while Russia remains a risky situation, many other emerging markets offer less risk and a more reliable opportunity going forward. There will most likely be greater volatility in these investments than we would expect to see in a portfolio comprising of large-cap U.S. companies or developed foreign companies. In fact, we experienced this volatility in the 1990s. Countries such as Malaysia, Thailand, Indonesia, Hong Kong, Singapore, North and South Korea,

Vietnam, and the Philippines are often referred to as the *tiger countries*. Their economies roared in the early 1990s.

After witnessing the phenomenal growth in the tiger countries, the average investor jumped in at the high. After exploding in value, the stocks in these countries underwent a major correction. Between July 31, 1997 and September 30, 1998, these markets declined more than 45 percent. What did most investors do then? They sold. This is another recent example of emotional buying at the high followed by emotional selling at the low.

The situation with the tiger countries is quite different than what we see in Russia today. For example, consider Hong Kong. There are more Mercedes-Benz automobiles in Hong Kong than in any other major city in the world. Hong Kong has more millionaires per capita than the United States. Its economy suffered in the late 1990s and fell onto rough times. But, having once enjoyed the good life, Hong Kong's people will work twice as hard to regain their previous status. We have that same sense of determination in our country. That type of determination helped us recover from our Depression in the early 1930s and every recession we've experienced since then. The tiger countries have all the key ingredients to experience the same degree of successful recovery in their economies. They continue to have low-cost, motivated, and well-educated workforces and governments that are committed to making their nation's businesses grow. Their currencies have stabilized and their markets are poised for continuing growth.

These are just two examples of emerging markets. The tiger countries look extremely promising, but Russia continues to be very risky.

History tells us that all stocks do not react the same way at all times. At times, we see emerging markets enjoying the best performance of the four equity classes. At other times, it will be the large-cap U.S. companies leading the way. If your equity portfolio is allocated between all four equity classes, it can be very rewarding as a long-term stock investment. By dividing your equity ownership among these various portions of the stock market, you can improve your long-term performance. Why? Because you always have some portion of your assets in whatever happens to be the best-performing equity market in the future. It is also to your benefit to periodically rebalance your portfolio. To rebalance, you sell your gains in the best-performing portion of your portfolio and reinvest those gains among the other sectors. In that way, you maintain the same risk in all sectors. You are also reducing the future volatility of your portfolio. By maintaining your original allocation, you don't go overboard in any one portion of the stock market.

There is one more important piece of the stock market puzzle. Each of the aforementioned stock classes has subclasses.

Equity Subclasses

In addition to the four main classes of stocks (U.S. large-cap, U.S. small-/mid-cap, developed foreign equities, and emerging markets), there are subclasses that further define various stocks.

There are three main subclasses you need to understand:

1. Value stocks

2. Growth stocks

3. Blended stocks

Throughout history, we have experienced periods when one of the four major classes of stock has dramatically outperformed the others. For example, in any given year, U.S. large-cap stocks might perform substantially better than U.S. small-/mid-cap stocks. But there can also be large differences in performance of stocks (or stock mutual funds) that invest in the same class. To explain, let's consider the performance of large-cap stock funds in the late 1990s. Some large-cap stock funds performed exceptionally well during the Giddy Years of the 1990s, only to plunge during the Gruesome Years of the early 2000s. Other large-cap funds (or individual stocks, for that matter) performed at a slower pace during the 1990s but held up fairly well during the Gruesome Years that followed. The difference in both performance and volatility of these large-cap funds was the result of what subclass of stock was used to build each portfolio. Some funds were composed of value stocks, while others consisted of growth or blended stocks.

VALUE STOCKS Value stocks are stocks of those companies that are reasonably priced in today's market. Think of them as bargain stocks. Some value stocks are so out of favor that they are bargain basement stocks or deep value stocks. One example of a deep value stock today is Phillip Morris (Altria Group). Here is a large, old, profitable company whose stock is so ugly no one wants to own it!

Yes, they manufacture cigarettes (and have litigation nightmares because of this). But they also own and manufacture products such as Kraft Foods. This company is a deep value stock and today's market price is deeply discounted. On January 27, 2003, the company changed its name to Altria Group, Inc. If the management were to break up the company and sell off the various businesses, the separate businesses would have a value greater than the price of today's Altria Group stock.

You may not want to own a tobacco stock for a number of reasons. In fact, you may not want to own any deep value stocks because, while they offer an opportunity for great returns, they also represent a great deal of risk. But what about normal, everyday value stocks? There are many great companies operating profitable (often boring) businesses. Many of these quiet companies are seldom mentioned in the financial press. A business making steady profits may not be in the headlines, but it can be a great company to own.

Many mutual fund managers focus their efforts on finding these value stocks for their portfolios. They are seeking quality stocks at bargain prices. For that reason they are called value money managers and they manage value-style mutual funds. What are these money managers looking for in a company? First, value-style managers are looking for companies with unrecognized value. They are looking for stocks trading at low market prices relative to their potential earnings. One example of a company's unrecognized value might be the company's superior management. The company might be in an industry going through major changes, but if it has great management, it can weather the storm and create fortunes for the owners (stockholders) of the company. A great historical example is Chrysler. Several years ago, it was questionable whether Chrysler would survive. In 1978, Lee Iacocca, creator of the Ford Mustang, was hired in an effort to turn Chrysler around. He had to beg Congress for loans and convince suppliers to reduce their prices and make other concessions to Chrysler. He also had to plead his case with the auto unions. He had to solidify the management team of the company. Iacocca was able to put all the necessary pieces together to turn the company around. At the time, the market questioned whether the company would survive. But those who invested in this stodgy auto manufacturing company were well rewarded.

Some value companies have strong name recognition. In many cases, their names and products dominate their industries. Three great examples come to mind: Coca-Cola, Gillette, and American Express. All three names have world recognition. This creates a competitive edge for each company in its particular industry. Let's consider Gillette. This company enjoys worldwide name recognition and dominates the shaving industry. It still owns all the machinery used in past decades to make its prior designs of razor blades and warehouses these old machines in Boston when not in use. Why? Many of those older-model, less expensive blades are manufactured for developing countries. Men in developing countries may not be able to afford the newest and latest blade design offered by Gillette, but they can afford the older model blades now manufactured in emerging countries where labor costs are relatively low. Remember, all of the development costs of these old machines were written off years ago. Therefore, the start-up costs are minimal when setting up an assembly line using this older equipment for a new market for these low-cost products.

Value-style money managers are always looking for the opportunity to buy great companies at a discount to their real value. Many value stocks pay a substantial annual dividend. This current dividend income can reward investors with a nice income while they wait for the market to recognize the value of the company. Phillip Morris/Altria Group, Inc., a deep value, heavily discounted stock today, is paying over 7 percent in annual dividends. Don't like cigarettes? Then look for dividend-paying, out-of-favor value stocks such as well-run banks' stocks. Many of these pay a higher dividend to their stockholders than they pay in interest to the bank CD holders. You have a choice: You can loan money to the bank and earn 2 to 4 percent in interest, or you can own the bank and earn that much or possibly more in current dividends. If you own the bank, you have the potential for rising dividends from rising bank profits and the potential for a rising stock price as the stock appreciates in value.

Careful, methodical research is the key to the success of value-style money managers. Typically, they approach stock buying as if they were buying the entire company. They want to know, "Is this a great company to own?"

If you were to buy a company, what would you want to know about the company before you bought it? Let's assume a clothing store is for sale in your town and you are considering purchasing the business. You would most likely seek out the answers to several questions. For example, you would check out the lease, especially if the location was critical. If you discover the lease is about to expire, with no chance of being renewed, you may well be less interested in the store. Next, you would probably talk to the employees. What if the key employees, including the tailors, were resigning to open up a new competing clothing store directly across the street? Again, this information would be a key factor in your decision. What about the quality of the inventory? If the inventory consisted of out-of-style double-knit polyester leisure suits from the 1970s, you'd have to be concerned about other details of this business. Perhaps the seller insists the company is very profitable. To check this out, you talk to the competition and the seller's suppliers. What if you discover the seller has a poor reputation and is in debt to most of his or her creditors? All these details are essential to your final decision. This same attention to fundamental research is the key to success for a value-style money manager.

Here is a tip to help you remember value-style money managers. Think of these managers as catfish. Catfish aren't necessarily built for speed, but they have other very important talents. Catfish carefully search for food in the murky waters at the bottom of lakes and rivers. They find delight in those morsels others often overlook. Their skill is in careful selection. Value-style money managers are recognized for their skill in buying. They have to make sure the companies they buy are only temporarily out of favor and not going out of business. Their stock selections typically pay dividends, so they have income while they wait for their stocks to be discovered by the rest of the market.

In summary, value stocks are often boring, often out-of-favor companies that can be quite profitable over time. Many experts consider Warren Buffett and John Templeton the top money managers of the twentieth century. Warren Buffett is the leading value-style money manager focused on U.S. stocks. John Templeton (now retired) was the leading value-style money manager focused on foreign companies. The Templeton mutual funds carry on his tradition.

Many of today's world-recognized money managers have devoted their financial careers to finding those companies that offer the best value. Seek them out!

GROWTH STOCKS There are other great companies whose stocks are called growth stocks. The key ingredient for a growth company is growth of earnings. Growth companies typically pay little if anything in dividends. They prefer to plow their profits back into the company for expansion and continued growth. As these companies grow in sales and earnings, they become more valuable, which pushes up the price of their stock in the market. A successful growth company typically trades at a higher price-to-earnings (P/E) ratio than a profitable value company. The growth investor is willing to pay more for the anticipated future growth of a growth stock than the boring current profits and dividends of a value stock. Growth companies may be large, well-established companies or smaller, newer companies. They are often the leading companies in rapidly growing industries. Peter Lynch was recognized as a leading growth-style money manager during the years he managed the Fidelity Magellan Fund.

Back in March of 2000 (the end of the bull market), the typical growth-style mutual fund had a portfolio of stocks with a P/E of over 40, while the portfolio of the typical value-style fund had a P/E of only 22.5. At that time, the growth-style managers were willing to pay almost twice as much for their portfolios, anticipating continued growth of earnings from their stocks.

Two leading growth industries today are the technology and health care industries. They have also enjoyed very favorable news coverage, as their new products are often very innovative and exciting to learn about. Many of the stories are about new companies. Unfortunately, many new start-up tech stocks are anything but safe! These smaller growth stocks often demand a P/E ratio up to five times greater than value stocks of proven companies. Please remember: It is always dangerous to invest in companies that are not making money. For every 11 hot new tech stocks coming to market, roughly 10 will fail. These are not good odds! Many of these new tech and biotech companies do not have a positive cash flow from sales. The only way they are creating cash is by selling more stock and borrowing more money. Since they are not yet profitable, the only way you as a stockholder can profit is if you can sell your stock to someone else who is willing to pay you a higher price for the right to own this company's possible future profits. New start-up companies are exciting, but their stocks can be risky to own. In fact, you don't have to buy technology-focused or biotech stocks from small, start-up companies in order to own growth stocks. There are many large, established growth companies from which you can choose.

The key to successful stock ownership is diversification, not dupli-cation. It is important to own both growth-style and value-style com-panies ranging from small-/mid-cap to large-cap in size. Often, an idea begins with a small start-up growth company. Then a larger, well-established growth company buys the smaller growth compa-nies. The larger growth companies have the capital to fully develop the idea or product and successfully bring it to market. The compa-nies that most likely will be the end users of the technological advances created by these growth companies will be the value com-panies. For example, General Motors, a value company, purchases new computer technology from growth companies. As a result, GM can upgrade the quality of its cars while improving efficiency. The company can reduce its costs and improve profits at the same time.

A money manager who specializes in growth stocks is called a growth-style money manager. The first thing he or she examines is the history of growth in earnings. The computer is an important tool for most growth managers because they can load the statistics of all the stocks in their universe into a database to search out those stocks that meet their criteria. For example, some managers are looking for small-cap companies with a recent growth rate of 25 percent or more to fit into an aggressive portfolio. Other growth managers are more conservative, perhaps seeking large-cap stocks with a more modest 15 to 25 percent growth rate history. Here are the names of a few of the large growth companies that led the bull market of the 1990s: Microsoft, Intel, Oracle, Qualcomm, Cisco Sys-tems, Amgen, and Amazon.com. At times, growth companies can be both exciting and rewarding to own.

Here is a tip to help you identify growth-style money managers. Think of them as falcons. These magnificent birds love speed and have no fear of heights. Growth-style managers are attracted to high-flying stocks that are rapidly growing their earnings. They are attracted to companies that are trading at higher P/E ratios than the average stock. They typically rely on computers to help them in their search for stocks that meet their buying criteria. Their skills are not so much in buying; rather, they use computers to help select their stocks. Their skill is in selling. When a growth stock fails to meet its projected rate of growth, the stock can plunge in value. A successful growth-style manager recognizes when it is time to sell a stock. It is time to sell when the company's current and projected growth rate no longer meets previous expectations.

Let's look at one very large growth company, Cisco Systems, to see how profitable growth stocks can be. In 1999, Cisco passed Microsoft to become the second-most valuable company in the United States. (General Electric was number one.) That year, the value of Cisco's stock was greater than $555 billion.

Everyone has heard of General Electric. But what do we know about Cisco? It first went public in 1990. The company was founded just four years earlier. Its stock exploded in price during the 1990s, enjoying annual returns of nearly 100 percent per year over that 10-year period. But it was a volatile ride. There were short periods (typically a month or two) within 8 of the 10 years when the stock price dropped 20 percent or more before quickly recovering and again surging in price. In 2 of the 10 years, Cisco's stock experienced major losses. The stock plunged 54 percent in 1994 and 38 percent in 1997.

From March of 1999 to March of 2000, Cisco's stock tripled in price. Its revenue grew 53 percent over the previous 12 months. This was explosive growth for the second-largest company in America. Analysts were anticipating that revenues would grow by 50 percent for calendar year 2000 and by more than 35 percent for the two years after that. Unfortunately, continued growth was not to happen, as the Gruesome Years of the early 2000s put an end to the 1990s bull market. Cisco peaked in early 2000 at over $75 per share. Today it trades around $15 per share.

In the future, growth stocks, including Cisco, will again be in favor. As you invest in future technology, make sure you are well diversified. The technology portion of your portfolio should include semiconductor, computer hardware, software, communications equipment, and Internet companies. If you are not experienced in these fields, find one or more top-quality growth mutual funds that will help you achieve this important diversification. Make sure you own both large caps and small/mid caps in the growth stock portion of your portfolio.

BLENDED STOCKS Some money managers don't fit either the value style or the growth style mold. Their style of management falls in between these two. They lean toward buying growth stocks, but they are unwilling to pay as high a price for a growing company as a growth-style money manager might. You might say they are looking for growth stocks at a reasonable price. They are often attracted to stocks of companies transitioning from being a value stock to becoming a growth stock. They are also looking for those growth stocks that are out of favor at the time.

At times, value stocks have dramatically outperformed growth stocks and vice versa. There have also been times when the blended-style managers have excelled in performance. The better mutual fund money managers have learned to focus on the one style of money management for which they are best suited.

Caution!

Some managers do not follow a disciplined approach. They change their portfolios from value stocks to growth stocks, from small stocks to large stocks, in hopes of being in the right place at the right time. It is difficult, if not impossible, to time the market successfully over a significant period of time. If you jump from one style to another and then back again, you must be right on every move to be successful. If you miss one move, it can cause disastrous results, creating wild swings in your portfolio performance. I do not know of even one money manager who has been successful at timing the market over a long period.

Realistic Expectations

Seek out money managers who are true to a specific investment style. This is an important step in controlling the risk of your portfolio. The best mutual fund managers select one investment approach and then stick with it. On any given day, the market may not appreciate their approach, but over meaningful periods of time they will reward investors because they followed a specific investment style (be it value, growth, or blended). History tells us there is no clear way to project whether growth stocks or value stocks will be the better performer in any given year. History also suggests it makes sense to allocate a portion of your equities to growth and a portion to value. You might also consider investing a small amount in a fund that utilizes the blended style of management. By allocating portions of your portfolio to these various equity subclasses, you are reducing the volatility of your overall portfolio without hurting your long-term performance. You may not experience the emotional highs of 100 percent + rates of return, but you will avoid the emotional despair brought on by 70 to 90 percent losses.

When Do You Buy What?

When should you buy small-cap companies? When should you sell your large-cap stocks? When should you own value stocks? Should you concentrate on growth stocks right now? What about foreign stocks? Are they in or out of favor today? My suggestion is to own them all at all times. This is called *asset allocation*. If you own individual stocks, make sure you own both value stocks and growth stocks. If you are using mutual funds, make sure the money managers you have chosen are focused on one specific style of management. Own several equity funds to make sure you are allocated with the various management styles as well as at least two of the four major equity asset classes. Make sure the equity funds you own are not duplicates of each other. Owning five large-cap growth-style funds is not diversification, it is only duplication.

The first four asset classes consist of equity markets. Stocks represent business ownership, providing investors with the opportunity to enjoy the profits that are possible as a result of owning successful businesses. As a stockholder of a publicly traded company, you have the opportunity to enjoy business ownership without being forced to own the entire company. You can enjoy a steady paycheck by working for your current employer and you can benefit from ownership in other companies (stocks) at the same time. That is a winning combination! If you are an aggressive long-term investor, this may be adequate diversification for your needs. But many investors want less volatility, less market risk, and greater predictability of future performance. To accomplish this, you should diversify your portfolio even further by allocating a portion of your assets to bonds, real estate, and even cash. Let's consider bonds.

Bonds

Bonds are loans. They can be loans to the U.S. government (government bonds), state and local municipalities (municipal bonds), corporations (corporate bonds), or foreign governments (foreign bonds).

Figure 3.1 is a simple illustration that shows the historical effects

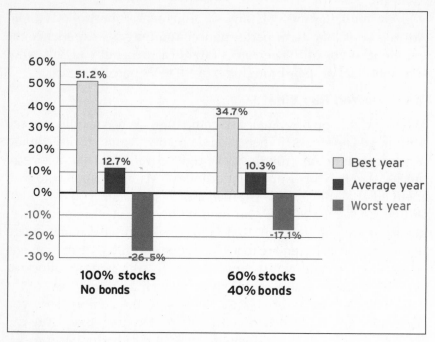

FIGURE 3.1   Fifty-year period from 1951 to 2000.

of adding bonds to a portfolio for additional diversification. The left side of the figure shows the returns of owning a portfolio that is 100 percent stocks. Over this 50-year period, the S&P 500 returned on average 12.7 percent. That is an excellent return, but there was a lot of volatility along the way. The best-performing year enjoyed a gain of 51.2 percent. The worst-performing year suffered a loss of 26.5 percent. It is the volatility that upsets the stomach, not the 12.7 percent average rate of return.

On the right side of the figure a blend of 60 percent in stocks and 40 percent in bonds is shown. The downside risk was reduced by over 30 percent, with the worst year being down 17.1 percent. Both the upside and the downside volatility were lower, creating a steadier, more predictable return. The average return over the 50-year period was a very respectable 10.3 percent. It is true that the total return was lower, but the volatility has been dramatically reduced.

Let's take a closer look at bonds. Just as we have seen subclasses in stock portfolios, there are also subclasses in bonds. Some are boring, but others are definitely not. Let's look at a few main subclasses of bonds.

U.S. GOVERNMENT BONDS These are the most conservative bonds available. The timely payment of interest and the return of principal at maturity are backed by the federal government. That doesn't mean there is no risk in owning U.S. government bonds. There are several risks:

- Income tax risk
- Inflation risk
- Market risk

Let's first consider the tax and inflation risks. Today's 30-year U.S. government bonds are yielding approximately 5 percent. If you are in the 30 percent bracket and are anticipating a 2 percent rate of inflation over the next 30 years, Table 3.3 shows the result.

If there is a surge in inflation, or an increase in your tax rates, you could see your profits disappear.

Next, let's look at how bonds react to changes in interest rates. When interest rates go down, bonds appreciate in value. Interest rates peaked in the early 1980s. As interest rates on U.S. government bonds declined from a high above 14 percent to a low below 5 percent, the bond market experienced its largest rally in history. But let's not forget there is market risk in owning bonds. If interest rates go up, existing bonds will decline in value.

Table 3.4 shows how small movements in interest rates will either increase or decrease the value of a $1,000 bond.

If interest rates increase by 1 percent (from 5 percent to 6 percent), the value of a 30-year bond will drop to approximately $871. That would be a loss of approximately 13 percent. (Keep in mind that you are earning 5 percent in interest, which will ease the pain of this drop in principal.)

TABLE 3.3

Net Rate of Return for Tax-Free Municipal Bonds	
Gross yield from taxable bond	5%
Inflation	Less 2%
Taxes at 30%	Less 1.5%
Net return after inflation and taxes	1.5%

TABLE 3.4

Interest Rate Change	5-Year Bond	20-Year Bond	30-Year Bond
+1.5%	$946	$897	$816
+1.0%	$964	$930	$871
+0.5%	$982	$964	$932
0	$1,000	$1,000	$1,000
−0.5%	$1,019	$1,038	$1,075
−1.0%	$1,038	$1,077	$1,159
−1.5%	$1,057	$1,118	$1,252

RISK VERSUS REWARD Because interest rates are at 41-year lows, we have to consider the risk of owning bonds versus the reward of owning bonds.

First, let's consider the reward side of owning bonds today. In the past, we saw interest rates on long-term U.S. government bonds drop from over 14 percent to under 5 percent. That nine-point drop in interest rates from 1981 to 2003 created an incredible bull market in bonds. Today's yield (roughly 5 percent) is relatively low, but we could see some additional appreciation if interest rates continue to drop. Mathematically, the most we could see interest rates decline is five points (from today's 5 percent to zero). That is highly unlikely. We might see a drop in interest rates to perhaps 3 to 4 percent over the next several years, but even that is questionable. If rates do in fact decline, there could be additional appreciation in bonds, but it is limited.

On the other hand, interest rates could go up. How high could rates go? No one knows, but remember, long-term government bond rates exceeded 14 percent in 1981. Is it possible we could see those exceptionally high rates again? Yes, but I don't believe it will happen. If it did, it would create a tremendous loss for today's bondholders. Table 3.5 clarifies the risk of owning 30-year U.S. government bonds that are currently yielding 5 percent. If interest rates increase in the near future, these bonds will lose a substantial percentage of their current value.

Today's reward for owning long-term U.S. government bonds is limited, while the risk is unlimited. Because interest rates are at 41-year lows, it makes sense to own bonds with shorter maturities.

TABLE 3.5

Future Interest Rates	Percentage Decline in 30-Year Bond Value
6%	−13%
7%	−24%
8%	−33%
9%	−40%

Consider owning bonds that mature in 5 to 10 years rather than the longer 20- to 30-year time periods. The interest paid on the shorter-maturity bonds is slightly less, but the volatility is minimized. The main reason for owning U.S. government bonds today is portfolio defense. Historically, when the stock market has dropped dramatically, worried investors have left the stock market and sought the safety of U.S. government bonds. That has been the pattern over and over. Most of us remember the Crash of 1987. As the stock market was experiencing record losses, the U.S. government bond market was experiencing record appreciation. We again saw the defensive value of owning government bonds during the Gruesome Years of the early 2000s. Let's look at just one year. In 2000, the Nasdaq suffered losses of 39 percent. The return on U.S. government bonds was a positive 21.48 percent. Who could have guessed that bonds could outperform the Nasdaq by over 60 percent in one year!

There are two relatively new types of government bonds you might want to consider. The first is called Treasury Inflation-Protected Securities (TIPS). These 10-year maturity bonds are designed to offer protection against rising inflation and rising interest rates. TIPS pay interest every six months and the principal is adjusted to account for inflation. Unfortunately, you are taxed each year on the interest and on the accrued addition to the bond principal, but you won't receive the accrued addition until the bond matures.

There is a second new choice called a Series I savings bond (I-bond). You can purchase only $30,000 worth of these bonds per year. They compound with inflation-indexed earnings for up to 30 years. With I-bonds, you don't pay taxes until you cash them in.

TIPS and I-bonds are relatively new. There is little history to indicate how they will perform in the long run. The current interest they pay is lower than that for other government bonds, but they could credit more if inflation rates increase dramatically in the years to come.

MUNICIPAL BONDS Municipalities such as states, cities, and counties issue municipal bonds ("munis"). The interest they pay is free from federal income tax. If you purchase bonds from municipalities within your state of residence, the interest you receive will be both federal and state income tax free. Munis are attractive for those investors focused on reducing their income tax risk. Historically, munis are second to U.S. government bonds when it comes to timely payment of interest and return of principal at maturity. Interest rates paid on munis are typically lower than those for U.S. government bonds, but they are very appealing to investors in high tax brackets. Table 3.6 shows an example of the net rate of return for munis today.

Tax-free munis offer a great buy for many of today's investors because the current yields are so close to taxable bond yields. The higher your tax bracket, the more attractive the net return on munis will be. Just keep in mind that there is market risk in all bonds, just as there is in other types of investments. If interest rates go up, there will be a drop in the market value of the bonds.

Never put municipal bonds in an IRA. There is absolutely no advantage to putting low-interest munis in a tax-free or tax-deferred program. Use U.S. government and/or corporate bonds in IRAs, because they pay higher interest rates.

QUALITY CORPORATE BONDS The yields on corporate bonds are normally greater than those for U.S. government and muni bonds because there is greater credit risk. The risk is that the issuing corporation may not be able to pay the interest when due or return the amount borrowed when the bond matures. Because they pay higher interest to investors willing to accept the additional credit

TABLE 3.6

Net Rate of Return for Tax-Free Municipal Bonds	
Gross yield from muni bonds	4.5%
Inflation	Less 2%
No federal income taxes	Less 0%
Net return after inflation and taxes	2.5%

risk, corporate bonds can be the most rewarding fixed income investment. For this reason, corporate bonds are rated according to credit risk. At one extreme, there are the highest-quality AAA corporate bonds; at the other end, there are low-quality bonds, often referred to as *junk bonds*.

HIGH-YIELDING CORPORATE JUNK BONDS Lower-quality, higher-yielding corporate bonds are loans to companies with lower credit ratings. These higher-yielding bonds are often called *junk bonds* because there is a greater risk of default. They pay a higher interest rate to compensate the bondholder for the additional risk of default.

Junk bonds have a greater risk of default, but they are less sensitive to interest rate movements than U.S. government, muni, and top-quality corporate bonds. Why? Junk bonds are already paying a higher rate of interest than the rest of the bond market, so they are far less sensitive to interest rate changes. Changes in the credit rating of the corporation issuing the bond have the greatest effect on the price of junk bonds. If the credit rating of the company improves, the junk bond price will appreciate. But, if the creditworthiness of the company drops, the price of the junk bond will drop. Junk bonds act more like stocks than bonds, because their value is so sensitive to the profits of the company. The ideal junk bond to buy would be one paying a high current interest rate that is on the verge of being upgraded as to its creditworthiness.

Let's take a look in Table 3.7 at just one year, 1999 (the last year of the most recent bull market), to see how different types of bonds can react in any given year.

Most bonds were not popular in 1999, as the country was enjoying the last year of a tremendous bull market in stocks. You can see that different sectors of the bond market reacted to different economic events that year. Junk bonds went up in value, as they reflected the positive stock market that year.

TABLE 3.7

Sector of the Bond Market	1999 Total Return
30-year U.S. treasuries	−8.61%
Municipal Bonds	−6.34%
Junk corporate bonds	+2.51%

One year later, government bonds enjoyed a positive total return of over 21 percent and muni bonds returned a positive 16 percent, as investors fled the stock market and rushed to the security provided by U.S. government and muni bonds.

In the case of junk bonds, where credit risk is involved, diversification is critically important. This is an area of bond management best left to the pros, such as mutual fund managers, who can carefully select, monitor, and diversify a portfolio of high-yielding corporate bonds.

FOREIGN GOVERNMENT BONDS You might also consider investing a small portion of your bond portfolio in foreign government bonds. Government bonds of developed countries, such as Great Britain, Germany, Switzerland, and others, offer a layer of protection in the case of a major drop in the value of U.S. currency. Historically, we have seen periods when the value of the U.S. dollar has dropped dramatically when compared to foreign currencies. During those periods, investors who owned foreign government bonds saw those bonds appreciate in value. It's not the current yield on foreign government bonds that makes them so attractive; it's the appreciation potential they provide during periods when the U.S. dollar drops in value. You might consider investing 5 to 10 percent of your bond portfolio in foreign government bonds.

Again, diversification and careful selection are most important. Consider mutual funds for their expertise in creating and managing a diversified portfolio of foreign bonds.

Real Estate

Real estate is one more investment sector you should consider as part of your asset allocation strategy. One way to participate is by owning several real estate investment trusts (REITs). A REIT is a publicly traded company that focuses on real estate rather than stocks and bonds. Some REITs own mortgages on homes and/or commercial property. These REITs have performed well over the last few years as the mortgages they own have appreciated as interest rates dropped. Other REITs, called *equity REITs,* own commercial properties. Equity REITs focus on one or more types of commercial properties, such as apartments, motels, shopping centers, offices, warehouses, and factories. The performance of REITs invested in commercial properties tends to lag behind corporate earnings.

REITs generally provide the investor with a fairly steady stream of dividend income. The average REIT currently pays slightly less than 4 percent in dividends. Many yield up to 8 percent and some yield even more. The income is not fixed, so it will change over time as the REIT management changes the properties in the portfolio. The dividend income and the total return are dependent on what type of real estate is involved. For example, apartment buildings appreciate the most when there are large numbers of young adults ready to leave their parents' homes. Shopping centers appreciate when retailers are enjoying record sales, as many leases are tied to the sales revenue of the tenants. Let's look at Table 3.8 to see the recent history and compare the performance of REITS to that of the S&P 500.

REITs, like bonds, don't track the stock market. At times REITs have outperformed the stock market, and at other times it has been the other way around. Table 3.8 shows how well REITs performed in recent years when corporate profits were suffering. REITs will probably trail the stock market in future years as corporate earnings get back on a profitable track.

Diversification is critically important when owning commercial real estate. Therefore, it makes sense to own well-managed mutual funds that specialize in REIT investments. Because REITs react differently than stocks and bonds, you should consider allocating 5 to 10 percent of your total portfolio to a few diversified mutual funds that specialize in REITs. Make sure the REIT mutual funds you choose aren't buying the same type of real estate. Remember, you want diversification, not duplication.

TABLE 3.8

Year	S&P 500	REITs
2000	−9.1%	+21.89%
2001	−15.5%	+11.89%
2002	−23.4%	+2.63%

Courtesy of Morningstar

Asset Allocation Models for Your Current Investments

There is no such thing as a perfect investment or a perfect asset allocation, but I suggest you start with one of the three following templates, especially for your current investments. If you are very conservative and looking for a portfolio that will provide current income, consider Figure 3.2 for your current investments.

In this conservative model, 20 percent is invested in large-cap U.S. stocks. Make sure you divide this portion into value- and growth-style stocks. If you are very conservative, consider 60 percent in value stocks and 40 percent in growth stocks. In this conservative allocation, 70 percent is invested in bonds. If you are very conservative, consider 65 percent in U.S. government bonds and the remaining 35 percent in high-quality corporate bonds. If you feel comfortable with a bit more risk, consider reducing the U.S. government bond portion to 55 percent and adding 10 percent in junk bonds. This income model is ideal for retired investors age 65 and over, because income is their primary concern. They need to continue growing a portion of their capital (20 percent) in large-cap U.S. stocks to meet future income needs.

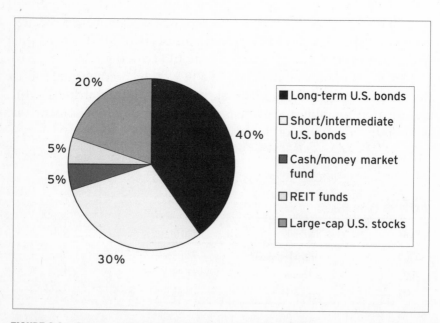

FIGURE 3.2   Conservative income asset allocation model.

If you are looking for more growth of your capital and less current income, consider the growth and income asset allocation model shown in Figure 3.3.

Divide both the large-cap and small-/mid-cap portions into both value and growth stocks. If you are using mutual funds, consider investing a portion with a manager who uses a blended style of managing stocks. If you use just value and growth styles, consider putting half in each. If you want to be a bit more conservative, put 60 percent in value stocks with 40 percent in growth stocks. Remember to divide your bond portions to include U.S. government bonds, muni bonds (for taxable investment accounts only), and corporate bonds. Because interest rates are at a 41-year low, consider reducing your exposure to long-term bonds. At this time, consider bonds maturing in 10 years. If you can accept a bit more volatility, add a bit of junk bonds to the equation. This model also includes 5 percent in REITs and 5 percent in stocks of developed foreign nations. A growth and income model is ideal for investors between the ages of 55 and 65. They can shift to an income model when they retire.

If you are more concerned about growing your capital and you are willing to accept more volatility to achieve greater returns over

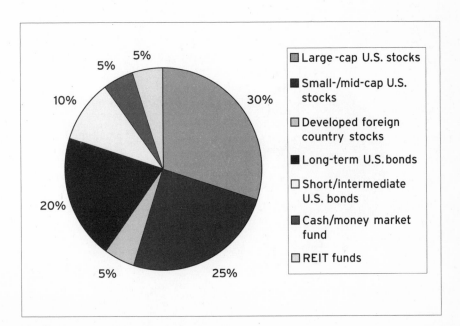

FIGURE 3.3 Growth and income asset allocation model.

time, consider the growth model shown in Figure 3.4. There are no bonds or real estate in this model. It is focused on stocks. To control the volatility and improve the return over time, it is important to split your equity portfolios into value and growth stocks, especially for the U.S. stock portions of this model. Most foreign market money managers follow the value style of management.

The growth asset allocation model will be subject to greater market volatility because it is 100 percent in stocks, but it also provides the greatest opportunity to build your capital over time. This model is ideal for investors younger than age 55 who have many years to build capital before retirement.

These three models should serve as your guideline. You can tweak one of the models to establish your personalized model if you choose to do so. Once your portfolio is established, avoid making needless emotion-based changes. Consider changes only if there has been drastic alteration in your tolerance for risk or in your need for immediate income.

These asset allocation models work because they minimize emotional decisions. Once you have established and funded your model, stay with it and give it time to work. As time goes by, you

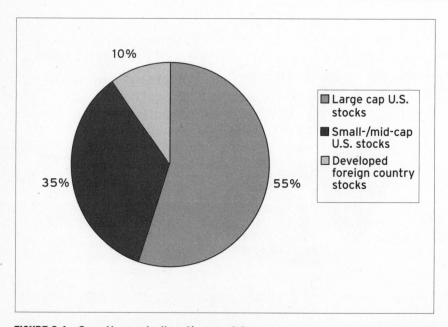

FIGURE 3.4   Growth asset allocation model.

will experience changes in your portfolio. For example, stocks may take off over the next few years with returns of 15 to 20 percent. If this happens, it will change the percentages each asset class represents in your model. You need to consider rebalancing your portfolio periodically to bring it back to your original allocation. In my example, you need to take your gains in the stock market and redistribute the proceeds to the other portions of your portfolio. History tells us that, over time, rebalancing can increase your return. Of greater importance, periodic rebalancing reduces your future risk, because you reduce your exposure to highly appreciated assets. Rebalancing forces you to follow an old rule about investing: Buy low, sell high.

These models are designed to work with lump sums of existing capital. There is a different strategy that will help you build capital with new investment dollars. It is called *dollar-cost averaging*.

Dollar-cost Averaging

Whether you already have a large investment portfolio or not, you need to continue building your capital. The best way to build new capital is with dollar-cost averaging. Asset allocation tames the market volatility of an existing investment portfolio. Dollar-cost averaging tames the volatility of future investments as you build your portfolio by investing on a periodic basis. History tells us that an aggressive portfolio of stocks creates the greatest investment opportunity over time. The problem has been the volatility and what that does to your emotions. Dollar-cost averaging makes it possible to invest in a stock portfolio and put that volatility to work for you rather than against you. This investing technique allows the investor to take advantage of volatility and turn it into profits.

Let's look at the part of a market cycle that sends chills down the spine of every investor—a severe down market. Figure 3.5 shows an extremely volatile period for investing. It illustrates an aggressive stock (or portfolio) beginning at $10 per share, dropping to a low of $1 per share before returning to $10 per share. Let's assume there are 100 shares of stock worth $1,000 at the beginning of this period.

This would be a very painful investment experience for most investors. The original investment was $1,000. During the second period of time (perhaps a month later), the price per share dropped to $5, reducing the account's value to $500. During the third period, the price plunged to $1 per share. This is where panic sets in.

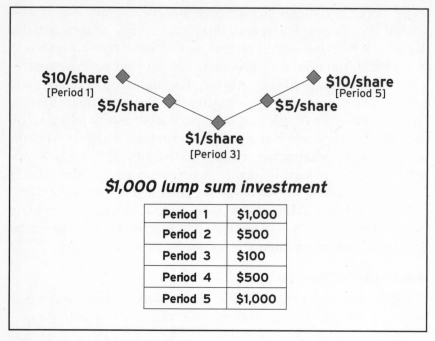

$1,000 lump sum investment

Period 1	$1,000
Period 2	$500
Period 3	$100
Period 4	$500
Period 5	$1,000

FIGURE 3.5 Severe down market.

History tells us that many would sell at a price below $10 per share just to get away from the volatility.

Some investors would weather the storm until they broke even. When the stock returned to $10 a share, they would most likely sell out, happy to get back their $1,000. The time period of this down market could be a few short months or several years. The longer the time period, the greater the emotional pain.

These down cycles can be very rewarding for investors if they invest periodically, using the technique of dollar-cost averaging illustrated in Figure 3.6.

Let's assume this illustration covers a period of five months. Rather than investing a lump sum, let's also assume investments of $200 were made each month. Ideally, every investor would love to invest only at the bottom of the market, but no one knows when that might be. With dollar-cost averaging, the market determines the best time to buy the greatest number of shares. In the first month, the stock (or mutual fund) is priced at $10 per share. A $200 investment would purchase 20 shares. In this example, the greatest

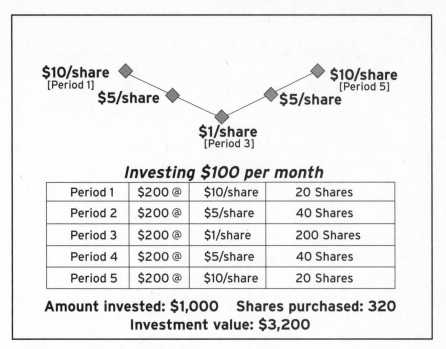

$10/share
[Period 1]
$5/share
$1/share
[Period 3]
$10/share
[Period 5]
$5/share

Investing $100 per month

Period 1	$200 @	$10/share	20 Shares
Period 2	$200 @	$5/share	40 Shares
Period 3	$200 @	$1/share	200 Shares
Period 4	$200 @	$5/share	40 Shares
Period 5	$200 @	$10/share	20 Shares

Amount invested: $1,000   Shares purchased: 320
Investment value: $3,200

FIGURE 3.6   Dollar-cost averaging.

number of shares was bought in the third month when the price was $1 per share ($200 at $1 per share buys 200 shares). By the end of this five-month period, the investor has accumulated 320 shares. The $1,000 invested over the period of time now has a value of $3,200. This simple example illustrates one of the best ways to invest periodically. It is a great strategy for building wealth in IRAs and qualified plans where you have the opportunity to add money on a periodic basis.

When will dollar-cost averaging not work? First, you must give it time. This market cycle must run its course, whether it is a few months or several years. If you stop your periodic/monthly invest- ing and liquidate your portfolio, you could easily sustain a loss. Second, it will not work if the stock you are purchasing does not recover from its low. In our example, if the stock stays at $1 you will have a substantial loss. For this reason, it is best to use this tech- nique with a diversified stock portfolio rather than one stock. Con- sider using a growth or growth and income portfolio for dollar-cost averaging. The growth account will be more aggressive than the growth and income account. These growth and growth and income accounts are available in investment products such as mutual funds, variable annuities, and variable life insurance policies.

To make sure dollar-cost averaging has the best chance for success, create a monthly investment program with the money withdrawn automatically from your checking or savings account. If your employer sponsors a retirement plan, you can participate by having funds automatically withdrawn from your paycheck. Automatic investing reduces the emotional decision-making process. Often, the best time to invest is when the news from the financial press makes you feel depressed. Keep in mind that only the market and history can tell you the best time to invest. Make the best of bad times with dollar-cost averaging.

Recovering from Substantial Losses

In recent years, many investors have experienced substantial losses in all or part of their portfolio. Unfortunately, most have no plan to correct the situation. I hear comments like, "There's not much I can do. I'll just have to weather the storm and wait until the market recovers." Others respond, "I can't deal with it! I don't even open up my monthly investment statements any more. It's just too depressing!" Let's look at this problem and create a realistic plan to repair the damage.

Let's assume a married couple invested $100,000 in aggressive high-tech stocks in the late 1990s. Unfortunately, these aggressive stocks peaked in early 2000. For example, the average stock listed on the Nasdaq plunged 70 percent in the Gruesome Years. In early 2003, the original $100,000 would have been worth only $30,000. If the couple does nothing, one of several things could happen:

- The stocks might recover as rapidly as 20 percent, 30 percent, or maybe even 40 percent per year.

- They could recover at roughly 10 percent per year (which the market has averaged over the last 75 years).

- They could recover at a much slower rate.

- Several of the companies could declare bankruptcy and the stock could become worthless.

Figure 3.7 paints a clear picture of how long it might take to break even if this couple takes a wait-and-see approach with these losses.

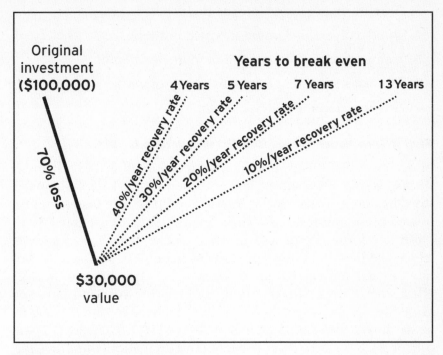

Original investment ($100,000)

Years to break even

4 Years   5 Years   7 Years   13 Years

70% loss

40%/year recovery rate
30%/year recovery rate
20%/year recovery rate
10%/year recovery rate

$30,000
value

FIGURE 3.7   Years to break even.

If they are lucky enough to consistently earn 40 percent per year, they will be back to breaking even in just 4 years. That is possible, but highly unlikely. Maybe their stocks will bounce back at the rate of 30 percent per year. If that happens, they can break even in just five years. At 20 percent per year, it will take seven years. If the recovery rate averages 10 percent per year, they will be back to $100,000 in 13 years.

Unfortunately, this picture is not the whole story. Historically, stocks that have dropped 70 percent or more tend to underperform the rest of the market going forward. Why? Losses of this magnitude indicate there are serious problems with the company (such as bad management) or major problems with the entire industry in which that company participates. Many of the stocks in the Nasdaq will take as long as 15 to 25 years to recover their losses.

This couple can sit and wait, or they can take action. I suggest following my four-step process to recover from large losses:

1. Turn the paper losses into tax-deductible losses.

2. Build a diversified, asset-allocated portfolio.

3. Continue to invest 1 percent or more per month.

4. Use tax-sheltered investments going forward.

Let's take a closer look at each step.

Step 1: Turn Paper Losses into Tax-Deductible Losses

In our example, this couple had a paper loss of $70,000. If these stocks are sold, the resulting loss is tax deductible. Let's assume the stock has been owned for at least a year. If so, the losses will be treated as long-term losses. Their first option is to use this loss to offset taxes due on the sale of other stocks that have long-term gains. The Jobs and Growth Tax Relief Act of 2003 reduced the tax rate on long-term gains to 15 percent. Perhaps this couple sold other stock with a $70,000 profit earlier in the year and have set aside $10,500 for taxes. By also selling the stocks with $70,000 in losses during the same year, they will save $10,500 in taxes (15 percent of $70,000 gain). This tax benefit can dramatically improve the starting point for the portfolio recovery. The couple has both the $30,000 in cash (received at the sale of the stock) and the tax savings of $10,500 that can be invested. In this example, that changes the starting point for recovery by over 30 percent.

Our investors may not have offsetting long-term gains to take at this point in time. They can then use this $70,000 loss to offset taxes due on ordinary income. Their current marginal tax bracket might be 30 percent or higher. If so, they can use $3,000 of the $70,000 loss as a deduction against ordinary income until it is exhausted. In our example, this couple would have a $3,000 annual deduction (saving them $900 a year in taxes) for over 23 years. It may take several years to get their tax benefits, but the tax savings is not limited to 15 percent.

The couple may end up using a combination of these deductions. For example, they might use $3,000 a year against ordinary income for the next five years. At that time, they may want to sell a portion of their portfolio that has substantial gains. They can then use the balance of the remaining losses to offset the long-term gains they take that year.

The key point to remember is that the tax savings created by taking your losses is the first step to recovery. Take advantage of the government's tax relief help.

Step 2: Build a Diversified, Asset-Allocated Portfolio

Use what you have learned in this chapter to build a new portfolio that is diversified and properly asset allocated based on your investment objective and your tolerance for risk. Use one of the three asset allocation models described earlier as your starting point.

Step 3: Continue to Invest 1 Percent or More per Month

This is an important step to rebuild your capital as fast as possible without taking on major investment risk. Take a second look at Figure 3.7, paying close attention to the 20 percent per year recovery line. If you can get your portfolio returning close to the 20 percent line, you can reduce your recovery time from 13 years to 7 years. That would cut your recovery time almost in half. So how do you get close to the 20 percent line without taking on a large investment risk? A diversified, asset-allocated portfolio should return roughly 10 percent over time. By adding 1 percent per month ($300 per month in our example), you are adding roughly 12 percent per year to your investment program. These additional monthly investments will bring your account growth close to the 20 percent line: half of it from portfolio performance and half from your continued investments. If you want to see exactly the power of my 1 percent rule, let's return to our example in Table 3.9.

As you can see, adding just 1 percent a month can help you speed up the recovery time for recovering from substantial investment losses. Even if your losses are 70 percent, you can be close to breaking even in 7 years and well ahead of the game in 10 years. If you want to recover in a shorter period of time, increase the monthly investment from 1 percent to 2 or 3 percent.

TABLE 3.9

Investment Amount	Rate of Return	Value in 7 Years	Value in 10 Years
$30,000 lump sum	10%	$58,461	$77,812
Plus $300 per month	10%	$36,285	$61,453
		$94,746	$139,265

Put two investment strategies to work in your recovery plan:

1. Incorporate asset allocation when reinvesting the initial $30,000 lump sum that will be available after selling your aggressive stocks.

2. Use the dollar-cost averaging strategy when investing the additional $300 each month.

This will be a winning combination for your road to recovery!

Step 4: Use Tax-Sheltered Investments Going Forward

If you control your taxes as you are rebuilding your capital, you can recover much faster. Again, let's assume our couple is in the 30 percent marginal tax bracket. They will be well ahead in the game if they use tax-favored investment vehicles such as IRAs, tax-deferred annuities, and additional contributions to their employer-sponsored retirement plans to rebuild their capital. We will talk more about these great investment options that are designed to help you build your capital in Chapter 8. The point to remember is that these government-approved tax-controlled investment options will speed up the recovery of your investment losses. Take advantage of this second tax benefit as you begin your portfolio recovery plan.

LESSONS AND STRATEGIES

1. A portfolio with steady performance can be as effective as an aggressive, volatile portfolio over significant periods of time.
2. Diversify your portfolio to reduce your risk. If you own individual stocks, consider owning no fewer than 10 different securities in at least six different sectors of the stock market. You want diversification, not duplication. The easiest way to create diversification is by ownership of mutual funds.
3. There are six asset classes from which you can chose to build your investment portfolio:
   - Large-cap equities
   - Small-/mid-cap equities
   - Developed foreign equities
   - Emerging markets
   - Bonds
   - Real estate

4. Your asset allocation should contain at least three of these six asset classes.

5. Divide your equity positions into both growth- and value-style stocks. If you are using mutual funds, select funds that give you exposure to both management styles.

6. Unless you are an aggressive investor, bonds should be part of your allocation.

7. Consider blending government bonds, municipal bonds, and high-quality corporate bonds. You can also add a small portion of junk corporate bonds and foreign bonds for additional diversification if you are comfortable with the additional risk.

8. Consider one of the three asset allocation models illustrated in this chapter as a starting point for your existing pool of capital: growth, growth and income, or conservative income model.

9. Once you have your portfolio in place, stick with it, rebalancing on a regular basis.

10. Use the dollar-cost averaging strategy to build your capital on a monthly investment basis. It is a great strategy for reducing the risk for future monthly equity investments.

11. If you have substantial losses in a portion of your portfolio, follow my four-step process to turn that situation around.
    - Turn your paper losses into tax-deductible losses.
    - Build a diversified, asset allocated portfolio.
    - Continue to invest 1 percent or more per month.
    - Use tax-sheltered investments going forward.

12. Asset allocation and dollar-cost averaging are logical, time-tested strategies that will help put your mind at ease and minimize emotional decisions.

Inflation Risk

Mistake 2: Failing to Plan for the Devastating Effects of Inflation

asn't inflation disappeared as a result of the Federal Reserve's watchful eye on interest rates? Wrong! Since 1900, we have had only 15 years without inflation. Seven of those 15 years occurred in the late 1920s and early 1930s. That period in history is referred to as the Great Depression. It should have been named the Great Deflation! It was a period of high unemployment and few dollars to spend. The prices of goods and services dropped dramatically during that period. In fact, the cost of living dropped seven years in a row! That leaves 85 of the last 100 years with inflation. Historically, there is better than an 85 percent probability of inflation, and inflation can create havoc with your long-term financial plan.

Rule of 72

The rule of 72 is a useful financial tool that can help you approximate how long it takes to double your money. Simply divide the number 72 by the rate of return your money is earning to approximate how long it will take to double your money. For example, let's assume you have three investments, the first returning 3 percent, the second returning 6 percent, and the last compounding at 12 percent. How long does it take for the investment compounding at 3 percent to double?

24 years to double your investment (at 3%)

Here is what we find for the lump sum of money earning 6 percent.

12 years to double your investment (at 6%)

The lump sum of money compounding at 12 percent grows much faster.

6 years to double your investment (at 12%)

Let's look at the effect of time on these three investments in Table 4.1.

How hard you work your money is one key to building capital over time.

The rule of 72 is also a useful tool in helping us understand the risk of inflation over time. For example, let's assume inflation averages 3 percent over a period of time:

3% Inflation over 24 years (the number of years for the dollar to drop 50% in purchasing power)

Think that's not important? Let's assume you are retiring at age 65. What is the probability that either you or your spouse will still be alive at age 95? I recently asked a leading insurance company about the life expectancies they anticipate in designing today's life insurance policies. For a 65-year-old couple in good health and able to qualify for life insurance, there is a 47 percent probability that one of them will still be alive at age 95. Life expectancy continues to increase. We added more than three decades to the average lifespan during the twentieth century! The fastest-growing segment of the

TABLE 4.1

Years	3% Return	6% Return	12% Return
Today	$1,000	$1,000	$1,000
6 years			$2,000
12 years		$2,000	$4,000
18 years			$8,000
24 years	$2,000	$4,000	$16,000
30 years			$32,000
36 years		$8,000	$64,000
42 years			$128,000
48 years	$4,000	$16,000	$256,000

TABLE 4.2

Rate of Inflation	Price in 30 Years
2%	$1.80
3%	2.40
4%	3.20
5%	4.30
6%	5.70
7%	7.60

U.S. population is individuals over the age of 85! These are today's actuarial probabilities. Should we experience any major medical breakthroughs, these life expectancy figures will spiral upward. Should you and your spouse retire at age 65, one of you could easily live to see 30 years of inflation. It's very possible you will live to see prices triple in your retirement years. Let's see the effect of various rates of inflation over a 30-year period. Table 4.2 projects the future cost of goods that cost $1 today, based on various average rates of inflation.

Remember the years of double-digit inflation (see Table 4.3)?

Let's assume you retired at the end of 1978 on a fixed income of $50,000 and you needed every penny of this income to pay your bills. Let's see the effect of inflation on this fixed income in Table 4.4.

After just three years of inflation, retirees found their bills exceeded their income by 39 percent!

What if inflation averages 6 percent over your retirement? Let's examine the effect:

12 years to double your cost of living (6% inflation)

Let's look at history in Table 4.5.

TABLE 4.3

Year	Inflation
1979	11.28%
1980	13.48%
1981	10.36%

TABLE 4.4

Year End	Bills
1978	$50,000
1979	$55,640
1980	$63,140
1981	$69,681

Inflation has averaged over 4 percent for the last 50 years. It has averaged over 5 percent in the last 30 years. Check out Figure 4.1 to get a real understanding of inflation.

In roughly 30 years, we've seen the cost of a pound of cheese increase 11-fold. The price of a pound of coffee has increased over fourfold. Buying a new car today easily costs over $23,000. That's the cost for a depreciating asset! Thirty years ago, the average home cost less than a new car costs today. But the home has gone up in value.

In 2000, inflation was 3.36 percent, followed by 2.8 percent in 2001 and 2.4 percent in 2002. The Federal Reserve Board, under the direction of Alan Greenspan, has been watching inflation carefully in an effort to keep it under control. (Note: they are trying to control inflation, not eliminate it.)

Your Future Rate of Inflation

The historical inflation numbers we just mentioned are average numbers. Your personal future inflation rate could be higher (or lower) than the averages you hear about in the news. For example, you may have children nearing college and you are frantically saving and investing for this near-term event. Historically, college

TABLE 4.5

Decade	Inflation Rate
1950s	2.11%
1960s	2.76%
1970s	7.86%
1980s	4.75%
1990s	2.80%

	1970s	Today
	34 cents	$3.78
	75 cents	$3.35
	4 cents	37 cents
	$2,853	$23,600
	$20,100	$132,900

FIGURE 4.1   Inflation erodes your purchasing power.

costs have increased at a pace far greater than the average inflation rate. During the last few years, inflation has averaged less than 3 percent, but college costs continue to soar. If you have more than one child headed to college in the next 10 years, base your planning on a personal inflation rate of 1 to 3 percent greater than average. In case you are wondering, a year at Harvard currently costs $35,000. We will look at projected costs in Chapter 6.

Energy prices are also up sharply. We saw these costs increase 10.7 percent in 2002, with continuing major increases in early 2003 before the conflict in Iraq. Often, you see or hear the news media quote the rate of inflation excluding the volatile costs of energy. This can lead you to believe that inflation is not a problem. But let me ask you: Do you not drive a car or heat your home? Look only at the total rate of inflation.

Perhaps you are in your fifties, with college costs behind you. Your personal inflation rate may be less than average. You are spending less, which means you are less affected by inflation, and saving more as you prepare for retirement.

Perhaps you have already retired. College costs are not a problem for you, unless you are helping to fund your grandchildren's education. But you may have other expenses that are growing at a rate exceeding the average rate of inflation. As our population ages, there is greater demand for all health-related care, from prescription drugs to nursing homes. Currently, the cost of these goods and services is far outpacing the average rate of inflation. Remember, the fastest-growing portion of our population is age 85 and over. Depending on your age and health, you and your spouse may need to project an inflation rate of 1 to 3 percent greater than what you hear in the news as average. Be prepared for a major shock if you are among the 14 million retirees over age 65 who depend on health benefits provided by a former employer. Many company plans already have a cost-sharing formula for prescription drugs. More than half of the companies polled by the Kaiser Family Foundation in 2002 that have a formula in place revealed they intend to increase the retiree's cost for prescription drugs. (Some companies in the poll don't currently have a cost-sharing formula. A third of these companies plan to introduce cost-sharing formulas within the next two years.) Even without these coming changes, retirees are already paying more for health benefits than working employees. Retirees are paying 26 percent of the total premium cost on average, while active employees pay only 13 percent on average at the same companies.

Earlier, we saw that inflation averaged 3.36 percent in 2002. Beginning in 2003, Social Security recipients saw their checks increase by only 1.4 percent.

Personal Rate of Inflation

All of us are at different stages in life, faced with different needs, goals, and challenges. It is important to predict your personal future rate of inflation and make plans to offset those anticipated future increases in expenses. But, before you make your prediction, let's look at how prices changed on many items in 2002. (See Table 4.6.)

You can see that the prices of many items decreased in 2002, especially for items manufactured overseas. These price reductions reflect deflation in costs of goods. But, at the same time, the price for many items was increasing, especially the cost of services. (See Table 4.7.)

Inflation affects all of us differently, based on how each of us spends our money in the future. Take a few minutes to project your personal rate of inflation, not just for next year, but also for the next 30 years. (See Figure 4.2.) Why 30 years? Listen to the advice of William Huff, an actuary with Safeco Insurance. If you are age 65, you need to plan for many years to come. Huff threw out the two

TABLE 4.6

Items that Decreased in Cost in 2002	
Computers	−21%
Computer software	−8%
Airline fares	−5%
TV sets	−11%
Watches	−3%
Appliances	−2%
Coffee	−3%
Clothing	−2%
Dishes and flatware	−2%

extremes, the 10 percent of retirees who die too soon and the 10 percent who live too long. His focus was on the middle 80 percent. According to Huff, men in this middle group need to plan for 32 years of inflation. Women need to plan for 33 years, which would be age 98.

Market Risk versus Inflation Risk

Many people consider market risk a bigger risk than inflation risk. This major misunderstanding has created the poverty among the elderly we see in this country today. Let's compare these two risks.

TABLE 4.7

Items that Increased in Cost in 2002	
Cigarettes	10%
Hospital services	9%
College tuition and fees	7%
Educational books	6%
Prescription drugs	5%
Legal services	5%
Car insurance	9%
Child care	6%
Cable TV	6%
Home repairs	4%

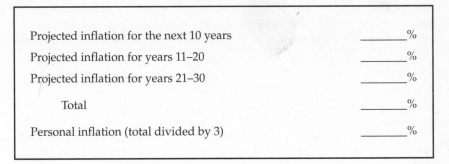

Projected inflation for the next 10 years	_____%
Projected inflation for years 11–20	_____%
Projected inflation for years 21–30	_____%
Total	_____%
Personal inflation (total divided by 3)	_____%

FIGURE 4.2   Personal inflation worksheet/projection.

Market risk can be controlled. Your actions have a direct bearing on controlling market risk, as we discussed in Chapter 2. Market risk reduces over time. Serious investors (as opposed to gamblers) should be investing for a minimum of five years. Few quality mutual funds with long-term track records have lost money over five-year investment periods. Look at the 10, 15, and 20-year track records of mutual funds. Time is your ally when it comes to controlling market risk. The longer the time period, the more likely your investment portfolio will be successful. Remember, your investment period is the rest of your life!

Inflation risk cannot be controlled. Remember, the government is not trying to eliminate inflation, but only trying to control it. You cannot control the country's rate of inflation. You might be able to modify your personal rate of inflation by carefully monitoring your spending habits. But, if you are faced with college costs or major medical costs and related health expenses, there is little you can do to control your costs. The risk of inflation increases over time, and it has hurt people much more than market risk. Since we cannot eliminate inflation, we must anticipate it will continue and plan accordingly.

Use either the rule of 72 or the inflation table per $1000 in Table 4.8 to help you determine your future income needs based on your personal rate of inflation.

Let's assume you have $1,000 to spend today. Let's also assume you anticipate your personal inflation rate will be 5 percent. You will need $1,629 in 10 years to have the same purchasing power that $1,000 has today. In 30 years, you will need $4,322 to buy the same goods that cost $1,000 today.

Do you think you might want a new car in 20 years? Assuming

TABLE 4.8

Inflation Rate	10 Years	20 Years	30 Years	40 Years
2%	$1,219	$1,486	$1,811	$2,208
3%	$1,344	$1,806	$2,427	$3,262
4%	$1,480	$2,191	$3,243	$4,801
5%	$1,629	$2,653	$4,322	$7,040
6%	$1,791	$3,207	$5,743	$10,285
7%	$1,967	$3,870	$7,612	$14,974

5 percent inflation, a car that costs $23,600 today could cost you over $62,000 in 20 years. Even at 3 percent inflation, the sticker price would be over $42,000. Other expenses related to your car, such as repair costs, taxes, and insurance, will also be increasing. Have you figured all of these increasing expenses into your retirement planning?

Do you think inflation might average 5 percent during 30 years of retirement? You will live to see prices increase more than fourfold during your retirement years. If inflation averages only 3 percent, you will live to see prices increase almost 2½ times! Do you have a plan to offset the effects of inflation?

LESSONS AND STRATEGIES

1. Remember, inflation never retires.
2. Inflation has averaged over 5 percent for the last three decades.
3. Don't underestimate inflation's effect on your future. Try to guesstimate your personal rate of inflation, and base your planning on this.
4. Use the rule of 72 or the inflation table to project your future needs.
5. The failure to anticipate continuing inflation has caused more financial ruin than investing in the stock and bond markets.
6. Your greatest risk is outliving your income.
7. Over the long term, the stock and bond markets are your friends, not the enemy! Investing in stocks and bonds provides the only solution to offsetting a lifetime of inflation. From 1919 through 2000, the stock market (as measured by the S&P 500) returned on average 10.82 percent.

Income Tax Risk

Mistake 3: Not Taking Advantage of the Opportunities to Control Taxes on Savings and Investments

Let me introduce you to the formula for building wealth: gross rate of return less taxes and inflation equals net rate of return. Watching your net rate of return is more important when you are in your thirties, forties, and fifties (when you are accumulating financial assets) than if you're in your sixties, seventies, or eighties (when you are spending financial assets).

Let's put some simple percentages to the formula for building wealth. (See Table 5.1.)

Now let's put dollars and cents into this formula. Let's see the impact on $10,000 invested long term for important needs such as a child's education or your retirement. (See Table 5.2.)

This is a very fragile formula. Any changes in the three variables can create havoc. For example, what if interest rates drop, taxes increase, and inflation increases slightly? Table 5.3 shows what could happen.

This combination of negative events would create financial suicide!

You can control two of the three variables in the formula: the gross rate of return and your current taxes. In the Chapter 4 you learned we have very little control over inflation but we can anticipate it and make plans to offset it. This chapter will focus on taxes.

TABLE 5.1

6%	Gross rate of return
−2%	Combined federal, state, and local income taxes at 33% rate
−3%	Rate of inflation
1%	Net rate of growth after taxes and inflation

TABLE 5.2

$600	Gross return at 6%
−200	Taxes at 33% (combined federal, state, and local)
−300	Inflation at 3%
$100	Real rate of growth on $10,000 investment

TABLE 5.3

4%	Gross rate of return of only 4%
−1.6%	If taxed at higher 40% combined tax rate
−4%	If rate of inflation becomes 4%
−1.6%	Net rate of *losses* after higher taxes and inflation

TABLE 5.4

Taxpayers Ranked by AGI	AGI Threshold	Percentage of Federal Income Tax Paid
Top 1%	$313,469	37%
Top 10%	$128,336	56%
Top 25%	$55,225	84%
Top 50%	$27,682	96%

Courtesy of IRS

You have three major ways to control income taxes on your investments. You can invest in assets that:

- Create tax-free income, either now or later
- Convert taxation from ordinary income tax rates to the much more favorable capital gains tax rates of 15 percent (or possibly as low as 5 percent)
- Defer income taxes to your retirement years, when your tax rates will most likely be substantially less than they are now

Tax Burden

Taxes are a burden for half of our population. The IRS released the figures in Table 5.4 based on taxes we paid in 2000.

As you can see, the top 50 percent of taxpayers paid 96 percent of the federal income taxes collected. Those with adjusted gross incomes (AGIs) under $27,682 paid only 4 percent of the income taxes collected by the IRS.

If you are in the top 50 percent, you need to look at ways to legally reduce your tax burden. Tax planning is not a one-year event. You will be filling out tax returns for the rest of your life. Take a long-term view on control of this permanent problem.

Income Tax Rates

Income tax rates are constantly changing. In fact, they were recently changed again in the Jobs and Growth Tax Relief Act of 2003. Let's review the new tax table effective for 2003 and 2004. (See Table 5.5.)

It is a progressive tax structure. Let's assume you are married. The first $14,000 of your taxable income will be taxed at 10 percent,

TABLE 5.5

Joint Return	Single Taxpayer	Tax Rate
$0–14,000	$0–7,000	10.0%
$14,000–47,450	$7,000–28,400	15.0%
$47,450–114,650	$28,400–68,800	25.0%
$114,650–174,700	$68,800–143,500	28.0%
$174,700–311,950	$143,500–311,950	33.0%
$311,950+	$311,950+	35.0%

Courtesy of IRS

the next $33,450 will be taxed at 15 percent, and so on. If you have earned income (your paycheck), you would love for it to be so large it puts some of your income into the top marginal tax bracket (which is now 35 percent). But what if you have taxable investment (unearned) income as well? Some of this unearned income (interest and profits from short-term stock trading) would be taxed at your top marginal rate, which, in our example, could be as high as 35 percent. For that reason, you need to watch your marginal tax rates carefully, especially if you are compounding this unearned income in a taxable account for the future.

Dividend Tax Rates Reduced

Stock investors have received tax relief on their dividend income. Under the new tax law, investors in the lowest two tax brackets (the 10 percent and 15 percent tax brackets illustrated in Table 5.5) will pay only 5 percent taxes on dividend income. Those investors fortunate enough to be in the 25 percent bracket or higher will now pay 15 percent in taxes on their dividend income. There are some dividends that do not qualify for the new tax breaks:

- Dividends from master limited partnerships (MLPs)
- Dividends from real estate limited partnerships (REITs)
- Dividends paid by preferred stocks
- Dividends paid by a small number of mutual funds, because they invest in the previously mentioned nonqualifying assets

Tax-Free Investments

There are four tax-free investments you need to consider. The first two are for you; the last two will help you accumulate and use dollars for your children's education.

- *Municipal bonds* pay interest that is federal tax-free. Consider municipal bonds, especially if you need income now or in the near future. Municipal bonds are loans to a state or local government agency. In return for loaning your money to this municipality, you are paid federal tax–free interest until the bond matures or the borrowed money is repaid. These loans can be relatively short in nature—say five years. It might be an intermediate loan of perhaps 10 years, or a long-term loan of 20 to 30 years. Usually, the shorter loans pay less interest. The interest earned on all municipal bonds is free of federal income tax. If you purchase a muni bond issued by a borrower within your state of residence, the interest will also be state income tax free. Currently, the rate of return on long-term tax-free municipal bonds is approximately 4 to 5 percent.

- *Roth IRAs* provide a great investment opportunity to build wealth for your future retirement, if you qualify. There are income restrictions. (See Table 5.6.)

  If you are married, your modified adjusted gross income (MAGI) must be less than $150,000 to fully benefit. If you are married and your MAGI is between $150,000 and $160,000, your contribution limits will be lower. If you are single, your MAGI must be lower than $95,000 to fully benefit from the Roth IRA. If single, your contribution limits begin phasing out at $95,000 and you will not be able to participate if you income exceeds $110,000. If your adjusted gross income is less than these limits, you and your working spouse can each invest in Roth IRAs. The following tables illustrate how much you and your spouse can contribute to IRAs each year. All earnings grow tax-free until retirement. At retirement, your Roth IRA withdrawals will be tax-free income. Unlike muni bonds, a Roth IRA makes it possible for you to have both tax-free compounding of assets and tax-free retirement income, without being restricted to a 4 to 5 percent rate of return! And now, because of the recent tax law of 2001, you and your spouse will be able to invest a substantial amount of money in Roth IRAs. (See Table 5.7.)

Catch-Up Contributions for People Age 50 and Over

The law also provides an important benefit for taxpayers age 50 and over. These taxpayers can make additional contributions,

TABLE 5.6

Status	Maximum MAGI for Full Participation	MAGI for Phase-Out of Participation
Married	$150,000	$150,000–$160,000
Single	$95,000	$95,000–$110,000

Courtesy of IRS

TABLE 5.7

Contribution Limits for Traditional and Roth IRAs for Taxpayers under Age 50	
Years	**Contribution Limit**
2002–2004	$3,000
2005–2007	$4,000
2008 and after*	$5,000

*After 2008, the contribution limits will adjust in $500 increments, based on inflation.
Courtesy of IRS

referred to as *catch-up contributions.* Table 5.8 shows the total contribution permitted for investors age 50 and over.

The next two tax-free investment opportunities can provide the funds for the education of your children or grandchildren. Briefly, they are:

1. *The Coverdell education savings account* (originally called an education IRA) offers you the opportunity to invest up to $2,000 per child for your children's education. These programs grow for your children without taxes and create tax-free income for education.

2. *The 529 college savings plan* offers a second opportunity to build savings for college education. This is a great program for grandparents to use to help provide savings for grandchildren's future college education.

TABLE 5.8

Traditional and Roth IRA Contribution Limits for Taxpayers Age 50 and Over	
Years	**Contribution Limit**
2002–2004	$3,500
2005	$4,500
2006–2007	$5,000
2008 and after*	$6,000*

*Adjusted for inflation.
Courtesy of IRS

You will learn more about these last two tax-free programs as well as other ways to save for this future expense in Chapter 6.

Tax-Converting Investments

It is possible to convert some taxation from ordinary income taxation to the more favorable long-term capital gains taxation. We have a tremendous tax incentive to build capital with stocks, stock mutual funds, real estate, and other investments that appreciate in value over time. Our gains (12 months or longer) are taxed at very favorable long-term capital gains tax rates. There are two great benefits to this:

1. There are no taxes due until the gain is realized.

2. The gain is taxed at either 5 percent or 15 percent, depending on your taxable income at that time.

These tax incentives encourage us to invest in areas where there is market risk we might not otherwise consider. Consider this: A stock or stock mutual fund that appreciates at more than 5 percent over time will be subject to the much lower capital gains tax of either 5 percent or 15 percent. An investment subject to ordinary income taxation, such as a bank CD or corporate bond, might earn an identical 5 percent return, but all of the gains (interest) would be subject to ordinary income tax rates of as high as 35 percent. Look back at the formula for building wealth. Cutting your tax rate on investment earnings from as high as 35 percent (the top bracket in 2003) to only 10 to 15 percent will have a dramatic impact on your wealth over time. Remember, the stock dividends you earn along the way are also taxed in the same favorable way as long-term capital gains.

Tax-Deferred Investments

Last but not least, tax-deferred investments need to be part of your plan. There are several opportunities to defer taxes to a later date. You need to consider four tax-deferred investments in particular, because they complement each other:

1. 401(k) plans, 403(b) plans, and other qualified plans

2. Traditional IRAs

3. Tax-deferred variable annuities

4. Variable universal life insurance

401(k) Plans

401(k) plans have become the qualified plan choice for most companies over the last 20 years. Let's assume your employer offers one. Pay close attention, because your retirement depends on it! Many employees are in shock over the drop in value they experienced in the Gruesome Years of 2000 to 2003.

These accounts are important for several reasons:

- Your personal contributions to the account are pretax dollars. (Most other investments you could make with these dollars would be with after-tax investments.) Let's assume you are in the 28 percent marginal tax bracket. Investing $100 in your 401(k) plan doesn't really cost you $100, because you are saving $28 in taxes. In effect, for every $72 you contribute, the IRS contributes $28 (the dollars you would have paid in taxes had you taken the $100 as salary). Think of it as a government matching program. For every 72 cents you put in the plan, the government adds 28 cents. For every dollar you put in the plan, the government adds 39 cents (or 39 percent). That is a great deal! The higher your tax bracket, the better the deal.

- Many employers match your contributions up to some point. Let's assume they match your first 3 percent. Their match doubles your investment that year and you haven't even begun to earn investment returns on this money!

- The earnings on your account compound without current taxation. Think of this as an interest-free loan from the IRS. You agree to pay the taxes later. But in the meantime you are earning profits on money you would have given to the IRS. This interest-free loan is very meaningful over time. Once again, think about the formula for building wealth.

There may be some limitations on building all of your wealth in your 401(k) plan. For example:

- Your employer may not sponsor a 401(k) plan.

- Your employer may not match much, if any, of your contributions.

- The quality of the investment selections in your 401(k) may be far below average.

- You may not be able to invest more than $13,000 (the annual limit in 2004).

- You must begin taking distributions by age 70½, whether you want to or not.

Traditional IRAs

If you are not covered by an employer-sponsored retirement plan, you can fully participate in a tax-deductible traditional IRA regardless of your income. The contribution limits are the same as the Roth IRA limits shown earlier in this chapter. For years 2002 to 2004, the contribution limit is $3,000 (under age 50) or $3,500 (age 50+).

If you are covered by an employer-sponsored plan, the tax deductibility of a traditional IRA contribution is limited, as shown in Table 5.9.

Remember, you can still participate in a traditional IRA regardless of your income level. It may not be a deductible contribution if you are covered by an employer-sponsored retirement plan, but you still enjoy the beauty of tax-deferred compounding.

Tax-Deferred Annuities

A third tax-deferred investment option is a tax-deferred annuity. A tax-deferred annuity is a product of the life insurance industry. There are two types of deferred annuities: fixed and variable. The fixed annuity provides a guarantee of principal by the issuing insurance company and a fixed rate of return. The variable tax-deferred annuities are more popular today. Instead of receiving a fixed rate of return, the buyer invests in professionally managed variable investment accounts within the variable annuity. These accounts are similar to mutual fund accounts, and are often managed by the same money managers who manage the most popular mutual funds. Tax-deferred annuities enjoy favorable tax treatment.

TABLE 5.9

Single	Married
Fully deductible if MAGI is under $34,999	Fully deductible if MAGI is under $54,000
Phase-out of deduction if MAGI is between $34,000 and $44,000	Phase-out of deduction if MAGI is between $54,000 and $64,000
No tax deduction if income exceeds $44,000	No tax deduction if income exceeds $64,000

Courtesy of IRS

The IRS tax code allows these products to compound your earnings without current taxation. Annuities enjoy this special tax treatment because they are designed to help investors accumulate capital for retirement income. If these assets are used prior to age 59½, they are subject to taxes and a 10 percent penalty tax because annuities are intended to be used for retirement income.

UNDERSTANDING TAX DEFERRAL One of the key advantages of saving money in qualified plans, traditional IRAs, and deferred annuities is tax deferral. Here's an anecdote to show the power of tax deferral. Let me introduce you to the Smiths and the Joneses. We will be talking about these two couples throughout the book, so let's begin by discussing their different approach to paying taxes. They are both age 45 and would love to retire in dignity at age 65. Each has $100,000 to invest today. They went separate ways and made different investment choices. They both found investments that would return 8 percent over the next 25 years, but the difference in their accounts was the timing of taxation. The Smiths' account was fully taxed each year at the combined federal and state tax rate of 31 percent. The Joneses' account was tax deferred. Figure 5.1 illustrates the power of tax control.

By controlling when they paid taxes, the Joneses were able to build a substantially greater pool of capital by age 65. The couple with the greatest pool of capital at retirement can create the greatest retirement income.

At retirement, the Smiths can call their investment source and instruct them to stop compounding the 8 percent. The future earnings of 8 percent can be mailed to them in their retirement years, with a 1099 each year, for a taxable retirement income of $23,430.

Meanwhile, the Joneses invested their $100,000 in a tax-deferred annuity. Over 20 years, they were able to compound their savings without taxes. At retirement, Mr. and Mrs. Jones can contact their tax-deferred annuity company and begin an income stream. Let's assume they elect to withdraw 8 percent per year from their $466,096 account. They can receive a taxable income of $37,287. The annuity can create the larger income because the capital account is larger. The type of annuity income being illustrated is called a partial withdrawal. It will be taxable income because the Joneses are withdrawing part of the accumulated and future earnings in their annuity that have never been taxed. This income option leaves the

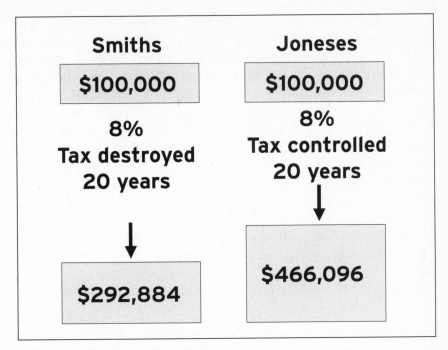

Smiths

$100,000

8%
Tax destroyed
20 years

$292,884

Joneses

$100,000

8%
Tax controlled
20 years

$466,096

FIGURE 5.1   Tax Deferral Makes a Difference

original investment ($100,000) intact in the annuity policy until all of the accumulated and future earnings are withdrawn. Should the Joneses withdraw all of the accumulated earnings, they can then withdraw their original $100,000 investment on a tax-free basis.

Let's assume both couples plan on retiring on the income generated by their respective accounts. The Smiths' retirement income would be $23,430 (8 percent on $292,884). Meanwhile, Mr. And Mrs. Jones would enjoy a much larger income of $37,287 (8 percent on $466,096). That is over $1,000 more income every month for the Joneses.

Let me tell you a little more about Mrs. Smith. She tends to be a jealous woman. During retirement, she notices that her neighbor, Mrs. Jones, is able afford a nice car, purchase new carpeting, and enjoy dining out one night a week. It doesn't take long for Mrs. Smith to have a serious discussion with her husband. She complains, "I don't know and I don't care where you have our retirement account. What I do care about is the fact it is not paying us enough income! You had better go to wherever this account is and say $23,430 is just not enough money. In fact, we need at least $37,287 every year so I can keep up with the Joneses!"

Mr. Smith knows how important it is to keep his wife happy, so he promises to get her the additional money each year. How does he create this extra cash? He begins spending part of their capital each year. The first year's cash consists of $23,430 earnings and $13,857 of principal, for a total of $37,287. Each year's payment will come less from earnings and more from principal. At this rate, it won't be long until the Smiths deplete their entire nest egg. What happens then? They may be forced to move out of the neighborhood. It is a sad story, but it happens all the time.

There is a moral to this story. Income tax planning is more important when you are building capital for retirement than when you are retired and creating income. Tax deferral does indeed make a difference.

Besides tax control, deferred annuities provide many additional benefits, such as:

- If the owner dies while the annuity is building, the heirs have an attractive death benefit guarantee. With variable annuities, the minimum death benefit will be at least equal to the amount that was invested. Many of today's most popular tax-deferred variable annuities have a death benefit guarantee that far exceeds this minimum guarantee. For example, many provide a death benefit equal to the greater of the original investment in the contract or the greatest value achieved in any year.

- Unlike life insurance, annuities do not require an insurance physical exam. This is a great benefit for people in poor health who want to provide some level of death benefit guarantees for their heirs.

- This asset avoids probate. Probate is a process of determining who will inherit your assets. If you own an asset jointly with someone else, such as your spouse, there is no probate process on that asset, as the asset will pass directly to the joint owner. But what if you are not married? What if you own some assets in a single name? If there is no joint owner, the asset must go through the probate process to determine who will inherit the asset. But annuity contracts allow you to name a beneficiary. The beneficiary or beneficiaries can inherit the annuity proceeds without the delay, expense, and notoriety of the probate process.

There are several retirement income options with annuities. Many of these income options provide lifetime income. We will look at additional annuity income options in Chapter 9, when we examine your best options for retirement income.

LUMP SUM SURRENDER OF AN ANNUITY CONTRACT Often I hear, "Tax deferral sounds good, but I'm just putting off the eventual taxation. I might as well just pay the taxes now and get it over with!" Let's see if that statement is true. Let's assume Mr. and Mrs. Jones need to surrender their annuity at the end of 20 years rather than using it for retirement income. The following is the math on this lump sum surrender:

$466,096 Annuity Value

($100,000 original investment plus $366,096 accumulated gains)

	$366,096	Taxable gain in the annuity
Less:	113,490	Taxes at 31% bracket
	$252,606	Gain after taxes
Plus:	100,000	Original investment
	$352,606	Annuity value after lump sum liquidation

This is the worst way to liquidate an annuity, because the Joneses would lose a substantial amount of their capital. But it is still better than paying taxes each year as the Smiths did. The Smiths have only $292,884, while the Joneses have $352,606 after liquidating their annuity. The Joneses are ahead by $59,722. Is this sleight of hand? How could the Joneses create this additional gain of almost $60,000? They took advantage of an interest-free loan from the IRS for 20 years! For 20 years, they made money on the taxes they would have paid had they been in a taxable account. This 20-year interest-free loan helped them build almost $60,000 more than the Smiths.

A lump sum surrender of a tax-deferred annuity is not in your best interest. You are far better off using one of the annuity income options when you retire and need income.

TAXATION DURING RETIREMENT YEARS Some critics of 401(k) plans, traditional IRAs, and tax-deferred variable annuities complain that the taxation will be too great during retirement. The income from these assets is taxed as ordinary income, not the more favorable capital gains tax rates.

Earlier, I said that income tax planning is far more important when you are in your thirties, forties, and fifties (when you are accumulating financial assets) than in your sixties, seventies, or eighties (when you are spending financial assets). Let's examine this taxation issue and see how it can impact your planning. While you are working, I hope your earnings push you into the top marginal tax bracket of 35 percent. Your taxable interest earnings and short-term trading profits are taxed on top of your earned income, meaning they will be taxed at your top marginal rate, which I hope is 35 percent.

Now, let's examine your retirement income. Once you retire, your primary income is made up of:

- Social Security income, which might be partially taxed
- Tax-free municipal bond income
- Tax-free Roth IRA distributions
- Dividends taxed at 5 percent or 15 percent
- Interest income, which is fully taxable
- Taxable distributions from qualified plans and traditional IRAs
- Taxable distributions from nonqualified annuities

Let's consider the taxation on your unearned retirement income. Assume your fully taxable unearned income is $100,000, coming from your qualified plans, traditional IRAs, and tax-deferred annuities. Here is the taxation on this taxable retirement income:

$100,000	Gross taxable unearned income
– 11,400	Standard deductions for married couple over age 65
– 6,100	Personal exemption for you and spouse
$82,500	Taxable income

For 2003, your federal income tax bill would be $14,245.

Our tax system is a progressive tax system. That means that the lowest portion of your income is taxed at the lowest 10 percent tax rate, the next portion is taxed at 15 percent, the following part at 25 percent, and so on. Only a portion of your income will be taxed at your top marginal tax rate. We know the total tax in our example would be $15,000. What is the overall effective tax rate?

$$\frac{\$14{,}245 \text{ total tax due}}{\$100{,}000 \text{ gross income}} = 14.2\% \text{ effective tax rate on gross income}$$

$$\frac{\$14{,}245 \text{ total tax due}}{\$82{,}500 \text{ taxable income}} = 17.2\% \text{ effective tax rate on taxable income}$$

Either way you look at it (as tax due on gross income or tax due on net income), the effective tax rate in this example is either 14 percent or 17 percent. That's not much different than paying a 15 percent capital gains tax rate on $100,000 of long-term gains taken during retirement. Don't be afraid to spend income from retirement assets that will be taxed at progressive income tax rates in retirement. It is better that you pay a 14 to 17 percent effective rate of taxation than your children or heirs paying a marginal 35 percent on these same dollars. Why will the heirs most likely pay more? This inheritance will be added to their other taxable income in the year they receive your tax-deferred assets, which will force them into higher marginal tax rates. (More on this later.)

Variable Universal Life

Variable universal life is the fourth great investment that can control your taxes, especially if your family needs the extra protection life insurance provides. Most investors are drastically underinsured. Interest rates have dropped from roughly 14 percent in the early 1980s to roughly 5 percent today. A widow in the early 1980s could earn 14 percent on a $100,000 life insurance policy, or $14,000 per year in income. Today, that same $100,000 policy can create only $5,000 in income. Variable universal life can help solve two problems at the same time:

1. Take care of your family if you die too soon

2. Take care of you and your spouse if you make it to retirement and need the cash values of the policy to retire as a lady and gentleman and not just an old couple

Variable universal life is similar to buying term insurance with a tax-favored investment account attached. The tax treatment is better than buying term insurance with a separate tax-deferred annuity. Here is how the cash values of life insurance are treated:

- It grows without current taxation, similar to an annuity or qualified plan.

- It can be accessed prior to age 59½ without a 10 percent penalty, unlike an annuity or a qualified plan.

- You can withdraw your investment in the contract tax free, unlike the annuity or the qualified plan.

- At death, the entire proceeds pass to your family income tax free, unlike the annuity and the qualified plan, which pass income-taxable gains to the heirs.

So, Which Is Better?

There are several choices for deferring your taxes while you are building wealth for your retirement:

- Qualified plans, such as a 401(k) plan

- Traditional IRAs

- Tax-deferred annuities

- Tax-advantaged universal life

And don't forget your tax-free investment opportunities, such as municipal bonds and Roth IRAs. Converting profits from ordinary income to the much more favorable capital gains tax rates is also a real plus in controlling your taxes. It's not really a question of which is better. These tax-advantaged investment choices actually complement each other!

LESSONS AND STRATEGIES

1. Remember the formula for building wealth. You can control both the rate of return on your investments and the taxation on these dollars.
2. Municipal bonds are great for immediate tax-free income.
3. Roth IRAs create tax-free retirement income in the future.
4. Traditional IRAs may or may not be deductible, but will help you build capital on a tax-deferred basis for retirement.
5. The Coverdell education savings account (formerly known as the education IRA) and the 529 college savings plans create tax-free dollars for your children's education. (More on this topic later.)

6. Appreciating assets, such as common stock, allow you to build wealth with no current tax, and the gains will be taxed at the favorable 5 percent or 15 percent capital gains tax rate when sold.

7. Your employer-sponsored qualified plan, such as a 401(k) plan, allows you to save on a pretax basis.

8. A tax-deferred annuity builds capital without current taxation and can create a guaranteed lifetime of income.

9. Variable universal life insurance provides tax-free liquidity before age 59½ and the largest possible income tax-free dollars for your family at your death.

10. All of these accounts build capital without current taxation to create the largest possible pool of capital for your future needs.

11. All of these great options should be considered.

12. A combination of at least three tax-favored programs is a great idea.

Educational Needs of Children and Grandchildren

Mistake 4: Not Deciding What You Want to Accomplish with Your Money

ollege costs have been doubling every 10 years. Will my children be able to provide my grandchildren with the same quality higher education I provided my children?" If you are a grandparent, you need to ask yourself this question. Perhaps you are a parent with young children, struggling with the question, "How will I afford a college education for my children?"

A college education is one gift no one can ever take away from our children or grandchildren. According to the U.S. Census Bureau, an education is the most important inheritance you can give your children or grandchildren. (See Figure 6.1.)

The average high school graduate can earn $1.2 million over his or her working years. A person with a bachelor's degree can earn $2.1 million. A master's degree is worth $2.5 million. The biggest difference is between a high school diploma and a bachelor's degree. That spread has been growing for the last 25 years, and it won't be long before the difference in earning potential is over $1 million.

It's not just a dollars-and-cents opportunity: A college education provides the opportunity to have a career doing something you can enjoy doing for decades. But it is going to be expensive. It is

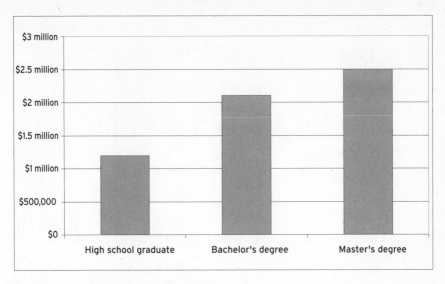

FIGURE 6.1   The value of an education.

estimated that by the year 2019, the cost of four years at a private college will be a staggering $301,442.

Let's see just how expensive this is going to be. Figure 6.2 compares today's college costs with the projected costs in 18 years. The lighter bars represent the cost of the average state university both today and in 18 years. The darker bars represent the cost for the average private university. These projections cover all of the main costs, such as tuition, books, supplies, and room and board.

Table 6.1 is a year-by-year chart to help you project college costs for children of various ages.

These projections are conservative and assume only a 5 percent annual increase in education costs. Unfortunately, the historical pattern has greatly exceeded 5 percent. It also assumes earning a degree in just four years. Over half of today's college students take five years to finish.

Adjusted for inflation, tuitions have risen 33 percent at private schools in the last 10 years and 40 percent at state universities. During the same 10 years, family income has increased only 12 percent. Many feel their children will get full scholarships, but unfortunately, this is also changing. In past decades, a college might extend full scholarships of $20,000 to five of the most needy

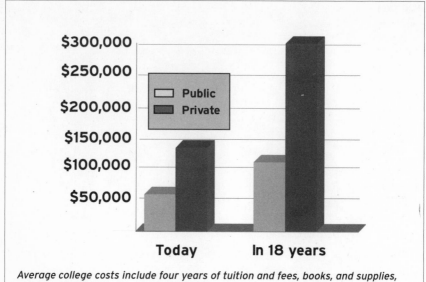

Average college costs include four years of tuition and fees, books, and supplies, room and board, transportation, and other expenses for the 2002–2003 school year, as stated by the College Board's Annual Survey of Colleges report. Projected costs assume a 5% inflation rate per year.

FIGURE 6.2   College costs.

students. The current trend is to give $5,000 to 20 students of middle-income families that are capable of paying the balance of the tuition. It costs the college the same $100,000, but each of the 20 middle-class students will be paying $15,000 (or a total of $300,000) in tuition. Many parents think of financial aid as scholarships. Unfortunately, 58 percent of financial aid comes in the form of student loans. The costs incurred with these loans actually increase the cost of an education.

More students are graduating from college with massive loan debt. According to data from the U.S. Department of Education, 40 percent of student borrowers are graduating with unmanageable levels of debt. The debt is considered unmanageable if debt payments require more than 8 percent of the borrower's monthly income. The average student loan debt has doubled in the last eight years. Paying off large college loans will have a major impact on the economic value of a college education.

Without planning, this expense will become almost insurmountable. However, if you plan ahead, you can discount this future

TABLE 6.1

Year	Public	Private
2003	$12,841	$27,677
2004	$13,483	$29,061
2005	$14,157	$30,514
2006	$14,865	$32,040
2007	$15,608	$33,642
2008	$16,389	$35,324
2009	$17,208	$37,090
2010	$18,068	$38,944
2011	$18,972	$40,892
2012	$19,920	$42,936
2013	$20,917	$45,083
2014	$21,962	$47,337
2015	$23,061	$49,704
2016	$24,214	$52,189
2017	$25,424	$54,799
2018	$26,696	$57,538
2019	$28,030	$60,415
2020	$29,432	$63,436
2021	$30,903	$66,608
2022	$32,449	$69,938

From Annual Survey of Colleges *(The College Board, New York, NY)*

expense by as much as 75 percent. This chapter focuses on how you can tame these future expenses, cutting college costs to as little as 25 cents on the dollar. Let's examine five specific plans designed to make it happen.

Investment Opportunities

There are several ways to plan ahead. Let's look at five approaches:

1. Custodial accounts
2. Coverdell education savings accounts (once known as education IRAs)
3. Prepaid tuition plans
4. Roth IRAs
5. 529 college savings plans

Custodial Accounts

For decades, parents and grandparents have been able to gift money to a child in an account designed for a minor child called either a uniform gift to minors account (UGMA) or a uniform transfer to minors account (UTMA). Many years ago, these accounts had significant benefits. In the Reagan years, when income tax rates were as high as 70 percent, it made tax sense for a wealthy taxpayer to gift to a child or grandchild who would be in a much lower tax bracket. The earnings on these accounts were taxed at the child's lower tax rate. There has been one additional change over the years. In the past, parents felt their children were responsible and would use the money in these accounts wisely (for a college education). Unfortunately, many of today's parents are far more concerned about the maturity of their children.

Today, custodial accounts have several major limitations:

- The tax rules have changed and these accounts are now subject to the "kiddie tax" rules. A child under age 14 pays no tax on earnings under $750. If the account has earnings between $750 and $1,500, those earnings are taxed at the child's rate of only 10 percent. But, if it is a sizable account, earning over $1,500 a year, the excess is taxed at the parent's top marginal rate, which can be 35 percent. For example, let's assume an $11,000 annual gift to this custodial account for 5 years. Assuming a 10 percent return, the account would be worth more than $67,000 in just five years. If the account earns over 2.2 percent in year six, the earnings would trigger the kiddie tax problem.

- The days of *Leave It to Beaver,* where Wally and the Beaver could be trusted to use this money wisely, have disappeared. The money in these accounts is the property of the child at legal age (either 18 or 21, depending on the child's state of residence). In August of 2001, a young man in Missouri took control of his custodial account money on his 21st birthday and spent every dollar in this account on lottery tickets. Easy come, easy go!

- Since these assets are in the child's name, it will be more difficult for the child to qualify for student aid, loans, and grants. The federal student aid program requires a child to use one-third of his or her savings each year toward college costs. The new college savings vehicles that have become available in recent years are far more attractive than custodial accounts.

Coverdell Education Savings Accounts (Once Known as Educational IRAs)

This education-planning vehicle has been available since 1997. Today, it is a tool to consider carefully. Prior to 2002, contributions were limited to $500 per year. Today, you can contribute up to $2,000 per year to a Coverdell education savings account (ESA) for each child. Here are the basic rules that apply to the revised Coverdell ESA:

- You can contribute as much as $2,000 per year for each child until age 18.
- Parents must have an income below $190,000 to take full advantage of the Coverdell ESA (their ability to contribute is totally phased out at $220,000).
- Single parents must have an adjusted gross income below $95,000 (phased out at $110,000).
- Contributions must be in cash and are not deductible.
- You can contribute to both a Coverdell ESA and a 529 plan in the same year.
- Distributions are tax free when used for tuition, books, fees, supplies, and room and board.
- Distributions used for other purposes (such as the purchase of a new car) are subject to ordinary income tax and a 10 percent penalty.
- The balance in the account must be distributed by age 30. To avoid paying the tax and the 10 percent penalty, the balance could be rolled to a Coverdell education savings account of another family member.
- This account can be used for elementary and secondary schools as well as post-secondary educational facilities (colleges, universities, and trade schools).

This is a great program, but there are a few limitations:

- Only $2,000 can be contributed to each child's account in one year.

- The joint filer's contribution amount is phased out when the taxpayers' modified adjusted gross income is between $190,000 and $220,000. Those fortunate enough to earn over $220,000 cannot contribute to a Coverdell ESA and should consider a 529 Plan.

- Penalties apply if the money in the account is used for purposes other than education expenses.

Prepaid Tuition Plans

Now let's look at the prepaid tuition plans that are available in many states. Here are the benefits of a prepaid tuition plan:

- The money compounds without taxes.

- You lock in tomorrow's tuition cost, regardless of inflation.

- The distributions are taxed at the child's income tax rate (probably 10 percent during college).

- It is easy for everyone, including grandparents, to contribute to the account.

- There are no earnings limitations to qualify.

Unfortunately, there are major limitations to a prepaid tuition plan, such as:

- You have no control over how the money is invested. It is like a defined benefit plan. You know only the benefit—the tuition—is prepaid.

- It covers only the tuition and required fees. At many schools, room and board is more expensive than tuition.

- If the child goes to college in another state, or chooses not to go to college, you may get back only your original contribution, with no investment return.

- These plans usually cover only state university tuitions, excluding all private universities in the state.

- Prepaid tuition plans can only be used for undergraduate studies. Assets in other plans can be used for both undergraduate and graduate school.

- The account must be used by a certain age (usually age 30).

- Either the account owner or the student beneficiary must be a state resident.

- Contribution limits for a prepaid tuition plan are much lower than for other 529 plans.

- Enrollment is limited to children under a certain age (typically 13 or 14).

Many states are facing financial difficulties with these plans because they have overestimated the investment returns they could earn on prepaid tuitions. They also underestimated the rapid increase in college costs in recent years. Every state is experiencing budget difficulties and few are prepared to meet these college tuition promises. Many states may not be able to meet the unfunded liabilities these plans are creating. If you have started one of these plans, carefully examine how your state plans to meet the obligations. Don't be surprised if the rules and promises change dramatically between now and the time your child goes to college. The changes will not be in your favor.

Roth IRAs

Roth IRAs can also be used for college costs. Here are the key rules regarding Roth IRAs:

- The most you can contribute in 2004 is $3,000 ($3,500 if you are age 50 or over).

- Contribution levels will increase to $4,000, but you will have to wait until 2005.

- Your spouse can also contribute, based on his or her age.

- There are earnings limitations. Roth IRAs are phased out at incomes of $150,000 to $160,000 for married couples and $95,000 to $110,000 for singles.

- The account can be invested in stocks, bonds, mutual funds, or other acceptable investments.

- The account grows tax free and the withdrawals are tax free if used for postsecondary education expenses.

There are significant limitations to using the Roth IRA for college expenses:

- These are your retirement dollars you are spending. Be careful! Withdrawals for college costs can't be added back to your Roth IRA at a later date.

- Because of the current $3,000 limitation, the account will not accumulate enough to cover the costs of college.

- It is not available to high wage earners.

529 College Savings Plans

Section 529 in the Federal Tax Code lays out the basic rules that allow each state to develop a tax-favored savings program for post-secondary education costs. The rules for these state-run programs are very liberal.

As a nation, our economic growth is dependent on the education of our children and grandchildren. Our economy is no longer based on farming or manufacturing. Rather, our future economic growth will be in technical fields, such as computer-driven industries and medical care research. A highly educated workforce is critical for the growth of our nation. There is also a demographic problem. Where is all the money? In the hands of Grandmother and Grandfather! How can we transfer the money from the grandparents to the grandchildren where it will be needed for education funding? The answer is the 529 plan.

For many people, the 529 plan is the best opportunity to save for future college costs. Here are the basic rules for the 529 plans:

- Section 529 of the Federal Tax Code makes it possible for each state to establish its own plan, as long as it meets certain federal guidelines. Almost every state has established a 529 plan.

- You can contribute up to $55,000 in any year. The IRS allows you to contribute your annual $11,000 gifts for the next five years in advance. If you are married, you and your spouse can jointly gift $110,000 per student this year. No other gift can be made in advance.

- There is a maximum you can contribute to a 529 plan, which varies from state to state. Most states permit contributions up to $200,000 or more. For example, the Rhode Island 529 plan allows contributions up to $265,620. These limits are indexed to inflation and will most likely increase each year. This maximum contribution is a combination of out-of-pocket contributions and earnings. Once the account reaches this limit, you cannot make additional contributions. (It should continue to grow in value as a result of investment performance. You just can't add any more to that child's account.)

- The earnings grow without taxes.

- The distributions, when used for postsecondary education expenses (college, trade school, junior college, graduate school, etc.), are tax free.

- These plans cover most college expenses, such as tuition, books, fees, supplies, and room and board. Transportation costs are not included.

- You can choose any state's plan. You do not have to be a resident of that state, and the child does not have to choose a college from that state. It is a very portable account. Since you can select any state's plan, you need to look carefully at who is managing the money.

- The main difference between the states' plans is how the money is invested. Most states have turned to the mutual fund industry and selected a professional money management company to manage the funds and take care of the administration of the accounts. You will recognize many of the names, such as American Funds, Putnam, Alliance, T. Rowe Price, Fidelity, TIAA CREF, Franklin/Templeton, and so on. Some states have elected to manage the money on their own. (Doesn't that sound scary?) You can select any state's plan. You do not have to be a resident of that state. Your state of residence may provide a small state income tax incentive to select your home state's 529 plan, but that should not be the way you choose a plan. Choose a plan with the money manager you want to entrust your funds with for the next 5, 10, or 20 years. The performance of a quality money manager is the key, so choose your state carefully.

- Each plan offers a choice of investment options, from aggressive to conservative. You must choose one or a combination of the investment choices available. Assuming a mutual fund management company manages the plan, each of the investment choices is typically a blend of several of their existing mutual fund accounts.

- These assets are not subject to estate tax. Wealthy grandparents can establish a 529 plan for each grandchild. The contributions and the growth on the account will not be part of the estate.

- The owner (for example, the grandparent) maintains all of the control. This is the only financial asset a wealthy individual can control and still have the value of the asset pass to the heirs free of estate taxes.

- The owner can even take the money back. If the owner takes money out of the 529 plan for any reason other than education, the gains withdrawn will be fully taxed and subject to a 10 percent penalty. The tax and penalty are only on the accumulated earnings.

- Some states allow a limited state income tax deduction. A few states will match the contributions up to some point for state residents choosing that state's plan.

There are no income limits for making contributions to a 529 plan. A custodial account allows each donor to gift up to $11,000 per child. Grandparents can jointly gift up to $22,000 per grandchild, using a custodial account. The 529 plan rules are different. The 529 plan rules allow the grantor to gift up to five annual gifts up front in one year. For example, let's assume the Joneses are grandparents. Together, they can gift up to $110,000 to each grandchild in a 529 plan this year. Why would they gift so much in one year?

- There are no gift taxes, even though they have exceeded the normal $22,000 gift limit.

- The assets in a 529 plan grow without taxes. No 1099s on each account.

- The accumulated earnings will pass to the successor owner estate tax free.

- The entire account will be estate tax free after five years ($22,000 per year will become tax-free). It will take five years for the entire $220,000 to be outside of the Joneses' estate.

- When used for secondary education, the withdrawals are income tax free.

- This is the only asset the Joneses can control and keep out of their estate at the same time.

OWNERSHIP CONTROLS WITH 529 PLANS There are three parties in a 529 plan account: the owner, the successor owner, and the student/beneficiary. The control of these assets remains in the hands of the owner for the owner's lifetime. The successor owner takes over the ownership rights after the original owner's death. The successor owner might be the original owner's spouse, the parent of the student/beneficiary, or the student/beneficiary. The owner has tremendous control over the 529 plan:

- *The owner chooses which state's plan will be used.* Again, the key difference between the various state plans is the investment choices available. You need to select the money manager you trust the most for the next several years.

- *The owner selects the specific investments within the 529 plan.* Each state provides several investment choices.

- *The owner controls the distributions from the 529 plan.* Let's assume the student wants to go to the number one party college in the country. If the owner does not approve, the owner does not have to pay. The owner controls all of the distributions.

- *The owner selects and can change the student/beneficiary on the 529 plan.* If one child completes college and there is still money remaining in the account, the owner can name a new student/beneficiary. This control is not available on a custodial account. There are some restrictions on who can be named as the new student/beneficiary on the 529 plan account: It must be a relative of the original beneficiary, such as a brother, sister, or cousin.

- *Unlike any other educational savings account, the owner can take the money back for his or her own use at any time.* This option makes the 529 plans unique.

IDEAL PLAN FOR GRANDMA AND GRANDPA The 529 plan is ideal for grandparents for several reasons:

- They always retain control of the money.

- They typically have pools of capital in reserve that could take full advantage of the income tax deferral opportunities.

- Prefunding can pay future college costs for as little as 25 cents on the dollar. For example:
  - $63,100 invested today in a 529 plan at 8 percent for 18 years can grow to $252,000, which is the projected cost of a four-year education at the average private college in 18 years. Every dollar invested today can create $4 for future college costs.
  - The elite colleges, such as Stanford, Yale, Georgetown, Tulane, Harvard, Duke, Princeton, and Cornell (just to name a few),

cost more than twice as much as the average private college. An investment of $100,000 today in a 529 plan will prepay $400,000 of those projected costs in 18 years.

- They may have large estates that need to be sheltered from estate taxes.

- They have the love and concern for their grandchildren.

- They can take the money back if they need these assets for personal use later in life.

The 529 plan does have limitations, such as:

- There is a cap on how much can be invested in each state's plan. The cap will be roughly $200,000 to $250,000 (it depends on the limits of the state plan you choose). This cap will grow over time as a result of inflation.

- The investment choices are limited. You cannot invest in individual securities like you can in a custodial account or a Coverdell education savings account. With the 529 plans, you must chose one or a combination of specifically named accounts (similar to mutual funds) in the state plan you have chosen.

- You can change your investment choices only once per year.

Recent Tax Law Change

There is a new wrinkle in the tax law that may have some value if you have not planned ahead for college costs. Under this new rule, you can write off up to $3,000 of college costs, even if you don't itemize your deductions. However, this new tax write-off has many limitations such as:

- It is limited to expenses for tuition and related fees, so it will not cover room, board, books, and other costs.

- It has limited value. For example, if you are in the 25 percent tax bracket, you will save 25 percent of $3,000, or $750. Remember, it is a tax deduction and not a tax credit. In this example, you still have to come up with $2,250.

- If you use money from a state prepaid tuition plan or a Coverdell ESA, or interest from savings bonds you cashed in to pay for school costs, you must subtract these amounts from your expenses to arrive at the deductible amount.

- The maximum deduction per year is $3,000. Even if you have three children in college at the same time, you can only deduct a total of $3,000.

- There are income limits to qualify for the deduction. As a parent, you lose the deduction if you are single and making more than $65,000 or if you are married and earning more than $130,000. This income limit will ease up just a bit in 2004 and 2005.

- This tax break may end in 2005. Congress will have to reapprove this deduction at that time.

- If you take this $3,000 deduction, you cannot use the Hope tax credit ($1,500) or the lifetime learning tax credit ($1,000). Sometimes a tax credit (which directly reduces your tax bill) is worth more than a tax deduction.

In short, this deduction is of limited value. It is not a good alternative to planning ahead for college costs.

Discounting Future College Expenses

Earlier, I suggested you could discount future college expenses by as much as 75 percent if you plan ahead. Let's look at one more example of this planning opportunity. Let's assume you have a newborn child or grandchild who would be entering a public university in 18 years. College costs for freshman year are projected to be approximately $30,000, and the total cost for all four years would be $129,300. An investment of $32,357 today into a 529 plan, hopefully returning 8 percent over 18 years, can create the $129,300 tax-free dollars for the college education. This preplanning has cut these future expenses by 75 percent.

Fidelity Investments recently completed a survey that revealed that 62 percent of grandparents are more than willing to help finance their grandchildren's college education. At the same time, only 27 percent of the parents were willing to ask for help. If you are a parent, speak up and ask for help. If you are a grandparent, let your children know you want to help.

A little help goes a long way. Let's assume there are two sets of grandparents enjoying the birth of a new grandchild. Each set of grandparents might be able to gift $10,000 to a 529 plan. Each set of grandparents should establish their own 529 plan, naming the newborn grandchild as the student beneficiary. Assuming the two

529 plans (with $10,000 each) grow at 8 percent over 18 years, there will be roughly $80,000 available for college needs. That would be a tremendous help to the parents in funding the college costs. Even in today's dollars, that college degree will be worth over $2 million in future earnings. What a fantastic gift! Remember, wealthy grandparents can each gift up to $110,000 to a 529 plan for each grandchild in one year. That gift would pay for Harvard and graduate school.

For many families, education financing requires a two-generation solution, with both parents and grandparents building assets in Coverdell education savings accounts (for private high school) and 529 college savings plans. Take advantage of your opportunity to discount these future expenses while sharing your wealth with those who mean so much to you.

LESSONS AND STRATEGIES

1. Plan ahead! With careful planning, you can discount future education expenses by as much as 75 percent.
2. Custodial accounts can trigger a substantial amount of tax while growing. Consider moving these assets to a 529 plan. You may incur some income (or capital gains) taxes now, but you are creating tax-free compounding and tax-free income in the future.
3. Consider the Coverdell education savings account, which allows you to contribute up to $2,000 per year per child, which can be used for elementary, secondary, and postsecondary education.
4. Look closely at the 529 college savings plans. Projected college costs seem insurmountable at first glance. Two generations (parents and grandparents) can work together to create the capital necessary for a four- or five-year college education.
5. Start as soon as possible. You have to start early if you want to reduce your out-of-pocket costs for college by up to 75 percent.
6. Set priorities. Driving a new car would be enjoyable, but nothing would make you happier than seeing your children or grandchildren graduate from college with neither of you being in debt.

PART TWO

THE KEYS TO MAKING INVESTMENT DECISIONS

The Risk of Outliving Your Income

The Number One Risk for Today's Investor

Comedian Henny Youngman once said, "I've got all the money I'll ever need—if I die by four o'clock this afternoon." We don't know exactly how long we will live, and that is why it is so important to carefully plan your retirement income for you and your spouse. The number one fear of investors today is (and should be) the fear of outliving their income.

So far, we have discussed four of the eight deadly mistakes investors make with their money. These mistakes have something in common: They deal with saving and investing. In case you forgot, let's review the first four mistakes:

1. They make investment decisions based on emotion rather than logic.

2. They fail to plan for the devastating effects of inflation.

3. They don't take advantage of the opportunities to control taxes on their savings and investments.

4. They have not decided what they want to accomplish with their money.

With this type of planning, we all make some mistakes. No one is perfect. There are just too many "moving parts" to create the perfect plan. We just need to hope the mistakes we make are not critical. Here is a sample of a small mistake: perhaps your youngest child is about to enter his or her last year of college and the tuition goes up by an unexpected 10 percent. It may come as a shock, but you can tighten your belt and pay that last year's tuition and you are done with this problem.

Some mistakes might be larger. For example, if you fail to establish any meaningful investment plan to build assets for a child's education, you will be forced to finance this cost at the last minute by arranging costly student loans and taking out an expensive second mortgage. That's not good planning, but at least you would have some options.

But when we delve into retirement income planning, a major risk must be addressed—the risk of outliving your income. You won't have last-minute options to create the large pool of capital necessary to provide you an adequate lifetime retirement income. You can't expect to win a national lottery just before you retire. It requires careful planning to make certain you and your spouse have adequate resources to retire as a lady and gentleman and not as an old woman and an old man.

The risk of outliving your income has been rising for several reasons. There are many pieces to the puzzle. The next four chapters will bring the parts into focus and help you prepare for important decisions you must make, such as when to begin taking Social Security benefits. These chapters will help you create a realistic plan to retire in dignity. First, we need to look at the facts.

Retiring Earlier and Living Longer

Let's look at some startling information revealed in the February 2000 issue of *The Journal of Financial Planning:*

- Forty-six percent of American men under the age of 62 are retired.

- Twenty-one percent of American men over the age of 70 are still working.

What about retiring early, at age 62 or earlier? I feel these statistics are going to change. Part of my concern is the dependability of Social Security projections and the trend of corporate retirement plans away from providing a lifetime pension income. But my major concern is our plunging personal savings rate. Back in 1982, the savings rate in America was 10.9 percent of take-home pay. As of January 2002, the savings rate had plummeted to less than 2 percent, and there is little evidence of it going back up. This is a serious problem as baby boomers expect to retire in just a few years. Rather than saving, they are spending more than ever, which is reflected in increasing credit card debt and record high personal bankruptcies. Some people use the excuse that they are investing less today because of concerns about recent stock market losses. You would expect them to save somewhere else or at least pay off their debt if they aren't going to invest. All I am seeing is more consumption.

The deadly combination of the recent stock market correction and increased consumer debt has produced the largest decline in inflation-adjusted household wealth since World War II! Christian Weller, an economist with the Economic Policy Institute in Washington, DC, reports that household wealth dropped $2.3 trillion (that's an unbelievable 8 percent drop) in 2000. Many investors find it difficult to make investment decisions today. They make statements such as, "There is nothing I can do. I'll just have to wait it out until the market rebounds." Others are saying, "I'm still planning to retire before age 65. I think I'll be able to squeak by. I can always get a part-time job at Wal-Mart if I have to." Unfortunately, retiring before you are financially prepared drastically increases the risk you will outlive your income.

There are two planning mistakes that are causing major retirement planning risk:

1. Using outdated mortality assumptions

2. Using aggressive investment return assumptions

We need to examine these assumptions carefully to find out why so many people run into financial difficulty in retirement.

Mortality Risk Assumptions

We need to know about historical life expectancy tables, because many financial products are tied to them. Throughout history, actuaries have created and updated these historical mortality tables. Let's look at the last 60 years. For example, one such table was created in the 1940s, based on life expectancies prior to 1940. This mortality table was heavily influenced by the fact that people born in the year 1900 had a life expectancy of only 47 years. The 1940 mortality table was updated to a 1958 table because people were living longer. In 1980, these tables had to be updated again. Why? People continue to live longer. Several new mortality tables are being created for the twenty-first century. Why? You got it—we continue to live longer and healthier lives. People born in 1900 had a life expectancy of only 47 years, while a person born in 2000 has an average life expectancy of 77 years. Average life expectancies have increased three decades in one century!

Part of this longer life span is the result of improvements in infant mortality. But that's not all that has been changing. Consider the improvements in retirement years. If your parents retired at age 62, they spent an average of 11 years in retirement. If you retire at the same age, you should expect retirement to last more than 20 years. That's almost twice the number of years your parents spent in retirement. Keep in mind that these numbers include retirees in poor health. If you enjoy average or better than average health at retirement, these numbers need to be adjusted upward.

Many financial instruments are based on the historical (conservative) 1980 mortality table, for example:

- The cost of life insurance policy premiums
- The lifetime monthly income options available from annuity policies
- Social Security retirement income benefits
- The retirement income distribution from defined benefit pension plans

Some financial events are based on newer 2000 tables. For example, in April of 2002, the IRS issued major changes for IRA distributions that reflect these new, longer mortality assumptions. We will look more closely at these financial events in following chapters when we examine how best to create retirement income.

Dare to be Age 100!

Allow me to introduce you to Marie Bremont. This French woman died on June 5, 2001, having celebrated her 115th birthday in April of that year. At the time of her death, she was considered the world's oldest person since the death of Eva Morris of Britain. (Eva died in November of the year 2000, just four days before her 115th birthday.)

Marie's story is quite interesting. During her working years, she worked in an artist supply store in France. In fact, one of her customers was Vincent Van Gogh, to whom she sold paint and canvas.

At age 90, Marie fell upon tough times. She never thought she would live that long and had outlived her savings. The one asset she had of value was her home. Her lawyer wanted to buy her property, but she was reluctant to sell her one remaining valuable asset. They entered into an interesting contract. He would pay her $500 per month for as long as she lived and she could remain in her home until death. Upon her death, the property would revert to the attorney and his family. In effect, she had purchased a lifetime income annuity. Her attorney had anticipated she would die within just a few years, but she lived until age 115. Now here is the important twist to the story: The attorney died in 1987, 14 years before Marie! His family went to court to try to get out of the contract. The judge ruled in Marie's favor, and the attorney's family had to continue her $500 monthly lifetime income until she died. Marie received over $80,000 from the deceased attorney's estate. What is the moral of the story? You need to understand mortality tables before you agree to pay someone an income for life.

The more current mortality tables project that a person born in 2000 has a life expectancy of over age 77. But age 77 is not the end of the road. Life expectancy is not the same thing as death expectancy. Remember, life expectancy means you have a 50-50 probability of still being alive. Life expectancy is not a fixed number. It continues to change. For example, let's look at a newly created IRS table that is used to determine the required distributions from qualified plans and IRAs at age 70½. The table assumes you are married and your spouse is 10 years younger. This age 70/60 combination reflects a joint life expectancy of 27.4 years. This means there is a 50-50 probability that one of you will be living at the older spouse's 97th birthday. If you are both alive at that point, your new joint life expectancy will be an additional 7.6 years. That's over age 100! Not only are we living longer, but the rate of improvement in life expectancies is also accelerating. Medical science continues to improve the outlook for longer life expectancies. The fastest-growing age group in this country is people age 85 and over.

There are over 50,000 people in this country over the age of 100. Let's meet Cleo Craig. On February 14, 2003, she celebrated her 113th birthday. She is the oldest living person in Illinois. Benjamin Harrison was president when she was born in 1890. The light bulb was a novelty that year. To this day, she is an avid Chicago Cubs fan; she remembers the Cubs winning their last World Series game in 1908. In

2003, her beloved Cubs made it to the seventh game of the playoffs. Maybe next year they can go all the way. Her mind is very active, as she reads the *Chicago Tribune* every day from cover to cover as well as every issue of *Newsweek*. She ranks 5th-oldest in the United States and 10th-oldest in the world. The oldest living person today is Kamato Hongo of Japan, who was born on September 16, 1887.

Many experts predict we will have over 1 million centenarians living in this country within 50 years. I believe that the quality of life during retirement will dramatically improve for people currently age 65 or younger. It is a demographic thing. Our population is aging rapidly as the older baby boomers near age 60. As a direct result, the amount of dollars being used to research the aging process is accelerating.

Medical Research on Aging

How long could we live? Let's begin by looking at just a few segments of the fascinating medical research being conducted on aging and longevity.

Telomere research is both new and exciting. In recent years, scientists have learned quite a bit about the aging process. Our bodies are made of X and Y chromosomes. At the tips of the Xs and the Ys are tiny "caps" that prevent our chromosomes from fusing together. These caps, called *telomeres*, have been described as being similar to the plastic ends of a shoestring. Each time a cell divides, the telomeres shorten. As a telomere reaches a minimum length, it causes the cell to stop dividing, and eventually the cell will die. This telomere aging process is considered by many experts to be the main factor in our current life span being limited to 115 to 120 years. The aging process of telomeres not only quantifies the length of our life span: It also affects the quality of life. The wearing out of telomeres is being recognized as the leading cause of Alzheimer's, cataracts, and other aging problems. This knowledge of telomeres is new and important. Now that scientists know a major cause of the aging process, solutions to many health problems might not be far behind.

Gene research is very much in the news today. In the year 2000, scientists identified the genes that make up life as we know it, including plant and animal life. In 2001, they discovered the human body consists of only 30,000 genes, much fewer than estimated. A single grain of rice has almost as many genes as a human. Cells produce proteins by reading information inside genes. Proteins act as the building blocks of life, the chemical messengers between cells and the other proteins. Armed with this improved knowledge of proteins, scientists believe they can finally solve the basic biochemical mechanisms underlying sickness and health. The speed of our improving medical knowledge is fascinating.

Stem cell research might also play a key role in our future. Scientists successfully grew human embryonic stem cells in the laboratory for the first time in 1998. John Gearhart, a pioneering researcher at the Johns Hopkins School of Medicine, was the first to isolate embryonic stem cells. In the same year, Dr. James Thomson, a biologist at the University of Wisconsin, announced he had grown human stem cells successfully. These embryonic stem cells are unique because these cells from an unborn fetus have not yet differentiated, or started on the path toward becoming nerve cells or liver cells or any other specific tissue in the body. Scientists believe these stem cells can be coaxed into becoming any type of human tissue. These cells can keep dividing and multiplying indefinitely in the laboratory. Think of all of the diseases that might be cured or kept in remission by replacing damaged cells with healthy cells grown in a laboratory. These cells can revolutionize transplant medicine; help people with diabetes, cancer, heart failure, Lou Gehrig's disease, Parkinson's disease, and spinal cord injuries; and the list goes on.

There is much discussion about stem cell research, because until recently scientists have focused on cells from unborn embryos. Political leaders are wrestling with the moral dilemma of the rights of an unborn child while scientists are seeking other methods to create stem cells without using the controversial embryos. Infigen Inc., a Madison, Wisconsin–based company, has been successfully cloning animals for years. Its research team is examining a revolutionary method of creating stem cells using adult cells by taking an adult cell back to its embryo-like state. The cells can then be turned into specialized cells, such as brain cells or heart cells. When these cells are transplanted back into the same adult, there hopefully will be no rejection because of the perfect genetic match. I'm confident we will hear more on stem cell research from Infigen and other companies such as Advanced Cell Technology and PPL Therapeutics PLC, to name just a few.

We must plan on living beyond historical life expectancies. Let me share with you some forward-looking life expectancy statistics. These are different than historical statistics. Life insurance companies are keenly interested in forward-looking life expectancy projections, which are critical to their pricing of life insurance and annuity products.

Let's assume you are married and 65. Let's also assume you are in average health. Average health means no history of heart disease, diabetes, or cancer. The forward-looking probability that either you or your spouse will still be alive at age 95 is 47 percent. What is the probability that you or your spouse will still be alive at age 100? The answer, according to a major life insurance company, is 25 percent. This means that, without any major improvements in medical technology, there is a 1-in-4 probability that either you or your spouse will be alive at age 100!

When I mention this in public seminars, many people respond, "My God! Who wants to live that long?" We tend to look backward. We remember the health of our grandparents at age 65. Many of them were physically worn out. They worked on farms or in factories. Their world was a world of physical labor, which began at a very early age. Most of us now work in offices, using our brain and not our brawn. This is adding to our life expectancy. We also enjoy better health care. Our grandparents never heard of cholesterol. Many died because they knew little, if anything, about nutrition.

We need to focus on forward-looking statistics and anticipate that both life expectancies and the quality of life will continue to improve as scientists find new solutions to further modify the aging process.

Cardiac Patients: Take Heart

The quality of life after treatment for heart disease has improved dramatically in the last 50 years. Back then, there were no coronary care units in hospitals. No one understood how high cholesterol could lead to heart attacks and strokes. In recent years, we have seen significant changes. For example, newly designed stents make angioplasty and bypass surgery more effective than ever before. Today's heart surgery is safer and far less traumatic. Surgeons can now repair and even replace heart valves or perform bypass surgery making only small incisions in the chest wall rather than the older method of open heart surgery. A new blood test that measures the C-reactive protein (CRP) level is a better predictor of heart attacks and strokes than tests for bad cholesterol. New drugs are available to strengthen a failing heart. New easy-to-use defibrillators are available for home use and are showing up in office buildings and public places, such as airports and airplanes. And this is just part of the good news.

Since 1950, mortality among adults age 45 to 64 fell nearly 50 percent as a result of declines in heart disease, strokes, and injuries. Deaths by injury have declined because of safety changes in auto design. Deaths by cancer have declined since the 1980s. Because of these dramatic changes, we need to carefully develop an investment plan that will provide adequate income during a long, healthy retirement.

Let's consider the improvements for people in all age groups. In 1950, 585 people out of every 100,000 in the United States developed heart disease. By 1999, the number had fallen to 268 out of every 100,000, a drop of over 45 percent. In 1950, 181 of every 100,000 people died of strokes and other cerebrovascular disease. By 1999, the number was down to 62 per 100,000.

Headline News

I was on a business trip in November of 2002, speaking to investment professionals in Florida. Part of my topic was creating lifetime income for investors. The newspapers that week helped me give a new meaning to the word *lifetime*.

Monday, November 18, 2002, Associated Press: "Doctors said Sunday that they had restored life to seemingly dead heart muscle by seeding it with cells borrowed from patients' own thigh muscles or bones." The article described how immature muscle cells, called *myoblasts*, obtained from the patient's thigh can be grown in test tubes until millions of cells are available for injection into parts of the heart that have died. In a report at the American Heart Association meeting in Chicago, Dr. Nabil Dib of the Arizona Heart Institute predicted these new techniques will someday replace heart transplants.

Wednesday, November 20, 2002, *USA Today*: "STENTS IN NECK CAN PREVENT STROKE. MAY MAKE CAROTID SURGERY OBSOLETE." The article pointed out that roughly 200,000 people in the United States have this difficult type of surgery every year. Using the newly designed stents and surgical techniques, doctors will no longer be required to make two six-inch-long incisions on the neck of the patient. The old technique required these incisions so the surgeon could carve out two inner layers of the carotid arteries in the neck.

Thursday, November 21, 2002, *USA Today:* "CANCER VACCINE SHOWS PROMISE. CERVICAL MALIGNANCY COULD BE WIPED OUT." Scientists have successfully tested a vaccine that brings them one step closer to eliminating the cause of the second-most lethal malignancy in women.

Thursday, November 21, 2002, *USA Today:* "GENE THERAPY BOOSTS HEART'S OXYGEN SUPPLY." A team of doctors headed by researcher Duncan Stewart of Toronto released their gene therapy results at the American Heart Association meeting being held in Chicago. Their findings suggest it is possible to introduce new blood vessels to damaged areas of the heart, thereby easing the pain caused by heart disease.

During the week after that business trip, on November 26, 2002, the Food and Drug Administration approved the first drug that successfully combats osteoporosis, the brittle bone disease that affects 10 million Americans. This new drug not only slows down the bone aging process, it also stimulates new bone formation. This is great news for women.

Why am I telling you all of this? To convince you that all age groups are living longer. Even if you are near or in retirement, your life expectancy is increasing. And those of you with health problems can also anticipate longer, more enjoyable, and productive lives. This is why we need to maintain a long-term perspective when it comes to investing.

Investment Risk

Depending on Bonds for Retirement Income

Many retirees make the mistake of selling all their stocks at retirement and investing the proceeds in bank CDs or bonds for income. Bonds are often referred to as fixed-income securities. That sounds like something every risk-averse retiree would want. But there are two major problems: inflation and taxes.

Consider this example:

5%	Bond (or CD) interest
Less 1.5%	Income taxes (a 31% combined federal and state income tax rate)
Less 2.5%	Average inflation rate projection
1%	Net rate of return

This may work in the short run, but it could have a devastating effect over 30-plus years of retirement. This is a very fragile financial formula. If interest rates decline, you have a serious problem: Your bonds or CDs could renew at lower interest rates, creating a lower retirement income. This is exactly what happened to many retirees who invested in CDs when they retired in the early 1980s. If you retired in those high-interest-rate years, you could have earned 14 percent on CDs. In short, $100,000 earning 14 percent created $14,000 of safe retirement income back in the early 1980s. But, as interest rates declined, those CDs (and bonds) renewed at lower interest rates. Many of those retirees are now earning less than 5 percent, or $5,000 per year. They have seen their income drop to one-third of their initial retirement income. At the same time, they have watched inflation reduce their purchasing power. Unfortunately, interest rates can continue to drop or stay at current low levels for many years.

If your personal rate of inflation exceeds 3 percent, you could have a serious retirement income problem. Since your capital is barely growing, any unexpected liquidation of capital (to educate your grandchildren, pay for medical expenses, repair the roof, take a trip to Europe, replace a car, etc.) could permanently reduce your capital, which will affect your future retirement income. Let's look at how prices have increased over a 31-year period for everyday items. (See Table 7.1.)

These are items we will be buying for the rest of our lives. In this 31-year period, these items have increased in cost fivefold! And stamps went up to 37 cents (a 9 percent increase) in July of 2002. As you can see, investing solely in bonds or CDs leaves no margin for error.

TABLE 7.1

Everyday Item	1970	2001
Stamps	$0.06	$0.34
Big Mac, fries and coke	$0.87	$4.68
Candy bar	$0.10	$0.50
Monthly magazine	$0.50	$3.27
Monthly fee for cable TV	$5.50	$34.96

Depending on Stocks for Retirement Income

Perhaps you are considering a portfolio made up entirely of stocks or stock mutual funds as the answer for retirement income. It may work, but it may not. Let's see what would have happened had you invested all of your retirement capital in the S&P 500 over the 30-year period from 1971 through 2000. The S&P 500 averaged a 13.2 percent rate of return over this 30-year period. Keep in mind that the S&P 500 index is a raw statistical set of numbers. It is not a product. Should you buy a product that mirrors the index, there will be fees and expenses. Also, since the stock market has been disappointing over the last few years, you might decide to base your assumptions on a more conservative 12 percent return rather than the historical 13.2 percent return. Based on a 12 percent average rate of return, what would happen if you began withdrawing 8 percent for retirement income with the idea of increasing the income by 3 percent a year to offset inflation?

Let's also assume you were planning on depleting your $100,000 by age 96. Surely you won't live past age 95! In Figure 7.1 you see the projections based on these assumptions.

This illustration shows the $100,000 account increasing for several years, as you would be withdrawing less than the 12 percent projected rate of return. In later years, when you withdraw more than you are earning, the capital decreases, until it runs out in 30 years.

Sounds like a good plan for 30 years of income. Have you seen illustrations similar to this? More important, does it always work? The S&P 500 averaged better than 13.2 percent during this time frame. Please look carefully at Figure 7.2 to get a better feel for the real world.

Figure 7.1 assumed a nice, steady, predictable 12 percent rate of return each and every year. This is not the case in the real world. In fact, there were several bad years for the S&P 500 index during this 30-year period. For instance, in 1973 we see the account has dropped $25,211 in value from the previous year. By the end of 1974, the account's value is down to $60,000!

What would you do at that point as a retiree (five years into retirement)? Would you go back to work at age 70? I doubt it. My guess is you would do the prudent thing: You would cut your future retirement income by at least 40 percent, because your capital would have

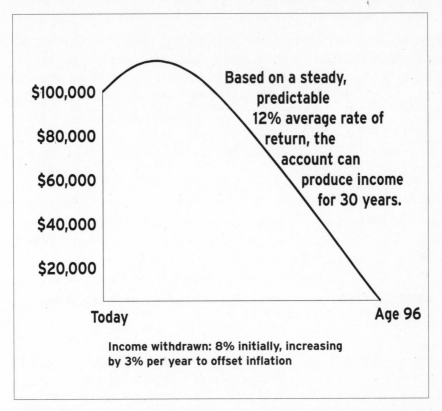

Based on a steady, predictable 12% average rate of return, the account can produce income for 30 years.

$100,000

$80,000

$60,000

$40,000

$20,000

Today   Age 96

Income withdrawn: 8% initially, increasing by 3% per year to offset inflation

FIGURE 7.1 Account value projection. (Courtesy of Wiesenberger, a Thomson Financial Company)

dropped from $100,000 to only $60,000. What would be happening to your marital harmony by this time? Would you spouse wait five years before voicing some concern about your investment assets? And, if you failed to act on this portfolio, would you continue to hear about it through the next 30 years?

This illustration shows the effect of market volatility on an index. Had I illustrated an indexed mutual fund (with lower investment results because of fees and expenses), the results would have been even more devastating.

I'm not playing a trick on you. I could have illustrated an even worse scenario by beginning in 1973, when the S&P 500 index was down over 17 percent, followed by 1974, which was down another 30 percent. The point is that no one knows when we will have down

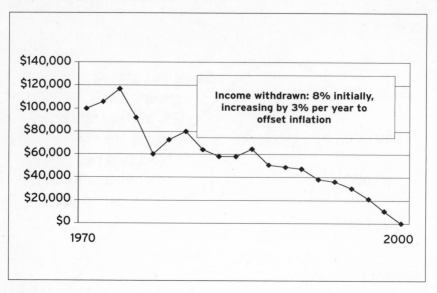

FIGURE 7.2 Actual values based on the S&P 500. (Courtesy of Wiesenberger, a Thomson Financial Company)

years in the market. History tells us we should anticipate two to three down years every decade. The S&P 500 has experienced negative returns in 9 of the last 35 years. That's roughly one of every four years. If your early years of retirement are down years and you are withdrawing an income of 6 percent or more each year, it could create permanent havoc in your investment portfolio. Is this what you want to look forward to in your retirement years? I don't think so!

Let's look at one more example to drive this point home. We'll begin by choosing a different time frame, beginning in 1973. Let's assume you began a lower income stream of 6 percent at retirement. Let's also assume you increased this income by 5 percent per year to offset the inflation we have experienced over the last 30 years. Figure 7.3 points out that the account (reflecting the S&P 500 index) is totally depleted in just 21 years.

In this example, the original investment of $100,000 decreased to less than $60,000 in just two years!

These illustrations have intentionally shown bad market conditions and aggressive income withdrawals to make a point: It is important that you understand the risk of withdrawing more income than your portfolio can produce!

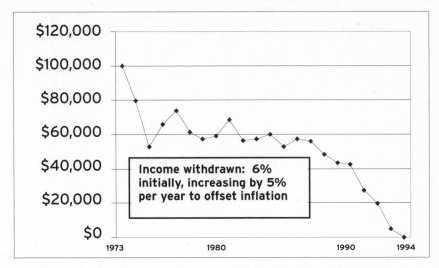

FIGURE 7.3   Based on the actual return for the S&P 500 index for 1973 through 1993. (Courtesy of Wiesenberger, a Thomson Financial Company)

Monte Carlo Simulation Models

For decades, mathematicians have been able to create performance models based on random historical timing probabilities. We have just reviewed specific time frames when you could have outlived your income if you were fully invested in the S&P 500 index. But other time frames should be considered. Some time frames would have been great. Some would have been fair. Some, as we have seen, would have been not so good.

How would various investment mixes affect your retirement income over various time frames? We should look at different investment portfolios, such as a portfolio of 60 percent stocks combined with 30 percent bonds and 10 percent cash. The answers are quite surprising. Depending on the historical years chosen, the results can be excellent or they can be devastating. Mathematically, you can determine the probabilities of success based on historical models reflecting these variables. These historical studies are referred to as *Monte Carlo simulation models.*

Let's see how we can put these Monte Carlo models to use. Assume your retirement nest egg is $1 million. Let's look at the probability of meeting your retirement income goals based on a portfolio of 60 percent stocks, 30 percent bonds, and 10 percent cash. What do you feel is a reasonable rate of income you should expect from this portfolio?

Let's assume you would like a 5 percent cash flow (increasing annually by 3 percent to offset inflation) for 30 years of retirement. Your initial retirement income would be $4,167 per month, for a total of $50,000 for the first year. Would you expect an 80 percent, 90 percent, or 100 percent probability that this increasing income will last for 30 years before you have completely depleted your principal? Surprise! When you consider all of the random past performance scenarios based on this 60 percent stocks–30 percent bonds–10 percent cash portfolio, the Monte Carlo simulations project you have only a 58 percent probability that this account will last for 30 years.

Before you get depressed, consider several important points. It is possible there may be a substantial amount of capital remaining in 30 years, if your timing is ideal. But remember, we've seen periods where the capital could be exhausted in just 21 years. There are important steps you can take to improve these probabilities, such as:

- Seek out active management versus inactive index mutual funds to reduce the volatility of your portfolio.

- If you elect inactive management (indexed mutual funds, for example), don't put all you eggs in one basket. Diversify!

- Diversify your portfolio by including real estate income trusts (REITs), bonds, foreign investments, large company stocks, and small company stocks for broader asset allocation.

- Withdraw less income in the early years of retirement.

- If possible, set aside six months to one year of income in a safe money market fund or a six-month CD. Use this account for income in a bad year, rather than liquidating your portfolio at its low point.

So what is the solution? Build more capital before you retire. Murphy's golden rule states, "He who has the gold makes the rules." Chapter 8 will focus on how to build more capital before you retire, to relieve the stress and strain of creating a lifetime of retirement income.

LESSONS AND STRATEGIES

Rules to Follow on Your Financial Journey

1. Plan on living to age 95 to 100. Remember, if you retire at 65, married, in good health, there is a 47 percent probability that either you or your spouse will still be alive at age 95.
2. Don't retire without a diversified portfolio. A portfolio consisting of 100 percent stocks is risky. Even adding bonds and cash does not guarantee you won't run out of money.
3. Be realistic in your income assumptions. Plan on initially withdrawing no more than 6 percent for income. If you want a high probability of not outliving your money, you need to be realistic in your assumptions.
4. A 5 percent initial income withdrawal plan dramatically improves the probability you won't run out of money.

Best Options for Building Capital

Whether you are building capital for your children's education or for your future retirement needs, bonds alone are not the answer. Stocks alone are not the answer. An indexed mutual fund is not the answer. What investment choices make the most sense?

Your first investment decision should be asset allocation. Asset allocation is the key to building your current pool of wealth. Over time, asset allocation will reduce your portfolio volatility and improve your rate of return. The key part of that statement is *over time*. Dollar-cost averaging is the key to adding to your current wealth. Combine asset allocation of your current investments with dollar-cost averaging of your future investments to grow your capital over time. A rising pool of capital must be today's priority if you want to retire as a lady and gentleman and not just an old woman and an old man!

New Income Tax Rates

As of 2003, there is a new income tax law, The Jobs and Growth Tax Relief Act of 2003, which includes several tax cuts. Even with this new tax law, tax deferral continues to make sense. If you can compound money without current taxation, you are already ahead. It is like having an interest-free loan from the IRS! Your capital grows faster because both your earnings and the money you would have paid in taxes are compounding. Yes, you owe taxes down the road, but look at the new tax law. Your tax rates are going down! Let's assume you were in the 30 percent marginal tax rate in the year 2002. Your tax rate on the same dollars will be only 28 percent in 2003 and later. This is great news for investors compounding money on a tax-deferred basis over the next several years.

Tax-Advantaged Retirement Planning

In Chapter 4, we discussed the burden of taxes on building capital, which eventually affects your retirement income. You may not be able to control inflation, but you certainly can control when and if you pay taxes!

Your first step is to take advantage of two major vehicles designed to help you build capital for retirement:

1. Your employer-sponsored retirement plan, such as a 410(k) plan, profit-sharing plan, or 403(b) plan

2. Your personal IRA

If you are under age 50, you can put as much as $13,000 into a 401(k) or 403(b) plan in 2004 (up to 15 percent of your income). You can invest up to $16,000 if you are age 50 or older. Your employer may match a portion of your contributions to your retirement plan. You need to make every effort to contribute at least the amount of dollars your employer matches.

The IRS provides you with a tremendous incentive to take advantage of this opportunity to build capital for your retirement. Remember, your contributions to an employer-sponsored qualified plan are pretax contributions. A part of every dollar you invest represents taxes you would have to pay if you took this money as salary. For example, if you are in the 25 percent marginal tax bracket, the IRS is contributing 25 cents of every dollar being contributed to the plan. Your contribution is 75 cents of every dollar. Your employer may also be contributing to your plan. Let's assume your earned income (salary and bonuses) is $100,000. If you are under age 50, you can contribute as much as $13,000 in 2004. In the 25 percent tax bracket, your $13,000 contribution has been subsidized by the $3,250 you save in taxes. Let's assume your employer matches the first 3 percent of your salary that you contribute to the plan. In this example, the employer will contribute $3,000 to your plan.

Think of your qualified plan opportunity as shown in Table 8.1.

Overnight your out-of-pocket investment has grown by almost 64 percent to $16,000, and you haven't even invested it yet!

Most qualified plans provide you with a selection of investment choices from which you can choose. You will be able to make changes in how your assets are allocated without incurring taxes. When you change jobs or retire, your contributions and some (or all) of your employer's contributions will be eligible for a tax-free IRA rollover, allowing you to continue the deferral of taxes until used for retirement income (after age 59½).

Table 8.2 illustrates how much you will be able to invest in your 401(k), simplified employee pensions (SEP), 403(b), or 457 plan in the years to come. If you are age 50 or older, you will be able to invest even more, as shown in the column on the right.

Salary Reduction Deferral Limits for 401(k), SEP, 403(b), and 457 Plans

Many businesses have established 401(k) plans for the benefit of their employees. These employer-sponsored retirement plans allow employees to contribute a portion of their salaries to the retirement plan on a pretax basis. Typically, these plans offer several investment choices. The earnings on the contributions grow tax deferred until withdrawn. Many plans are designed so that the company can match some portion of the contributions made by the employee.

A 403(b) plan is similar to a 401(k) plan, but it is available only to employees of nonprofit organizations such as schools and hospitals. SEP plans are designed for small businesses. These plans establish IRA accounts for each participant as the funding vehicle for the plan. Sole proprietors, partnerships, corporations, and tax-exempt organizations can establish SEP plans. A 457 plan is available for government employees. These payroll deduction plans help employees in the public sector save for retirement. All of these plans make it possible for investors to accumulate substantial

TABLE 8.1

$9,750	Your out-of-pocket cost
$3,250	Taxes you would have paid (IRS contribution)
$3,000	Employer's contribution
$16,000	Total invested in your qualified plan account

TABLE 8.2

Year	Contributions Up To Age 50	Contributions Age 50 and Over
2003	$12,000	$14,000
2004	$13,000	$16,000
2005	$14,000	$19,000
2006	$15,000	$20,000

Courtesy of IRS

assets for retirement. Table 8.2 shows how much you can set aside in these various plans.

This table illustrates the maximum you can contribute to these retirement plans. Remember, your employer might also be adding to your account!

The Economic Growth and Tax Reconciliation Act of 2001 simplified the contribution calculations for 403(b) plans. There used to be special maximum exclusion allowance calculations to compute what you could invest in a 403(b) plan, but they have been eliminated. The new schedule of what you can contribute is shown in Table 8.2. Under the new rules, up to $40,000 might be added to your 403(b) account through a combination of your contribution and your employer's additional contributions.

Some companies provide a retirement plan called a SIMPLE-IRA. This type of qualified retirement plan is ideal for many small businesses. With these plans, the underlying asset is an IRA, which in effect keeps the plan simple. Each employee opens an IRA account. The employer must also contribute by either matching dollar for dollar or matching up to 3 percent of the employee's compensation. The maximum contribution limits for this type of plan are shown in Table 8.3.

All of these plans are indexed to inflation after the year 2006. In short, it is most likely that contribution limits for all of these various plans will continue to increase. Remember, all of these plans are powerful tools for building retirement capital because:

- These are pretax contributions, so the IRS helps subsidize your initial contributions.

- The account can grow rapidly, because you pay no taxes on the gains as the account is building.

TABLE 8.3

Year	Contributions Up to Age 50	Contributions Age 50 and Over
2003	$8,000	$9,000
2004	$9,000	$10,500
2005	$10,000	$12,000
2006	$10,000	$12,500

Courtesy of IRS

- Your employer may also be contributing to the account, helping your account grow even faster.

Many of you will become millionaires simply by taking full advantage of the opportunity to build capital in your employer-sponsored qualified plan. When changing jobs, pay close attention to this employee benefit. A million-dollar qualified plan account balance is worth a lot more at retirement than a gold watch!

IRAs

The second retirement vehicle you need to examine is an IRA. There are four different types of IRAs:

1. Traditional (or standard) IRA

2. Roth IRA

3. Coverdell education savings account (formerly known as the education IRA)

4. Rollover IRA

Both the traditional and Roth IRAs are opportunities for you to build substantial assets for retirement. The Coverdell education savings account is an opportunity to build dollars for your children's or grandchildren's education. This was covered back in Chapter 6, where we focused on building assets for education. The rollover IRA is a special IRA that allows you to roll over (transfer) assets received as a distribution from another retirement plan, such as a 401(k) or 403(b) plan, without paying taxes. This allows you to continue deferring the taxes on money accumulated in qualified plans. Rollover IRAs are ideal IRAs to establish when you change jobs or retire. Unfortunately, most young workers fail to take advantage of the rollover opportunity when they change jobs.

Let's see how important this rollover opportunity is. Assume a 30-year-old is changing jobs. He has $10,000 in his 401(k) plan. If he cashes it in (assuming he has to pay 25 percent in taxes), he will have only $7,500 to spend. Unfortunately, this is what most people do. But what if this money is rolled over to an IRA to continue growing without taxes? Ten thousand dollars, invested without taxes at 8 percent for 35 years, will grow to almost $148,000. If it compounds at 10 percent, it will be worth over $280,000 at retirement! What is more important, having $7,500 to spend one time at age 30 or building $280,000 by retirement, which can create twice as much income for every year you spend in retirement? IRA rollovers make sense, even with small amounts of money. We will talk more about rollover IRAs when we address estate planning issues in Chapter 12.

Let's focus on the two IRAs that are designed to build capital as a complement or an alternative to a qualified plan:

1. Traditional (standard) IRA

2. Roth IRA

You might be able to select either type of IRA (or both) as an asset-building account. Let's first see what the traditional and Roth IRAs have in common:

- Both grow without current taxes.

- Your investment choices are the same (mutual funds, individual securities, CDs, etc.).

- You must have earned income (i.e., wages, tips, bonuses, or taxable alimony) in order to contribute.

- The amount you can contribute each year is the same. The contribution maximum is increasing in the years to come, as illustrated in Table 8.4.

TABLE 8.4

Year	IRA Contribution Under Age 50	IRA Contribution Age 50 and Over
2003–2004	$3,000	$3,500
2005	$4,000	$4,500
2006–2007	$4,000	$5,000
2008	$5,000	$6,000

Courtesy of IRS

After 2008, the contribution limits will adjust in $500 increments, based on inflation. As the contribution limits increase, IRAs will play a more important part in accumulating assets for retirement income.

When you are age 50 or older, you can contribute more to an IRA. The 2001 tax law included a catch-up provision to encourage older workers to save more for retirement.

■ A nonworking spouse can also establish an IRA as long as the working spouse earns enough to qualify. For example, let's assume you and your spouse are both over the age of 50. As long as one spouse earns $7,000, you and your spouse can each contribute $3,500 into IRAs in years 2003 and 2004.

■ Contributions must be made by April 15 of the following year.

What a Difference Time Makes

If you are under age 50, you can contribute up to $3,000 between Roth and traditional IRAs this year. And what a difference time makes! Let's assume you average an 8 percent rate of return.

Table 8.5 assumes that you make your contributions at the beginning of each year, rather than waiting until the end of the year. You can see that a 35-year-old can accumulate $575,584 by investing at the beginning of each year. Let's assume you are age 35 and you wait until the end of the year to make your contribution. You would have $54,467 less at retirement. That is almost 10 percent less at retirement if you wait until the last minute to make your contributions each year.

The calculations in Table 8.5 reflect the maximum contributions made each year according to the rules as defined in the Tax

TABLE 8.5

Current Age	Years Investing	Retirement Value If Funded at Beginning of Each Year
35	30	$575,584
40	25	$379,262
45	20	$245,648
50	15	$134,819
55	10	$74,886
60	5	$25,528

Reconciliation Act of 2001. The table also includes the full catch-up contribution in the year the individual turns age 50 and every year thereafter.

If you are married, double these figures. IRAs provide 35-year-old couples the opportunity to become millionaires before age 65.

Differences between Traditional and Roth IRAs

There are several differences between these two types of IRAs. You need to look at both before you determine which might be best for you. Let's look at the Roth IRA first. You and your spouse must have an earned income less than shown in Table 8.6 to make contributions to a Roth IRA. The contribution is not deductible, but it builds tax-free and creates tax-free income at retirement. The Roth IRA has a special appeal to young workers. After five years, both the contributions and $10,000 of earnings can be withdrawn without triggering taxes or the 10 percent penalty tax if the monies are used for a first-time home purchase. This special accessibility provides a great incentive for young couples to participate in a Roth IRA. The Roth IRA also allows tax-free, penalty-free withdrawals for college education costs. As discussed earlier, it's not a good idea to rob your retirement account to pay for your children's education. There are other options, such as a 529 college savings plan, that might be a better plan for accumulating money for college needs.

Many teenagers and college students are creating Roth IRA accounts. Let's assume a student is working part-time and earning $3,000. The student can contribute that $3,000 to a Roth IRA. The student can use money other than his or her earnings to make the contribution to the Roth IRA. For example, the parents or grandparents can make a $3,000 gift to the child, which can be used to make the Roth IRA contribution (assuming the child earned $3,000 that year working part-time). If the child earned only $1,000, then only $1,000 can be contributed to the Roth IRA. Keep in mind that people are living longer. The Roth IRA's ability to compound money

TABLE 8.6

Income Limits for Roth IRA Contributions	
Single Filers	$95,000–$110,000
Married Filers	$150,000–$160,000

Courtesy of IRS

without taxes and create a tax-free retirement income provides investors of all ages a tremendous opportunity to build financial security. Table 8.6 illustrates the modified adjusted gross income (MAGI) limits for contributing to the tax-free Roth IRA.

Let's assume you are married, both in your 50s, with a MAGI under $150,000. You and your spouse can each contribute up to $3,500 to Roth IRAs each year through tax year 2004. You'll be able to contribute more in 2005 and later. If your MAGI is between $150,000 and $160,000, your contribution limits will be lower. If your MAGI exceeds $160,000, you and your spouse cannot contribute to the Roth IRA.

Now let's look at the traditional (standard) IRA. Contributions to a traditional IRA might or might not be tax deductible. Let's first look at the three cases when they can be tax deductible:

1. If neither spouse is covered by an employer-sponsored plan

2. If you are a low wage earner covered by an employer-sponsored plan

3. If only one spouse is covered by an employer-sponsored plan

If you fall into one of these three categories, you will enjoy an up-front tax advantage and your account will grow without taxes until retirement. The income withdrawn from a tax-deductible traditional IRA is fully taxable when received.

If neither you nor your spouse is covered by an employer-sponsored plan, there is no income limitation. Regardless of how much you make, you can each contribute to a tax-deductible IRA.

If you are covered by an employer-sponsored plan, it is possible you may not be allowed a deduction for contributing to a traditional IRA. The deductibility depends on the level of your income. Table 8.7 shows the income limits for deductibility of traditional IRA contributions if you are covered by an employer-sponsored plan.

For example, in 2004, a married couple with an MAGI over $75,000 will not be able to deduct contributions to a traditional IRA if they are covered by employer-sponsored plans. If their income falls between $65,000 and $75,000, only a portion of their contributions will be deductible. It will be fully deductible if their income is under $65,000.

What if one spouse is covered by a qualified plan and the other is not? There is a different set of rules. Here are those rules:

TABLE 8.7

Year	Single Filer	Married, Filing Jointly
2003	$40,000–50,000	$60,000–70,000
2004	$45,000–55,000	$65,000–75,000
2005	$50,000–60,000	$70,000–80,000
2006	$50,000–60,000	$75,000–85,000
2007	$50,000–60,000	$80,000–100,000

Courtesy of IRS

- In tax year 2004, the deduction for the covered spouse is phased out when the MAGI is between $65,000 and $75,000. This changes in future years, as you can see in Table 8.7.

- The deduction for the working spouse not covered by a plan is phased out when the MAGI is between $150,000 and $160,000.

The traditional IRA might be the best choice if:

- Your employer does not have a qualified plan. (You can contribute to a tax-deductible IRA no matter how much you earn.)

- You make too much to qualify for a Roth IRA. (Large wage earners can contribute to a traditional IRA. It might not be tax-deductible, but it will enjoy tax-deferred growth until age 70½.)

- You are starting after age 50, with less than 15 years to invest before retirement. (A small traditional IRA account at retirement will not trigger much taxable income.)

- You need the tax deduction to help you reach the contribution limits. Remember, if you are in the 25 percent marginal tax bracket, the IRS is helping you contribute 25 cents of every dollar to your tax-deductible traditional IRA. (The immediate tax benefit provides a major incentive to contribute.)

- You anticipate little or no taxable income in retirement. (For example, your employer might not sponsor a qualified plan, so you will have no taxable income from qualified plans when you retire.)

- You are within five years of retirement and anticipate needing income from the IRA as soon as you retire. (Roth IRA contributions are subject to a five-year holding period in order for the income to be tax free.)

The Roth IRA is very appealing if:

- Your earnings are under the income limitations. (Maximum of $160,000 for married couples or $110,000 for single filers.)

- You start early and build a large account by retirement age.

- You want tax-free income throughout retirement.

- You are saving for a first home purchase and want access to your Roth IRA assets without triggering taxes or a 10 percent penalty.

- You might need to tap into your IRA for your children's education. (You can withdraw your original contribution in the Roth tax free, leaving the earnings to grow.)

- You want to avoid the requirement to begin distributions by age 70½. (There are no requirements to take distributions from a Roth IRA by a certain age.)

Choosing the Right IRA

You may want to refer to Table 8.8 from time to time to make sure you are maximizing your IRA opportunities.

Choosing the Right Combination of IRA and Qualified Plan Participation

You may want to refer to Table 8.9 from time to time to figure out your combination of IRA and employer-sponsored qualified plan.

The numbers shown for years 2007 and later will be adjusted in $500 increments to offset the effects of inflation.

IRAs and qualified plans are two great building blocks for building capital for future retirement income, but they do have limitations, such as:

- The amounts you can contribute to an IRA are limited.

- You may earn too much to contribute to either a tax-deductible traditional IRA or a Roth IRA.

- Your employer might not match any of your personal contributions to the employer-sponsored qualified plan. If the company does match, it might be only 1 to 3 percent of your salary.

- Your contribution to a qualified plan is limited. For example, your contribution to a 401(k) cannot exceed $13,000 in the year 2004 if you are under age 50.

TABLE 8.8

| Questions | Traditional IRA | | Roth IRA |
	Deductible Contributions	Nondeductible Contributions	Nondeductible Contributions
Contribution for 2004?	$3,000	$3,000	$3,000
Deductible contributions?	Yes	No	No
Income limits apply?	Yes	No	Yes
Contributions limited by employer plan participation?	Yes	No	No
Maximum age limit for contributing?	Yes	Yes	No
Earnings tax deferred?	Yes	Yes	Yes
Withdrawals tax free?	No	No	Yes
Distributions required at age 70½?	Yes	Yes	No

- The qualified plan may be designed to favor the highly compensated older employees of the firm. It may be of limited value to younger, lower compensated employees.

- The company-sponsored retirement plan may have poor investment choices.

- Many smaller companies do not offer a qualified plan.

You most likely will need to go beyond these two plans to find the complete solution for you and your family. If you need to

TABLE 8.9

| Tax Year | Traditional and Roth IRAs | | 401(k), 403(b), and SEP | | Simple | |
	Under 50	Age 50+	Under 50	Age 50+	Under 50	Age 50+
2003	$3,000	$3,500	$12,000	$14,000	$8,000	$9,000
2004	$3,000	$3,500	$13,000	$16,000	$9,000	$10,500
2005	$4,000	$4,500	$14,000	$18,000	$10,000	$12,000
2006	$4,000	$5,000	$15,000	$20,000	$10,000	$12,500
2007	$4,000	$5,000	$15,000	$20,000	$10,000	$12,500
2008	$5,000	$6,000	$15,000	$20,000	$10,000	$12,500
2009	$5,000	$6,000	$15,000	$20,000	$10,000	$12,500

complement your qualified plan and IRA, consider variable life and variable annuities as part of the solution. They will provide many important tax advantages to help you build capital for retirement while providing additional benefits for you and your family.

Variable Universal Life

This investment provides:

- Multiple tax advantages to help you build capital for retirement.
- A broad selection of professionally managed investment portfolios from which to choose.
- Flexibility in product design and investment selection.
- Unlimited contributions. (You can design a plan that allows you to contribute $50,000 or more each year, if you can afford it.)
- Relief from requirements that you have earned income to participate in a program with multiple tax advantages.
- Relief from complicated rules and regulations such as the ones with IRAs and qualified retirement plans.

Many investors are looking for these benefits and even more. Wouldn't it be great if your plan also provided:

- A choice of methods to access your investment account before age 59½ on a tax-free basis, without triggering a 10 percent penalty tax
- Additional income tax–free benefits for your family should you die prematurely

If you want these benefits, you need to look at the latest in life insurance products as part of your plan. Today's modern life insurance policies can be a tremendous complement to a qualified plan and/or an IRA. Let's review the basics of insurance and then investigate the tax advantages of variable life.

All life insurance is term insurance. You can buy a life insurance policy designed to provide only a death benefit for your family. It is called term insurance. But you have other choices. You can also choose a policy that provides a death benefit (term insurance) and also a second benefit, a forced savings account. Policies that provide the forced savings (or cash value) are often called permanent insurance. Permanent insurance sounds so rigid! Some designs are rigid, such as the traditional whole life. The forced savings (cash value) of the traditional whole life design pays a fixed return on the cash value (typically a fixed rate of return between 2 and 4 percent). It may also pay a dividend to supplement the guaranteed fixed rate of return. Both the premium and the guaranteed rate of return on the cash value are fixed (rigid). Fewer people are buying the traditional whole life design, because it is too rigid and too conservative.

However, there are alternatives. You can choose a policy building a variable savings (much like a mutual fund). Policies that provide a variable rate of return on the cash values are usually called *variable life* or *variable universal life*. The Variable universal life design provides the greatest flexibility.

The cash flow (premium) into a variable universal life policy can be designed to meet your needs and objectives. You can alter the premium flow after you begin the plan. It can be designed conservatively or very aggressively. I personally recommend the plan be designed conservatively (with investment assumptions of 8 percent or less). If you earn more than 8 percent, that's great; you get to enjoy those additional earnings. But if you design your plan with an aggressive investment assumption of 12 percent, but earn less, you will fall short of meeting your goals. If you design the policy with aggressive assumptions and fail to meet them, you will run into trouble maintaining the policy in later years. In simple English, you may have to contribute substantially greater premiums in the future to keep the insurance in force. A conservatively designed variable universal life policy will enable you to maintain the insurance coverage for life (if you want it that long) and build substantial cash value for retirement or emergency needs.

Since variable universal life (VUL) plans are the most flexible, let's focus on this design. Most of the insurance companies that offer variable universal life policies hire successful mutual fund money managers to run these variable cash value accounts. Many recently designed VUL policies offer a broad choice of money managers, so you can select from different money managers. For example, a VUL policy might give you access to multiple money managers such as Janus, Fidelity, American Century, MFS, Putnam, Lord Abbott, Alliance, and others. You can mix and match accounts managed by these money managers to create the portfolio you want, all in one package.

These variable cash value accounts are different than mutual funds because of the unique tax advantages they provide. First, the cash value (whether you choose fixed or variable) builds without current taxation. No annual 1099! If you are in the 33 percent tax bracket, your account is building 33 percent faster because all taxation is deferred. This is the same tax deferral feature that makes employer-sponsored 410(k) plans and IRAs so attractive. This tax deferral feature is one of the reasons you need to consider variable life as part of your plan. But, unlike the case for qualified plans and IRAs, life insurance premiums and the resulting cash values have no contribution limits. If you can afford a $50,000 annual premium, a variable universal life policy can be designed to accommodate that yearly cash flow. For example, Figure 8.1 assumes a $5,000 annual premium policy.

The cash value is accessible in two different ways, without incurring taxes or a 10 percent penalty tax. Liquidation of traditional IRAs and qualified plans prior to age 59½ would trigger ordinary income tax and a 10 percent penalty tax. The cash values in a variable life policy can be accessed without triggering taxes and penalties by way of:

- *A policy loan.* Loans might help you get through a short-term financial need, such as college education for your children or temporary unemployment. The insurance company will charge interest until the loan is repaid. The idea is to repay the loan as soon as you can to continue building tax-deferred capital for retirement. The loan option provides you with liquidity at any age, without triggering taxes or the dreaded 10 percent penalty tax. The net cost of these policy loans is typically 1 to 2 percent.

- *First-in-first-out partial withdrawals.* The tax code allows you to cash in or surrender part of your insurance policy for part of the cash

FIGURE 8.1 Benefits of variable universal life insurance.

surrender value, income tax free. Let's assume your premium is $5,000 per year for the next 20 years, for a total of $100,000. Let's also assume the variable cash value grows to $183,000 because of your wise investment choices. You can make a partial withdrawal up to your cost basis of $100,000 without triggering income taxes, the 10 percent penalty, or any insurance company loan interest charges. This partial withdrawal is in reality a surrender of part of your policy, and the death benefit will drop substantially. For that reason, any decision to use this provision should be carefully considered. This provision might best be used at retirement, when the need for the family insurance death benefit might be dramatically reduced. You might want to pull out all of the money you put into the policy ($100,000), tax free, to invest elsewhere for retirement income. You might then wish to keep the smaller remaining policy for estate planning reasons. (See Figure 8.2.)

Additional Tax Advantages

Should you no longer need any life insurance when you retire, you have two helpful tax-advantaged options to liquidate the policy for the entire cash surrender value:

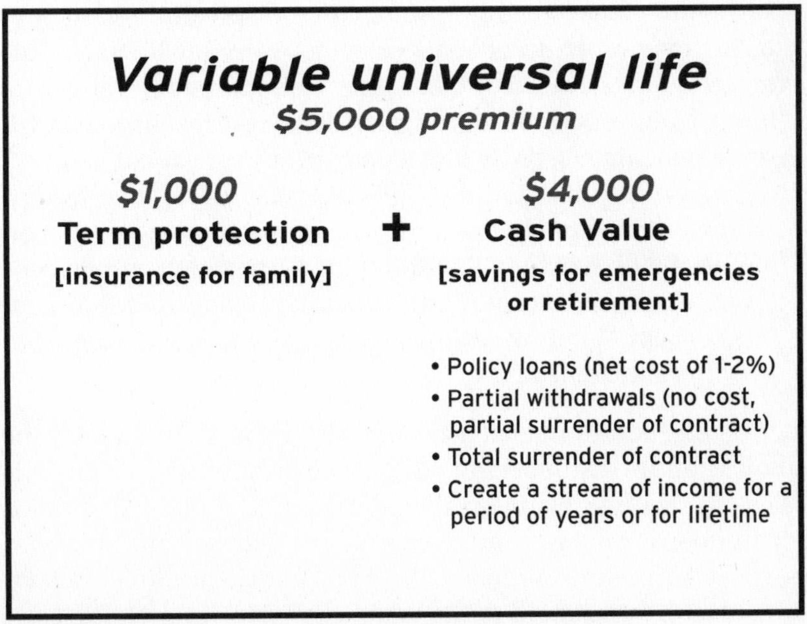

Variable universal life
$5,000 premium

$1,000
Term protection
[insurance for family]

+

$4,000
Cash Value
[savings for emergencies or retirement]

- Policy loans (net cost of 1-2%)
- Partial withdrawals (no cost, partial surrender of contract)
- Total surrender of contract
- Create a stream of income for a period of years or for lifetime

---

FIGURE 8.2   Withdrawals from variable universal life policy.

1. You can cash in the policy for the lump sum cash surrender value. You will have to pay taxes on the gains over your cost basis, but this is not as bad as it might seem at first glance. Remember, the cost basis is the entire premium, which includes the cost for the insurance protection provided for your family had you died prematurely. Again, let's assume the annual premium is $5,000. For simplicity, let's assume $1,000 of the $5,000 is needed each year for the cost of the insurance protection (the term insurance). The remaining $4,000 is invested in the cash value accounts. The cost basis is not just the $4,000 contributed to the cash value, but rather the entire premium of $5,000. Let's assume the $5,000 annual premium is paid for 20 years. The cost basis would then be $100,000. Let's also assume the cash value contribution of $4,000 per year grows at 8 percent for the 20 years, creating a cash value of $183,000. Should you cash in the policy at retirement, only the gain over the entire cost basis ($83,000) is taxable. In effect, you will be writing off the $20,000 you spent for insurance protection before you pay taxes. If you buy pure term insurance (no cash value), the cost of insurance will never be a deductible expense.

2. You can annuitize the cash values. Rather than taking the cash surrender values in a lump sum, you can spread the cash payments over a period of years or even over your lifetime. This makes more sense than taking the cash surrender value in a lump sum, especially if you plan to invest the proceeds for retirement income. Why lose a portion of your capital to taxes? Keep your capital (and the IRS's deferred taxes) invested for retirement income. In this way you are still earning profits on monies you have not yet withdrawn as income. You will continue to control taxes until the account is exhausted. More on this concept of annuitization (creating an income stream from your investments) later.

There is one additional tax advantage, but it is reserved for your family. The entire death benefit paid to the beneficiaries of the policy is income tax free. Had you elected to purchase a term insurance policy from one company and a separate tax-deferred annuity from the same or a different company, the gains in the annuity would be income-taxable when paid to the beneficiary. Not so with the variable universal life policy!

Variable cash value may seem more complicated than IRAs and qualified plans. Part of the reason is because other issues need to be considered:

- Do you need the life insurance coverage? If you are single and have no dependents, don't spend money on life insurance. You would be paying for a death benefit you don't need.

- Can you afford the higher premium of variable universal life? Perhaps term insurance is all you can afford at this time. The affordable answer might require a combination of two policies: a low-cost term policy (to take care of your family) and a tax-efficient variable universal life policy (to take care of both your family and yourself in retirement).

- Assuming your employer provides a good-quality retirement plan, are you participating in it? Most likely, participating in the qualified plan should be your first choice.

- Have you looked into IRAs? If not, consider this option. It might be an attractive option for you.

- How close are you to retirement? If you are under age 55 with family insurance needs, you should consider variable universal life as a way to build for your retirement while providing protection for your family. If you are within 10 years of retirement, other investments should be considered for building your retirement capital.

- Do you have a large estate that will be subject to estate taxes? Variable universal life is a great tool for estate planning. We'll discuss estate planning later.

- Can you invest on a periodic basis? To get all the possible tax advantages of variable universal life, you need to commit to regular, periodic premiums. Remember, it will help you build capital over time. You need to be patient and give your funds time to grow.

The ideal candidate for annual premium variable universal life (VUL) is an investor who is:

- Age 50 or less
- In a high income tax bracket (25 percent or larger)
- Already contributing to a corporate-sponsored retirement plan and an IRA

- In need of life insurance to protect his or her family

- Able to invest more money every year than existing qualified plans and IRAs allow

- In reasonably good health and able to medically qualify for the insurance

If you and your spouse meet these guidelines, by all means consider variable universal life as part of your program to build assets for retirement while providing important life insurance benefits for your family at the same time.

Variable Tax-Deferred Annuities

Many investors who are in their fifties and sixties have discovered that tax-deferred annuities are a great vehicle for building capital to create future retirement income. Also, many retired investors are purchasing deferred annuities because of the tax control on savings they might need many years down the road. In fact, there is now approximately $5 trillion invested in tax-deferred annuities. The majority of today's investors are choosing variable annuities rather than the fixed annuities. The same world-class money managers who are overseeing mutual fund and variable universal life accounts are typically managing similar variable annuity accounts.

Tax-deferred variable annuities provide:

- Access to world-class money management

- Tax-deferred buildup of capital

- The ability to transfer money between investment account choices without triggering income taxes

- Freedom from rules as to how much you can invest

- A broad choice of income options at retirement

- Estate planning benefits

These are tremendous benefits that help us build our wealth for our retirement. But annuities also take care of our families. Let's revisit the Smiths and Joneses to better understand the family benefits. Remember Joneses invested $100,000 in a tax-deferred annuity. The Smiths invested their $100,000 in a taxable investment account. By controlling taxes, Mr. and Mrs. Jones were able to build an additional $173,212 in capital. The Figure 8.3 reminds us how important it is to control taxes.

The largest pool of capital at retirement can create the largest retirement income. As we learned earlier, the Joneses could withdraw 8 percent of $466,096 or $37,287 per year for income at retirement. The Smiths could withdraw 8 percent of $292,884, which creates only $23,430 in income.

Annuity Benefits for the Family

There are some additional benefits to tax-deferred annuities. Most (but not all) variable annuities also provide a minimum death benefit guarantee, such as a guarantee that the beneficiaries will receive at least the amount that was invested in the contract.

Many annuities also guarantee a death benefit equal to the greatest yearly anniversary value. Let's assume Mr. Jones is the insured (annuitant). Let's also assume the annuity has grown to $120,000 as of the first-year anniversary. This becomes the new minimum death benefit guarantee. Let's further assume the annuity value drops in the middle of the second year to $90,000 and Mr. Jones dies. His

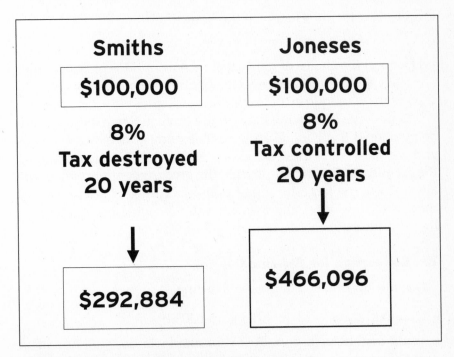

FIGURE 8.3 **Tax-controlled versus taxable investments.**

family receives the minimum death benefit guarantee of $120,000. Assume the Smiths' $100,000 alternative investment account also suffered a similar loss. Mrs. Smith will inherit only $90,000.

Some tax-deferred annuity contracts guarantee a minimum annual increase in the death benefit, such as 5 percent per year, regardless of investment performance. Again, let's assume $100,000 was invested. Let's also assume the first year's performance results in a 15 percent loss. The account value would be only $85,000 at the end of the first year. If the contract guarantees a 5 percent minimum increase in the death benefit, it would provide $105,000 to the heirs. If the performance exceeds the 5 percent guarantee, the death benefit would reflect that gain. Let's assume the $100,000 has enjoyed a 15 percent gain in the first year and the value is $115,000. The heirs will receive this greater value as the death benefit.

Some critics complain that annuities have higher fees than mutual funds. That is true. The question should be, "Are the additional fees worth it?" The benefits of annuities include:

- No 1099s while building capital for retirement
- More capital for retirement
- Protection for your family at the same time
- A broad choice of retirement income options

I also feel the choice of retirement income options provided with annuities will be more appreciated in the years to come. We will discuss these unique income options in Chapter 9.

You do have to watch what you are buying. Some annuities are being offered that contain an incredible number of expensive bells and whistles. All of these extras add additional costs. For example, the annuity contracts that provide the greatest death benefit guarantees have the largest internal costs. Talk to your advisor about these add-on features and their costs. If it is not important to have these additional benefits, don't pay for them.

Tax Conversion for Building Capital

So far, we have looked at pretax investing:

- Qualified plans, such as 401(k)s and 403(b)s
- Traditional IRAs (especially if your employer does not provide a qualified plan)

We also looked at tax-free investing:

- Roth IRAs (if you can qualify)
- Municipal bonds

And we examined tax-deferred investing:

- Nondeductible traditional IRAs
- Variable universal life
- Tax-deferred annuities

Now let's focus on tax conversion opportunities for building capital for future retirement income.

Tax Conversion

The tax code provides investors with tremendous tax advantages when investment dollars are used to purchase stocks and stock mutual funds. The gains on these appreciated assets sold after one year are taxed at the lower long-term capital gains rates of 5 or 15 percent. This tax conversion from ordinary income tax rates to the lower long-term capital gains rates is a tremendous benefit.

The 5 percent capital gains rate is paid on gains by taxpayers in the lowest two income tax brackets. If your marginal tax bracket is 10 percent or 15 percent, your capital gains tax rate is only 5 percent.

Capital appreciation enjoys tax deferral until the asset is sold. Many investors hold stocks for 5 to 10 years or even longer. There is no question that investing in common stocks entails more investment risk than buying bank CDs. But, given time, tax deferral and tax conversion—investing in the ownership of the best-run companies in the world—will be rewarding for investors building capital for retirement.

Controlling taxes is critical for building capital over time. Tax deferral is the most important part of tax control. Remember, if you are in the top tax bracket of 35%, you will build your capital 35 percent faster by taking advantage of your opportunities to control your taxes while building capital for future retirement income.

In Chapter 9 we will explore how to best create retirement income from these assets. Read carefully: The security of your retirement income is dependent on it!

LESSONS AND STRATEGIES

1. Take advantage of your employer-sponsored qualified plan. Take advantage of the increases in the amount you can contribute in the years to come.
2. Choose the IRA that is right for you. It might be the traditional or the Roth IRA.
3. If you are under age 50, consider variable universal life as a tax-favored savings vehicle to supplement your qualified plan and IRA contributions, especially if you need to provide income tax–free benefits for your family.
4. If you are age 55 or older, consider tax-deferred annuities to complement your investment program. You will enjoy tax-deferred savings and multiple retirement income options.
5. Hold stocks for the long term. Your profits will be taxed at the more favorable capital gains tax rate rather than ordinary income tax rates.
6. Think in terms of combinations of these investment vehicles for building capital for your retirement.
7. Remember to set priorities for you and your family.

Best Options for Retirement Income

arah Knauss of Harrisburg, Pennsylvania, died on December 30, 1999, just missing the beginning of the twenty-first century. Her age? 119, which qualified her as having been the oldest United States citizen in the *Guinness Book of World Records*. Her daughter, age 97, survives her.

Let's examine what you must do to create and preserve your financial health for a long, enjoyable retirement.

Conservative Sources of Retirement Income

There are four possible retirement income sources that are based on conservative assumptions:

Mandatory Plans

- Social Security
- Defined benefit pension plans

Voluntary Plans

- Immediate-income annuities
- Other qualified plans and IRAs

These four retirement income sources are conservative for two key reasons:

1. The income they can provide is based on historical (conservative) mortality assumptions. There are numerous mortality tables, but two that are the most commonly used are the 1980 commissioners standard ordinary (CSO) mortality table (used to design the premium structure of life insurance policies) and the 1983 annuity table (used to compute the income paid out to annuitants electing a lifetime income option).

2. These retirement income sources can provide you an income you cannot outlive!

Mandatory Plans

Let's first address the two most conservative programs: Social Security and defined benefit pension plans. These two retirement sources are the most conservative because:

- They are not voluntary plans. You cannot elect not to participate in a defined benefit plan if your employer provides this type of retirement income plan. Social Security contributions are mandatory.

- Your employer is also contributing to both of these plans.

- You have no choice as to how the money is invested. With Social Security, the government promises to pay your retirement benefits. With defined benefit plans, your employer guarantees the benefits. (The Pension Guarantee Corporation in Washington, DC, ensures the retirement benefits to retirees should an employer be unable to meet the obligations.)

- You know in advance what your monthly retirement benefits will be.

- The monthly income checks are the same each month. (The checks might increase over time to help offset the effects of inflation.)

- There are no benefits provided for children or grandchildren. The benefits are available only to you and your spouse. This limits the obligations as well as the costs and the risks of these plans.

For many retirees, Social Security is a major source of retirement income, so let's start there.

Social Security Decisions

Earlier, we discussed life expectancies and the trend for continuing improvements in life expectancies. Let's look at Social Security benefits, which, again, are based on historic mortality tables. According to the most recent calculations from the Social Security trustees, they are projecting a shortfall by 2013. They expect to fund full benefits until the year 2034 and only about 75 percent of the benefits beyond that year. Today, we have three workers contributing to Social Security for every retiree withdrawing income from the plan. In less than 30 years, it is projected there will be only one and a half workers for every retiree. You have to expect that there will be changes in the way this system operates, but it will most likely survive today's challenges to provide some degree of benefits for future generations.

Social Security is critically important to many of today's retirees. Social Security benefits are currently providing 63 percent of the income of today's retirees. In fact, Social Security is currently creating 90 percent or more of the income of almost one-third of today's retirees.

Let's assume Social Security will be there in one form or another for your retirement. The major changes you will see in the next several years are as follows:

- It pays to wait until normal retirement age (age 65+) rather than beginning early Social Security benefits at age 62.

- You might consider delaying your initial Social Security benefits until as late as age 70.

Full Social Security retirement benefits no longer automatically begin at age 65. It now depends on your date of birth. For example, if you were born in 1937, you will qualify for full benefits at age 65. If you were born one year later, in 1938, you have to wait until age 65 and two months. Born in 1939? You'll have to wait until age 65 and four months. For those born in 1940, the magical age is age 65 plus six months. Add two months for each year you were born after the year 1937 to find the normal age at which you can retire at full Social Security Benefits. If you were born between 1943 and 1954, full retirement age is age 66. If you were born in 1960, you have to wait until age 67! Why? We continue to live longer.

EARLY BENEFITS AT AGE 62 There are two reasons you might consider taking reduced benefits as early as age 62:

1. You are in very poor health, with a short life expectancy.

2. You have so little in savings that you cannot financially survive until age 65+ to qualify for full benefits.

CONSIDERING PART-TIME WORK AFTER AGE 62? Many of us are tempted to take early retirement with the idea of finding some type of less stressful part-time employment. A 1998 survey by the AARP revealed that 80 percent of baby boomers want to work in retirement, but in a more flexible framework. But there is a major drawback if you begin Social Security at age 62 and then find employment: For every $2 you earn over $11,280, you will lose $1 of Social Security benefits. Let's look at an example. Assume you elect early Social Security and, based on your previous earnings, you are entitled to $14,000 per year. Assume also that you find work that pays you $21,280 per year. You would lose $5,000 of your Social Security benefits. Let's assume you earned the maximum wage base amount during your working years. In the year 2000, you would have been entitled to the maximum benefit of $1,241 per month ($14,892 per year) at age 62. If you retired at age 62 and found part-time employment paying you $41,064 or more, you would lose all of your Social Security Benefits until normal retirement age.

What if you were an average wage earner until age 62? You would qualify for $853 per month ($10,236 per year). If you found part-time work that paid you $21,280, you would lose $5,000 (almost 50 percent) of your Social Security benefits until normal retirement age. If the job paid $30,000, you would receive less than $1,000 per year from Social Security. Therefore, if you plan to continue working after age 62, it is best to delay the beginning of your Social Security benefits.

If you wait until normal retirement age to begin your Social Security payments, you can work and earn any amount without a penalty. Keep in mind that your Social Security checks will be much larger if you wait until normal retirement age to begin taking benefits.

TAKING BENEFITS AT EXACTLY AGE 65 The full retirement benefit at age 65 is no longer the case. Let's assume your normal retirement age is

67. If you begin benefits at age 65, you might lose a portion of your benefits. If your wages are less than $25,000, your benefits will not be cut. If you earn more than $25,000, you will begin losing benefits. From age 65 until normal retirement age, you will lose $1 of Social Security Benefits for every $3 you earn over $25,000. Let's assume you earn more than $82,320 per year from age 65 until normal retirement age. Unfortunately, you will not receive Social Security benefits because you will be earning too much.

NORMAL BENEFITS AT AGE 65+ Why should you wait until normal retirement age to start Social Security? First, you can continue to work and earn any amount without a penalty. We are living longer, healthier lives. Using conservative mortality tables, the average life expectancy for 65-year-olds is now age 81 for men and age 84 for women. I stress the word *average* because, at age 65, half of all males and females are in better than average health. If your health is average or better than average, you have a much longer life expectancy. The Social Security literature says, "If you begin payments at the early age of 62, the payments are roughly 20% lower than had you waited until normal retirement age (65+)." There is another way to look at this. If you wait roughly three to four years, your benefits increase by 33 percent per year, for life! Some people suggest, "Take payments at age 62, because you can invest those early payments and create more value." If you do indeed invest those early payments each month for the three to four years and earn an excellent after-tax return, the break-even age is approximately age 77. You will be far ahead of the game by waiting until normal retirement age to begin your Social Security payments if either you or your surviving spouse lives past age 77. Waiting just three to four years increases your benefits by 33 percent for the rest of your life! Remember the forward-looking life expectancies? A couple age 65, in good health, has a 47 percent probability that at least one of them will be alive at age 95!

If you wait until normal retirement age to begin your benefits, you will also have a better hedge against inflation. For example, let's assume the early benefits are $14,000 per year and the normal retirement benefits are $18,620 at age 65. Let's assume benefits are increased by 3 percent per year to offset inflation.

Remember the Smiths and the Joneses? Guess which couple chose the early Social Security benefit at age 62? Yes, the Smiths.

Their initial benefit at age 62 is $14,000. In year two, the Smiths' early retirement benefit would increase by $420, whereas the future normal benefit that will be available for the Joneses increases by $559 per year. This doesn't seem like much if we are looking at only the first increase in benefits. Over time, however, there is a wide difference in benefits. The Joneses elected to wait until normal retirement age (65) to begin taking Social Security benefits. Their first check was for $20,347.

In Table 9.1 we see the difference in benefits at age 65. In 10 years (age 75), the difference has grown to $6,784. By age 80, the difference is $7,866 and increasing. This means that by age 80, there could be a difference of over $650 per month in income from Social Security. Waiting until normal retirement age to begin taking benefits provides a better hedge against long-term inflation. Remember, inflation never retires.

TABLE 9.1

Year	Beginning at Age 62	Waiting Until Normal Retirement Age
1 (Age 62)	$14,000	$0
2	$14,420	$0
3	$14,853	$0
4 (Age 65)	$15,298	$20,347
5	$15,757	$20,957
6	$16,230	$21,586
7	$16,717	$22,233
8	$17,218	$22,900
9 (Age 70)	$17,735	$23,587
10	$18,267	$24,295
11	$18,815	$25,024
12	$19,379	$25,775
13	$19,961	$26,548
14 (Age 75)	$20,560	$27,344
15	$21,176	$28,165
16	$21,811	$29,010
17	$22,466	$29,880
18	$23,140	$30,777
19 (Age 80)	$23,834	$31,700

WAITING UNTIL AGE 70 If you are married, it might pay you to wait as long as possible to begin Social Security benefits. You might even consider waiting until age 70. Why? First, you can earn any amount of income and not lose any of your benefits. Second, if you were born in 1943 or later, your yearly Social Security benefit increases 8 percent per year for each year you wait after age 66. If you wait until age 70, that is a 32 percent increase over age 66 benefits. The benefits will also be substantially greater for your surviving spouse. Remember, wives tend to outlive their husbands by several years. The further you defer your benefits, the greater the income that will be provided to a surviving spouse. If your spouse is five or more years younger than you, consider delaying your Social Security benefits until age 70 to provide the largest spousal benefit.

Pay close attention to your Social Security benefit projections, which are mailed to you each year by the Social Security Administration. You should receive your annual statement a few months before your birthday each year.

Defined Benefit Pension Plans

If you work for a company that provides a defined benefit pension plan, read this section carefully.

As recently as 1985, there were 114,000 defined benefit pension plans covering employees. As of January 2003, there were only 32,500 defined benefit pensions plans remaining, covering 44 million participants. Currently, only one out of five working family heads is covered by a defined benefit pension plan. These numbers do not include union pension plans, which provide their members with similar retirement income benefits. If neither you nor your spouse is covered by a defined benefit pension plan or a union-sponsored pension plan, you can skip this portion of the chapter.

Defined benefit pension plans provide the retiring employee with a lifetime of income. Large corporations might choose to self-insure these lifetime incomes to retirees, or the employer can elect to purchase immediate-income annuities to meet these obligations. Smaller companies often rely solely on immediate-income annuities to provide the employee lifetime income benefits.

Let's look at the three most common lifetime income choices you will have at retirement:

1. Life-only income (no benefits for a surviving spouse)

2. Life with 50 percent to the surviving spouse

3. Life with 100 percent to the surviving spouse

In Table 9.2, let's put some numbers to these options so you can better understand your monthly income choices:

Most of these plans do not permit a lump sum distribution at retirement: The employee must elect one of the income options. Most employers stress the second option, which is the one the government prefers you choose, because it provides some income for the surviving spouse. In our example, this option pays a monthly income of $850 while both the retiree and his or her spouse are alive. The surviving spouse receives 50 percent of this income ($425) for life. In fact, if you want to choose the life-only option, your spouse must sign forms acknowledging the fact that he or she will receive no survivor income.

There are six key points to consider:

1. The greater the benefit for the surviving spouse, the lower the initial retirement income.

2. In effect, you are buying insurance for the surviving spouse with the difference in pension income.

3. Should your spouse predecease you, you will most likely have to continue the same income option, even though there will be no benefits paid to anyone after your death.

4. For example, let's assume you elect the second option, paying you $850 per month. Let's also assume your spouse dies first. You cannot change your pension option to the life-only option, which would have paid you $1,000 per month. With most plans, you are out $150 per month for life, paying for a

TABLE 9.2

Income Option	Monthly Income While Both Are Alive	Monthly Income for Surviving Spouse
Life only	$1,000	$0
Life with 50 percent to surviving spouse	$850	$425
Life with 100 percent to surviving spouse	$700	$700

benefit no one will ever receive. Read the fine print of your plan description to see if you have any options should your spouse predecease you.

5. If you are in poor health, you should consider the third option, which buys the most insurance for your spouse. It may not be the cheapest or best way to buy insurance, but it might be the only way to provide for your spouse if you are in poor health and unable to buy life insurance.

6. If you are in good health, you should purchase your own personal life insurance. You can pay for your personally selected insurance by using part of the life-only pension income to pay the premium cost.

Purchasing Your Own Insurance

If you are in good health, you need to consider this planning tip to create an estate for your children and grandchildren. Remember, all of the pension options provide benefits solely for the retiree and the surviving spouse. There are no benefits paid to the rest of the family. Here is a plan worth considering:

- Find out how healthy you are by applying for life insurance. Most retirees can qualify for insurance. Remember, insurance companies are in the business of selling life insurance, not refusing to write life insurance policies. They don't expect a retiree to have the health of a 20-year-old: They only expect you to be as healthy as the average retiree.

- Determine how much insurance you need to purchase to provide income for your surviving spouse. Let's assume you want to create a plan that will provide $700 per month, or $8,400 per year, to your surviving spouse. Assuming your surviving spouse can create a 5 percent income stream, you will need to purchase $168,000 of insurance. Buy your insurance as soon as you can. The cost will be much lower if you purchase the insurance at age 55 rather than waiting until age 65.

- Make sure your life insurance is in place before you elect your pension option. If you cannot qualify for life insurance, you should not elect the life-only pension option. If you can't qualify for insurance, you need to consider a pension option that provides adequate survivor benefits for your spouse.

- Assuming you have adequate insurance in place, elect the life-only pension option when you retire, because it provides $300 more income every month for life. Use a portion of this $300 per month additional income to fund the insurance that will provide benefits for your spouse as well as your children or grandchildren.

- Consider establishing a life insurance trust to own this insurance policy. The trustee can be instructed to provide $700 per month to your surviving spouse for life. The trust might also provide the trustee with the power to invade the principal of the trust for the benefit of the spouse should there be special needs, such as adjustments for inflation, long-term care costs, and other emergency needs.

- When your surviving spouse dies, the balance in the trust will be distributed to your children or heirs both estate and income tax free.

- This plan is flexible. If your spouse predeceases you, there are several options as to what you might do with the insurance policy:
  - Cash it in for the cash surrender value
  - Convert it to a smaller paid-up policy for the children or heirs
  - Continue to fund the insurance for the benefit of the children or heirs

This plan provides greater flexibility for both you and your spouse. You and your spouse can decide how much insurance you need to purchase and the trust can provide important flexibility in providing for your spouse.

Don't wait until retirement to create your plan. The sooner you design and begin to implement your plan, the better your retirement will be. If there is a good chance you will be working for your current employer until retirement, begin creating your plan now!

Both Social Security and defined benefit plans are basic building blocks for retirement income. Remember, they don't provide enough retirement income for retirees to maintain their standard of living. Neither is intended to be your only source of retirement income. Let's see how you can supplement these benefits.

Voluntary Conservative Retirement Income Sources

With each passing generation, we see Social Security and defined benefit pension plans playing a smaller role in creating retirement income. We need to find meaningful ways to supplement these plans if we truly want to retire in dignity. Let's now look at the next three most conservative retirement income sources available:

1. Annuities

2. Qualified plans (other than defined benefit plans)

3. IRAs

These potential income sources have four things in common:

1. They are voluntary. In most cases, you can elect to contribute or not. (No one has to buy an annuity.)

2. You have some control over how the money is invested.

3. You have more income options when you retire.

4. You can leave a legacy to your children, grandchildren, or favorite charities or elect to spend all the money.

Immediate-Income Annuities

Many of us are somewhat familiar with tax-deferred annuities and how they can play an important part in building capital for retirement. But few know how to get money out of a tax-deferred annuity. Let's focus on how best to use your tax-deferred annuities for conservative retirement income.

We first met the Smiths and the Joneses when they were age 45 and investing $100,000. Both couples earned an 8 percent rate of return. The Smiths chose a tax-destroyed account (paying taxes on their profits every year). Because of taxes, their account grew to only $292,844 in 20 years. The Joneses invested their $100,000 in a tax-controlled deferred annuity. By controlling taxes, the Joneses built an account worth $466,096 at retirement. Earlier we learned that both couples could spend only the interest they earn each year from their respective accounts. Table 9.3 shows the retirement income both families would enjoy should their two accounts continue to earn 8 percent throughout retirement.

Both of the incomes are taxable income.

The Joneses created their income using an annuity income option called a partial withdrawal. Partial withdrawals are taxable as long as there are earnings accumulated in the annuity. Basically, their income is composed of the accumulated and future earnings in their annuity contract. These earnings are taxable income as they

TABLE 9.3

	Capital at Retirement	Earnings in Retirement	Income in Retirement
Smiths	$292,884	8%	$23,431
Joneses	$466,096	8%	$37,288

are withdrawn. If the Joneses withdraw more than their accumulated earnings, they will receive a return of their original principal. A return of the original principal is tax free.

The Smiths' income is also taxable even though they paid taxes each year as they built their account. At retirement, they notify their investment institution to stop compounding the taxable earnings and start mailing the future earnings to them as income. The Smiths' retirement income checks come with a 1099 every year.

Assuming both couples spend only the earnings of 8 percent on their accounts, the Joneses have $13,857 in additional income every year. This additional income is more than $1,000 per month! Over 30 years of retirement, that's $415,710 additional income, all created by controlling the taxes on their initial $100,000 investment while it was building for 20 years before they retired. The Joneses have 59 percent more retirement income than their neighbors, the Smiths. Both incomes are taxable, but the Joneses are the happier retirees!

You may be wondering how this will affect the children or heirs of Mr. And Mrs. Jones when they inherit the annuity. First of all, the children will be happy that their parents enjoyed $13,857 additional retirement income every year they were alive. (In short, that's $13,857 the children didn't have to provide their aging parents every year.) When the children inherit the annuity, they will have to pay income taxes on the accumulated gain in the annuity. Assuming the Joneses' children have to pay taxes at the rate of 31 percent on the $366,096 of deferred earnings built up in the annuity, they will have $352,607 after taxes. The Smiths' children don't owe any income taxes, but they inherit only $292,884 ($59,723 less). The annuity has provided substantial benefits for the Joneses' children.

Family Planning Hint

The Joneses' children would receive even more if they received their annuity inheritance over 10, 20, or 30 years as income rather than as a lump sum settlement. More on this estate leveraging technique later.

Let's take a second look at the Smith family's situation. The Smiths' children might not inherit the $292,884 shown earlier. To understand why, let's remember Mrs. Smith's jealous nature. In order to keep up with the Joneses, the Smiths began invading their principal in order to create a cash flow that was identical to that of the Joneses. Unfortunately, at this accelerated rate of withdrawal, the Smiths' account will be depleted in just a few years.

Like the Smiths, too many retirees do not have enough capital to enjoy the luxury of simply living on the earnings of their investments. They begin eating into their investment capital. Often, the result is disastrous.

Your Important Annuity Income Options

It makes sense to look at the other income options available with annuities for two reasons:

1. You may need substantially more income from this asset.

2. You might want to control the income taxes on your retirement income to create more spendable income.

Let's return to the story of the Jones family. They built $466,096 in their tax-deferred annuity by age 65. One option would be to cash in (liquidate) the annuity as a lump sum settlement. Should they do so, the results would be:

$466,096	Annuity value
Less 113,490	Taxes (31% tax bracket × $366,096 tax-deferred gain)
$352,607	Value of annuity after lump sum surrender

This lump sum distribution is not the Joneses' best option, but it is better than had they paid taxes along the way as the Smiths had done. Even after taxes, the remaining annuity value of $352,607 is greater than the Smiths' $292,884. This was possible because the Joneses took advantage of an interest-free loan with the IRS.

But, for most investors, it makes no sense to cash in an annuity at age 65 for a lump sum payout. Why should the Joneses lose $113,490 of their retirement capital? It makes more sense either to withdraw only the future earnings during retirement or to slowly liquidate the annuity principal over an extended period of time. Don't just control taxes until retirement; continue to control taxes throughout retirement.

Most retirees need to strive for level taxation through their retirement years. That is why most do not take a lump sum distribution from their qualified retirement plans, IRAs, or tax-deferred annuities.

Additional Annuity Income Options

Whether you are electing an income option from a tax-deferred annuity or purchasing a new immediate-income annuity when you retire, you have a wide variety of additional income choices that will provide more income than merely withdrawing the earnings each year. For example:

- You can elect to have the annuity value paid to you for a specific number of years, usually between 5 and 30 years. This is called a designated period payout.

- You can elect to have the account value paid out to you as an income stream that is guaranteed for life. You can choose to have the lifetime income paid out over one or two lifetimes. (Married couples usually choose to have the income paid out over two lives.) These lifetime income options are referred to as life only or joint life only income options.

- You can select lifetime income options that combine the first two options, creating an income for life while guaranteeing payments for a minimum number of years whether you are alive or not. For example, you might choose joint life income with 10 years certain. This option would pay you and your spouse an income for life. Should you both die in less than 10 years, the beneficiaries (typically your children) will continue to receive the income for the balance of the 10-year minimum period. In this way, someone is guaranteed to receive at least 10 years of income; hence the phrase *10 years certain*. It is a form of a minimum guarantee for the various lifetime income options. Let's examine these income options in greater detail.

All of these income options are available for both fixed and variable annuities. The income begins right away in an immediate annuity, whereas the income option can be selected at some future date in a deferred annuity. Once the income begins, the rate of return on a fixed annuity does not fluctuate. Therefore, with a fixed annuity, the income options provide a fixed cash flow for the payout option chosen.

There are more income options with a variable annuity. The income options can be fixed (as the fixed annuity provides) or variable (reacting to market performance of the accounts chosen). We will look at specific examples later in this chapter to see how these options might work for you.

Designated Period Options

If you and your spouse are in poor health, or if you don't like the concept of lifetime income, you can elect to have the annuity paid out to you over a specific number of years. For example, you can chose any time frame from 5 to 30 years. This is called a *designated period option*. You can choose either a fixed income payout or a variable income payout for the time frame you designate. Let's take a closer look at the 30-year time frame.

30-YEAR DESIGNATED PERIOD FIXED INCOME PAYOUT In Chapter 7, we talked about the risks associated with relying on an unchanging income stream over a number of years. We looked specifically at the risks associated with taking an unchanging income stream from a variable investment portfolio. The Monte Carlo simulations revealed a high probability that your principal (and therefore your income) might not last 30 years. A fixed annuity paid out over a designated time frame provides a 100 percent probability that the fixed income will continue for the period chosen. Again, you can choose any period of time from 5 years to 30 years, knowing that the insurance company guarantees those payments for the period of time you chose. These designated period fixed income options are available on both the fixed and variable deferred annuities.

With the variable annuity, the income will vary each year, but it is guaranteed to last for the designated period of time elected. The variable annuity might create more or less income than the fixed annuity.

Let's return to our example. The Joneses' tax-deferred annuity has grown to $466,096 by age 65. Let's assume they select the 30-year designated period income option. Let's also assume they elect a fixed income payout. They will receive an income that is partly a return of their account value (⅟₃₀ of $466,096) and partly future earnings. A fixed annuity guarantees the rate of return for the entire payout period selected. Today's fixed annuities credit approximately 5 percent in the payments of 30-year payouts. This option would provide the Joneses a fixed income of $34,789 per year for 30 years. Part of each payment will be a tax-free return of a portion of their original investment in the contract. For the Joneses, $3,333 (⅟₃₀ of $100,000) of their annual income is considered tax free as a return of principal. Here is the breakdown for the Joneses' annual income should they choose a 30-year designated period income option:

$31,466	Taxable accumulated and future earnings
Plus $3,333	Tax-free return of original investment (⅟₃₀ of $100,000)
$34,789	Total annual fixed income for 30 years

One of the biggest advantages of slowly liquidating the annuity over a period of years is that the portion remaining in the annuity continues to earn investment returns until it is paid out. The Joneses' deferred account of $466,096 would pay out a total of $1,043,670 over 30 years. In effect, they will earn $366,096 while building their capital from age 45 to age 65 and then earn an additional $577,574 during the 30-year payout phase.

There is a second important tax benefit concerning this annuity income option. Not only will the income be level, but the taxation will also be level. The accumulated interest earnings and the future credited earnings will be paid out in equal installments. The 1099s are the same each year for the entire 30-year payout period selected.

Any other investment account liquidated in equal installments over 30 years would not receive level taxation. For example, let's assume the Joneses sold their home and agreed to finance it for the buyer. Most of the early mortgage payments would be taxable income for the Joneses. Only in the last years of the mortgage would the Joneses have tax relief, as the final payments would be mostly tax-free return of borrowed principal. An immediate-income annuity can create a similar cash flow and provide the additional advantage of level taxation each year for 30 years.

There are several advantages to this fixed 30-year designated period payout income option:

- The income is guaranteed to be the same each year for the entire 30-year period.

- A portion of each payment will be tax free as a return of the original investment in the contract.

- The portion remaining in the annuity continues to earn interest until the final payment is distributed.

- The income is taxed exactly the same every year for the entire 30-year period.

30-YEAR DESIGNATED PERIOD VARIABLE INCOME PAYOUT If you choose a short payout period, such as five years, the fixed payout option makes sense. If you choose a long-term payout, such as 30 years, you need to consider a variable payout, which can earn more than a fixed rate of 5 percent to help offset inflation. Let's once again consider the Monte Carlo simulations we looked at earlier. Those simulations were first revealed following a groundbreaking study by three professors at Trinity University in San Antonio. The study by Philip Cooley, Carl Hubbard, and Daniel Walz measured the returns of stocks and bonds from 1926 through 1995 and revealed how difficult it is to create an income of 6 percent or more and achieve more than a 50 percent probability of having the income last for 30 years, especially if the first few years of the retirement income suffer investment losses.

The variable annuity can solve this income problem. The variable annuity can provide you a 100 percent probability of income for 30 years via a variable designated period payout. Under this payout option, the variable annuity will pay out $\frac{1}{30}$ of your account value each year, adjusted for portfolio performance. It is not providing a fixed income. The variable annuity is providing a variable income that will last exactly 30 years.

Let's return to the story of the Jones family to see how this variable income option can benefit them. Based on an 8 percent assumed rate of return, their $466,096 could provide a 30-year variable income of

$41,402 per year. If future returns are greater than 8 percent, the income will increase. If the returns are less than 8 percent, the future income will be less than $41,402. The income will vary each year, but it will last for exactly 30 years.

If you think future investment returns will average 5 percent or less, purchase a fixed-income annuity. If you feel you can earn more than 5 percent over the next 30 years, think variable-income annuity. Don't know which way to go? Split your capital and buy both a fixed and a variable annuity for income.

The designated period payout income options provide more income and better tax control than a lump sum payout. Remember, you can choose anywhere from 5 to 30 years for your designated time frame to liquidate your account. Is it possible to outlive the income provided by a designated period payout? Yes! What if you retire at age 60 and your spouse is age 55? Is there a high probability at least one of you will be alive and needing income for more than 30 years? Yes! To create a lifetime of income, consider a lifetime annuity payout.

Lifetime Income Options

Annuities are the only financial instrument that can provide you an income composed of principal and earnings with a guarantee that you cannot outlive the income.

Because we are living in a low-interest-rate environment, we need to consider these lifetime income options carefully. The life insurance industry has been offering conservative fixed lifetime income solutions for generations. Perhaps your parents are enjoying a fixed pension income, guaranteed for life, created by a defined benefit pension plan. Unfortunately, fewer and fewer companies are offering defined benefit plans to their current employees, because these plans require a substantial corporate commitment. Instead, corporations are offering programs like 401(k) plans, where all of the investment decisions are placed on the employee. You are indeed fortunate if your employer provides a combination of both types of retirement plans.

The insurance industry has the expertise to develop products where life expectancy is involved. Their knowledge of life expectancies has enabled them to develop not only life insurance products but also defined benefit payout options for corporate plans and lifetime annuity income options, which any consumer can create within an annuity. Insurance companies combine the use of historical life expectancy tables and their actuarial experience to design a choice of income streams the retiree cannot outlive.

Annuities will play a significant role in the lives of the 77 million baby boomers born between 1946 and 1964 for three main reasons:

1. Concern about the solvency of the Social Security entitlement program

2. The fact that we are not saving enough for retirement

3. The probability that we will live a long time in retirement

According to Michael Stein, CFP, the author of *The Prosperous Retirement* (Emstco, 1998), the trend toward increasing longevity should continue for the next 20 years. This means the life expectancy of 65-year-olds could increase by 25 to 30 percent.

Just to make life challenging, the insurance industry gives us even more choices on how to create retirement income. Both deferred and immediate annuities, whether fixed or variable, offer two lifetime income options:

1. A lifetime income for two lives

2. A lifetime income for one life

If you are married, chose option 1. If you are single, divorced, or widowed, chose option 2.

Annuities typically use the 1983 annuity mortality tables to determine what they will pay out to annuity owners electing a lifetime payout. Remember, life expectancy is not the same as death expectancy.

For simplicity, let's consider a single person electing a lifetime payout option. Based on the 1983 annuity table, a 65-year-old male has a life expectancy of 18.63 years. Based on this historic table, he has a 50-50 probability of being alive at age 83. Some annuitants will die prior to age 83 (the "early diers"). Fifty percent of income annuitants should live past age 83 (the "long livers"). Both groups are guaranteed an income for life. Insurance companies base the lifetime income stream on this actuarial basis (paying out all of the principal plus investment return) over 18.63 years. All of the annuitants choosing a lifetime income payout will receive an income for life.

Assuming you are married, you have several joint life income options. The most popular options are:

- *Lifetime income with 100 percent to the surviving spouse.* This option provides the most income for your surviving spouse, but the least income while both are alive. That's the trade-off. If your spouse is much younger and you are concerned about providing the most income for him or her, you need to consider this option.

- *Lifetime income with 75 percent to the surviving spouse.* This option creates more income while you are both alive, but provides less income for the surviving spouse. The surviving spouse receives only 75 percent of the initial income amount.

- *Lifetime income with 50 percent to the surviving spouse.* This option creates even more income while both are alive, but provides the least income to the surviving spouse. The surviving spouse receives only 50 percent of the initial income. This option will appeal to those retirees who intend to travel (spend) more while they are both alive and in good health.

These are the most common options, but other joint life income options are often available.

A fixed lifetime income annuity will appeal to you if:

- You are in average or better than average health

- You desire a fixed income to cover your fixed expenses in retirement

- You do not want to worry about the investment risk

- You want an income you cannot outlive

Unfortunately, this tends to get confusing. Let's compare some examples to clarify the differences in these fixed guaranteed lifetime income options. In Table 9.4, let's look at a married couple, age 65, with $100,000 to invest, wanting a fixed income they cannot outlive.

TABLE 9.4

Income Option	While Both Are Alive	Surviving Spouse
Lifetime income with 100% to the surviving spouse	$7,562 per year	$7,562 per year
Lifetime income with 75% to the surviving spouse	$8,002 per year	$6,001 per year
Lifetime income with 50% to the surviving spouse	$8,497 per year	$4,248 per year

Let's see what the income would be if the couple waited until age 70 to purchase their immediate fixed-income annuity. The income per year will be much higher, because their life expectancy is shorter. If they wait until age 70, their $100,000 investment can create the following income they cannot outlive. (See Table 9.5.)

With lifetime income options, the key to remember is life expectancy. For example, let's take a closer look at the lifetime income with 100 percent to the surviving spouse option. For a married couple, age 65, we know the income will be $7,562 per year for life. Using the historical 1983 annuity mortality table, this couple's life expectancy is projected by the insurance company to be 25.47 years. Let's round it off to 25 years. The total expected return is $192,609. (Multiply the annual income by the average life expectancy to determine the total expected return.)

Over the first 25 years, this couple will receive an income composed of $\frac{1}{25}$ of their $100,000 investment and a fixed rate of investment return. In this example, the internal rate of return is fixed for life at roughly 6 percent. Once again, the annual lifetime income is fixed at $7,562 per year. Over the first 25-year period, $3,925 (or 52 percent) of the income represents a tax-free return of the original investment. The balance of the income ($3,637 or 48 percent) is taxable investment return. Over the first 25-year period, the couple will enjoy level taxation. The 1099 will be the same each year for the first 25 years. Had this money been invested anywhere else, the taxation would be different. Had the couple loaned this $100,000 to a trusted friend, with the borrower promising to repay the loan in equal installments over 25 years, their early years of income would be mostly taxable income. The final years of their income would be mostly tax-free return of principal. There is economic value in having level taxation for the first 25 years of retirement.

TABLE 9.5

Income Option	While Both Are Alive	Surviving Spouse
Lifetime income with 100% to the surviving spouse	$8,179 per year	$8,179 per year
Lifetime income with 75% to the surviving spouse	$8,779 per year	$6,584 per year
Lifetime income with 50% to the surviving spouse	$9,474 per year	$4,737 per month

Remember, with their lifetime-income annuity, the couple has a 50 percent or better probability of outliving the total expected return. They are guaranteed an income they cannot outlive. The income they receive after the first 25 years is fully taxable. Why? They have had their entire investment in the account returned to them during the first 25 years. Income created after that point is pure profit, fully taxable.

The couple is now age 90. Based on forward-looking mortality projections, they have almost a 50 percent probability that one of them will still be alive at age 95. One or both could easily live to age 100 or beyond. Earlier, we divided annuitants into two groups: the early diers and the long livers. The money left in the legal reserves by the early diers creates the income provided to the long livers.

The lifetime annuity income options (fixed or variable, providing income for one or two lives) will maximize your lifetime guaranteed stream of retirement income.

Negative Press Concerning Immediate Annuities

For many years, there has been negative press concerning annuitization. Let's review the criticisms.

"BUT THE INSURANCE COMPANY CAN STEAL MY MONEY!" Some people have commented, "The life insurance company steals my money if I die early." That is not the case! These dollars are legal reserves that remain invested to provide the guaranteed lifetime income for all of those who live longer than the average life expectancy. Earlier I referred to annuitants as either early diers or long livers. The early diers (those who die before reaching average life expectancy) leave their remaining principal in the legal reserves of the insurance company to provide a guaranteed lifetime income for those annuitants who are long livers (those living beyond average life expectancy). Remember, all of the annuitants were guaranteed an income for life.

"BUT LOOK AT ALL THE MONEY I COULD LOSE!" Let's again consider our 65-year-old male who invested $100,000 in a life only immediate-income annuity. Let's assume he is run over by the proverbial concrete truck while on his way to the bank to deposit his first annuity income check. His estate is out $100,000, right? Not necessarily. Let's assume this annuity is not part of a qualified plan. There are two important tax ramifications on this nonqualified asset at his death:

1. The unrecovered cost basis is an income tax–deductible loss.

2. There will be no estate taxes on the annuity.

INCOME TAX-DEDUCTIBLE LOSS   When the heirs file the final income tax return of the deceased annuitant, they can declare the unrecovered cost basis in the immediate annuity a tax-deductible loss. In the case of an early death, the deductible loss could be substantial. If the man in our example dies right after purchasing the life only immediate-income annuity, the estate has a $100,000 tax-deductible loss. But what if he died on January 3 with only two days of reportable income? The heirs will not lose the deduction. They can refile up to five years of the deceased's previous tax returns to apply the loss against earlier years of taxable income, creating a tax refund for the heirs.

If this man's death occurs after age 83, there will be no deductible loss. He has lived average life expectancy and has recovered all of his investment in the annuity contract in the form of income. There is no loss.

ESTATE TAX CONSIDERATIONS   Estate taxes can be as high as 48 percent in tax year 2004. The life only income options, whether they pay income for one or two lives (single life only or joint life only), leave no value in the estate for estate tax purposes. For wealthy individuals, all life only income options eliminate the largest beneficiary, the IRS, from receiving any taxes on this type of annuity. The heirs might recover as much as 35 percent by way of income tax deductions, and they are avoiding estate taxes of as much as 49 percent.

The combination of income tax deductions (because of unrecovered cost basis in the annuity) and estate tax avoidance (on the life only annuity) makes this income option a very attractive income source for many wealthy investors. Many annuity investors don't need the income generated by the annuity. Each year, this income can be gifted to the children for the purchase of life insurance. The annuity income can be used to create an estate (with life insurance) that will be both income and estate tax free for the heirs.

This income option is not just for the wealthy. One of the greatest benefits of choosing a lifetime income option is that the income continues for life, even after the original investment has been depleted. This can be a great option for those who retire with little capital who need to maximize their lifetime income. Let's consider our 65-year-old male with $100,000 to invest. Let's assume he needs a fixed income for as long as he lives. Currently, a life only option would pay him monthly checks totaling $9,500 per year. Sixty percent of this income will be tax free for the first 20 years of income. What other vehicle can create this much tax-favored income guaranteed for life? It's not a question of, "Look at all the money I could lose." Those who elect this income option say, "Look at all of the income I can generate for life!"

The life only options are ideal for investors enjoying average to excellent health. Those in poor health should elect the designated period payout options, which create an income for the stated number of years elected. Remember, you can chose a period from 5 to 30 years. Assuming you elected the 30-year designated period income stream but died in the fifth year, your heirs would get the remaining 25 years of the income stream.

LIFETIME INCOME COMBINED WITH PERIOD CERTAIN There is an additional series of income options you can consider. This series combines the lifetime income options (for one or two lives) with the period-certain options. These options are referred to as the life with period-certain options. For example, let's assume a 65-year-old couple elects a joint life annuity with 100 percent to the surviving spouse with a 10-year period-certain guarantee. This couple is guaranteed a lifetime income for as long as either is alive. There is also a minimum guarantee that these income payments will be made to someone for a minimum of 10 years. If this couple dies at the end of year 1, their named beneficiaries (children) will receive the 9-year balance of the 10-year minimum guaranteed income stream.

Adding the period-certain provision to a lifetime income option will reduce your income checks. It may make little difference if you are a young age 65 and add only a 10-year certain guarantee of income. If you add a long period-certain provision, such as a 30-year period, it will drastically reduce your monthly income for life.

Compare the income generated by the life only options and the life with 10-year certain options. If there is little difference in income, choose the life option with a 10-year certain provision. It will give you added peace of mind in making your annuity income decision.

Think in combinations. You may want some income guaranteed for life with the balance paid out over a specific number of years. As we have seen, there are income options available that combine these two features, such as life with 10 years certain. It's all about choices and combinations. Again, seek professional advisors who can help you create a plan to meet your needs.

"WHAT ABOUT INFLATION?" In addition to being able to choose between the designated period options, the life only options, and the life with period certain income options, you also get to select the type of income that best meets your needs:

■ Fixed income (for one or two lives)

■ Variable income (for one or two lives)

You can consider combinations of the two. If you are concerned about inflation, you need to consider investing at least a portion of your capital in a variable annuity for retirement income.

Designing a Variable Immediate Annuity: 3 Percent, 4 Percent, 5 Percent, 6 Percent, or Other

Creating income using a variable annuity is quite different than creating an income stream from a fixed annuity. With a fixed immediate-income annuity, the insurance companies are offering a fixed lifetime retirement income based on an internal rate of return of approximately 5 to 6 percent. They are paying this fixed lifetime of income (part principal and part fixed investment return) based on the assumption that they can invest your annuity dollars at a rate of return equal to or exceeding the guaranteed rate they are paying you. They are guaranteeing your fixed income stream whether they meet their investment assumptions or not. The guaranteed income from a fixed annuity is also based on historic life expectancies. They are guaranteeing these fixed lifetime payments, regardless of changes in life expectancies or investment returns.

The whole concept of variable annuitization is probably new to you. Let's make sure you understand the lifetime income options available through variable annuities. These variable income options are available if you want income from a tax-deferred variable annuity or are purchasing an immediate-income variable annuity.

Let's assume you are retiring today and purchasing an immediate-income variable annuity. Variable annuities allow you, the consumer, to determine the investment risk and reward you want built into your annuity income stream. Part of each annuity payment will be a return of your original investment (premium) in the contract. The second key ingredient in a variable annuity income payout is the rate of return earned by your portfolio. No one knows exactly what future investment returns will be. As you design the income stream you will receive from a variable annuity, you need to assume some rate of investment return to begin your stream. To calculate your initial income, you have to select an assumed investment return (AIR). Fixed annuities today offer an internal rate of return of roughly 5 to 6 percent, which they are guaranteeing for the life of the contract. With variable annuities, the consumer designs the income stream by selecting the AIR of the contract.

Most variable annuity contracts give you a choice: 3 percent, 4 percent, 5 percent, or 6 percent AIR. Since the actual rate of return in the future is unknown, you select an AIR that will be used in calculating your retirement income. If you are conservative, choose the 3 percent AIR design. You will get an income that is partially a return of your original investment in the contract and the investment return of your portfolio. Let's assume you and your spouse are both age 70, with $100,000 to invest. Let's also assume you select the joint Life with 100 percent to the survivor income option, which will provide a lifetime income for you and your surviving spouse. Based on historical tables, you and/or your spouse have a life expectancy of 20.6 years. Let's also assume you selected the conservative 3 percent AIR. Using today's mortality tables, your first payment will consist of 1/20.6 of your principal, plus your selected AIR of 3 percent. Your total first year income would be $6,000 ($500 per month). Every year that your portfolio's actual return exceeds the assumed return, your income check goes up. If the actual return equals your assumed rate of return, there is no change in your check. If the portfolio's return is less than your assumed rate of return, your check will go down.

Selecting a 3 percent AIR is the most conservative design for a variable-income annuity. Think of the AIR as a hurdle for the money managers you have selected. Every time they clear that hurdle, your income checks go up. Let's assume you selected the 3 percent AIR and the actual return is 9 percent. The money managers have cleared the hurdle by 6 percent. The greater their performance over the hurdle, the greater the increase in your check.

Let's compare this to the high-end assumption, an AIR of 6 percent. The first payment will be much larger, because it is created by a return of part of your initial investment and a 6 percent assumed investment return. The total cash flow in the first year is $8,016 (roughly 8 percent). But the performance hurdle is much higher. The money managers must clear a 6 percent hurdle for you to get a raise in your income. If they earn exactly 6 percent, there will be no increase in your income. If the performance is less than 6 percent, your income checks go down. If your actual return is 9 percent, your check will go up, because you have cleared the 6 percent hurdle. But the increase in income will not be as much as it would have been had you chosen the conservative 3 percent hurdle.

Let's look at Table 9.6 to see how these two income options compare. Let's assume $100,000 is invested in an immediate-income variable annuity to provide a joint life with 100 percent to the surviving spouse income for a couple age 70. Let's also assume a 9 percent investment rate of return.

The income from a 3 percent AIR annuity starts low and increases every time the investment portfolio you have chosen earns more than 3 percent. This conservative design provides the best opportunity for

TABLE 9.6

Age	3% AIR	6% AIR
70	$6,000	$8,016
71	$6,350	$8,243
72	$6,720	$8,476
73	$7,112	$8,716
74	$7,526	$8,963
75	$7,965	$9,216
76	$8,430	$9,476
77	$8,921	$9,745
78	$9,441	$10,021
79	$9,991	$10,304
80	$10,574	$10,596
85	$14,037	$12,183
90	$18,635	$14,007
95	$24,738	$16,104
100	$32,841	$18,516

increasing income down the road. The 6 percent AIR design creates more income initially, but it provides less growth of income. Think of the 3 percent design as the tortoise and the 6 percent design as the hare. And think in terms of combinations. For example, this $100,000 could be split in two:

1. Fifty thousand dollars in a 3 percent AIR designed annuity to provide a modest initial income while creating the best hedge against long-term inflation.

2. Fifty thousand dollars in a 6 percent AIR designed annuity to create a greater cash flow in the early years of retirement while providing the opportunity for more modest growth in income down the road.

The use of a variable annuity as part of your conservative lifetime retirement income should appeal to you and your spouse if:

- You are in average or better than average health.

- You feel you can earn more than 3 to 6 percent on a diversified professionally managed portfolio over time.

- You are concerned about the long-term effects of inflation on your retirement income.

Buying Opportunities

You will have many opportunities to purchase immediate income annuities throughout your retirement years. Here are just a few of those occasions:

- When you need to reposition low-yielding assets to create more retirement income.

- When you need to maximize the income from a limited amount of capital.

- When you need to maximize your cash flow for a period of years, perhaps to cover long-term health care needs.

- If and when you want to create a retirement income stream using the cash surrender value from a cash value life insurance policy (assuming you no longer want to keep the life insurance coverage in force).

- When your employer provides you a defined benefit pension plan. If so, you will need to make a decision as to how to take the lifetime income from the pension. Basically, you are deciding which annuity income option is best for you and your family.

- When you take distributions from your IRA, qualified plan, or 403(b) plan at or before age 70½.
- When you need to create more cash flow for gifting to your children and grandchildren in order to reduce the size of your estate.

Whether you are poor, middle class, or rich, the cash flow you can create from annuities can play a significant role in meeting your income and estate planning needs. With the pressures on the Social Security system and the dramatic decrease in defined benefit retirement plans, future retirees will need both fixed and variable annuities for dependable retirement income.

Qualified Plan and IRA Distributions

Let's now look at the third source of conservative lifetime retirement income—your qualified plan and/or IRA.

Every investor knows he or she must start taking qualified plan and IRA distributions by age 70½ to avoid the nasty 50 percent penalty tax in addition to the regular tax if you fail to meet the required minimum distributions. Let's assume you wait until age 70½ to begin an income stream from your IRA. You will have three main income choices that can provide you and your spouse a lifetime income.

IRA Distribution Option 1: Recalculation Using an Investment Portfolio

This is the option you hear the most about. The IRA distribution laws were revised in 2001 to simplify the old minimum distribution rules, which were very complicated. You had to choose distributions over one life or two lives, and you had to elect to recalculate or not recalculate the life expectancies each year. The new rules simplified the process. Under the new rule, everyone, married or single, can use the joint life recalculation method shown in Table 9.7.

You can buy stocks, bonds, CDs, mutual funds, or any other permitted investment asset. Most retirees think taking the minimum distributions sounds great. By taking the lowest possible distributions in the early years, you create the lowest taxable income for many years. Let's assume you are married and both you and your spouse are age 70½. The new rules allow you to assume your

TABLE 9.7

Age	Minimum Distribution Divisor
70	26.2
71	25.3
72	24.4
73	23.5
74	22.7
75	21.8
76	20.9
77	19.2
78	18.4
80	17.6
85	13.8
90	10.5
95	7.8
100	5.7
105	4.1
110	2.8
115 and older	1.8

Based on IRS minimum distribution table

spouse (or other beneficiary) is 10 years younger than you. There-fore, the new minimum distribution rules are based on a joint life expectancy of age 70 (you) and age 60 (your beneficiary).

Under the new rules, almost every retiree will use Table 9.7 to determine the minimum required distributions at age 70½. Remember, this is a government table, and it is not necessarily an accurate mortality table.

Each year you must withdraw the minimum required that year in order to avoid the 50 percent penalty tax. Let's assume your account was $100,000 on December 31 of the year you turned age 70½. You must withdraw 1/26.2 of the account to avoid the penalty tax. Each year, you must withdraw a larger portion of the account. For example, by age 85, you must withdraw 1/13.8 of the account value that year. This table applies to most retirees, but there is one exception. You can elect to use a different table that allows for a lower distribution rate if you are married and your spouse is more than 10 years younger than you.

TABLE 9.8

Age	Distribution	Balance
70	$3,817	$105,183
71	$4,157	$110,492
72	$4,528	$115,908
73	$4,932	$121,408
74	$5,348	$126,986
75	$5,825	$132,590
76	$6,344	$138,179
77	$6,875	$143,740
78	$7,486	$149,190
79	$8,108	$154,509
80	$8,779	$159,636
81	$9,502	$164,501
82	$10,281	$169,025
83	$11,047	$173,190
84	$11,944	$173,833
85	$12,814	$179,934
90	$17,624	$184,080
95	$21,732	$163,033
100	$22,333	$116,424

NINE PERCENT INVESTMENT RATE OF RETURN Let's assume you have $100,000 in your IRA and you elect to use the new minimum distribution table at age 70. Based on an assumed investment return of 9 percent, your required minimum distribution income stream would be as seen in Table 9.8.

As you can see, the income starts low at $3,817. If your investment return is exactly 9 percent each year, the income will increase each year and the principal remaining at age 100 will be $116,424. But there are several things to consider in this approach to distributions at 70½:

- The income is quite low in the early years—less than 4 percent on your $100,000.

- Any year you have an investment return different than 9 percent will have an impact on the account balance that year, which in turn will have an impact on your income every year from that point forward.

SIX PERCENT INVESTMENT RATE OF RETURN Let's take a second look at the new minimum distribution rules in Table 9.9 and the importance of investment return. This time, let's assume your investment return is only 6 percent per year. We get a totally different income picture with this lower investment rate of return.

As you can see, lower returns can have a major impact on your IRA account. In the 6 percent return example, the income at age 85 was $8,256, versus $12,814 in the 9 percent example. In the 9 percent return example, the account balance peaked at age 94 and dropped each year thereafter. In the 6 percent example, the account balance peaked at age 81 and declined each year from there.

VARIABLE INVESTMENT RETURN In today's world, there is no way to earn a guaranteed 9 percent rate of investment return. We all know

TABLE 9.9

Age	Distribution	Balance
70	$3,817	$102,183
71	$4,039	$104,275
72	$4,274	$106,258
73	$4,522	$108,112
74	$4,763	$109,836
75	$5,038	$111,388
76	$5,330	$112,742
77	$5,609	$113,897
78	$5,932	$114,799
79	$6,239	$115,448
80	$6,560	$115,815
81	$6,894	$115,870
82	$7,242	$115,581
83	$7,554	$114,961
84	$7,928	$113,930
85	$8,256	$112,510
90	$9,764	$98,912
95	$10,311	$74,941
100	$9,017	$45,463

that volatility increases as we seek to earn a higher overall rate of return. So let's examine what happens if our investment return varies from our anticipated 9 percent rate. Let's assume we experience a minus 10 percent return in year six, followed by a 0 percent rate of return in year seven. Let's also assume that in year 12, we again experience a minus 10 percent return. (See Table 9.10.)

Any variation in investment rate of return affects both the income stream and the account balance of your IRA. IRA distribution planning at age 70½ is serious business! You must follow the required minimum distribution rules or be faced with a 50 percent penalty tax for failure to take the required minimum distribution. These rules require you to take distributions even in down market years, which dramatically affects your IRA balance and future stream of income.

To better understand the effect of these minimum required distribution rules, let's compare the variable illustration (Table 9.10) to the 9 percent rate of return illustration (Table 9.8). The 9 percent illustration shows a minimum required distribution of $9,502 at age 81. The variable illustration would require only $7,102 at age 81. That would be a 25 percent difference in income at age 81.

Let's also compare the right-hand columns, which illustrate the balance remaining in the IRAs. At age 81, the 9 percent illustration shows an account balance of $164,501, versus $100,278 in the variable

TABLE 9.10

Age	Investment Return	Distribution	Balance
70	9%	$3,817	$105,183
71	9%	$4,157	$110,492
72	9%	$4,528	$115,908
73	9%	$4,932	$121,408
74	9%	$5,348	$126,986
75	−10%	$5,825	$108,463
76	0%	$5,190	$103,273
77	9%	$5,138	$107,430
78	9%	$5,595	$111,504
79	9%	$6,060	$115,479
80	9%	$6,561	$119,311
81	−10%	$7,102	$100,278

table. This $64,223 difference in the account balance affects several things:

- There is $64,223 less capital available to meet emergencies.
- There is $64,233 less capital to create future retirement income.
- There is $64,233 less inheritance for your heirs.

Is this recalculated income stream really the best option for you and your spouse? Perhaps it is, but remember:

- It creates a low income in the early years of your retirement.
- If it is invested at a conservative 6 percent rate of return, the distributions will decrease in later years as you are forced to take out more principal to meet the minimum required distribution rules.
- Be conservative in your investment return assumptions.
- Every year of negative returns will dramatically impact the future income distributions.
- It is important to implement an asset allocation strategy to reduce the volatility of your portfolio.

You have other distribution options that might create a more meaningful retirement income. Let's look at two of those options.

IRA Distribution Option 2: Fixed Lifetime of Income (Annuitization)

We have just reviewed the minimum required distribution rules. But many of us need or want to maximize the income we receive from our IRAs for a number of reasons:

- We don't want to drastically reduce our standard of living in the early years of our retirement.
- We do not have enough capital to create the income we need.
- We do not want a volatile retirement income.
- We do not want the IRS to be the largest beneficiary of our IRA.

Your IRA and/or qualified plan assets are the most difficult assets to preserve and pass to the next generation. Under current law, these assets are subject to both estate taxes and income taxes. The combined taxes on large estates can be as high as 67 percent, leaving as little as 33 percent to your heirs. More on this tax problem later.

You should consider investing some of your IRA dollars in an immediate fixed-income annuity. We covered this unique contract in detail earlier in this chapter. You can purchase an immediate fixed-income annuity inside your IRA when you are ready to begin taking income (even as late as age 70½ or later).

Based on the historical 1983 annuity mortality table, a retired couple, age 70, has more than a 50 percent probability that at least one of them will still be alive at age 90. The Table 9.11 is based on this 1983 table.

Because we are living longer than the 1983 chart indicates, we need to at least consider the possibility of purchasing an immediate-income annuity inside your IRA. Let's look at a $100,000 immediate fixed-income annuity designed to pay you and your spouse an income for life. Your income will be $8,139 per month, guaranteed for life. If you and/or your surviving spouse are alive at age 105, you will still be receiving your $8,139 monthly annuity check.

IRA Distribution Option 3: Variable Lifetime of Income (Annuitization)

Here is a relatively new concept to consider. In recent years, the insurance industry has quietly introduced a new product called an immediate-income variable annuity. They have been so quiet about introducing this retirement income vehicle that few people have even heard about it and few financial advisors fully understand it.

TABLE 9.11

Attained Age	Probability of Being Alive at Attained Age		
	Male	Female	Joint*
70	92.3%	95.6%	98.6%
75	80.3%	88.8%	95.5%
80	64.8%	77.9%	88.5%
85	45.2%	61.3%	74.3%
90	25.2%	39.7%	51.1%
95	10.9%	18.9%	25.5%
100	3.1%	6.2%	8.4%

*Probability that either the husband or the wife will still be alive at attained age, based on the 1983 historical mortality table.
Based on individual annuity mortality rates from 1983 Society of Actuaries tables

There are several reasons an immediate-income variable annuity makes sense inside an IRA when you need to begin taking income:

- We are living much longer than the historical mortality tables assume we will.
- Inflation never retires.
- This product guarantees an income for life.
- If designed conservatively (based on a 3 percent, 4 percent, or 5 percent AIR), it should create an increasing lifetime income, providing a hedge against inflation.
- It is an ideal vehicle for implementing asset allocation and automatic rebalancing to reduce the volatility of your retirement income.

Immediate-income variable annuities were covered earlier in this chapter. If you skimmed over that section, go back and let it sink in.

What Do You Need?

A rising lifetime of income. An income you and your spouse cannot outlive. You need to maximize your lifetime of income.

An immediate-income fixed annuity would pay you (and your surviving spouse) a fixed income for life. This makes sense for part of your retirement income. Unfortunately, the income from a fixed annuity is like the income from a defined benefit pension plan in that the income is fixed and will not offset inflation. Remember: If inflation averages only 3 percent, we will see prices double in only 24 years. You need a retirement income that will at least double over your retirement years. Income maximization using an immediate-income variable annuity can be part of the solution.

Should you choose a fixed income or a variable income? Should you select a lifetime income with 100 percent or 75 percent or 50 percent to your surviving spouse? There is no right answer. When in doubt, seek help from a competent financial advisor. You need to look at all of your sources of retirement to determine what might be best for your family. You should consider combinations. You don't have to choose just one IRA option.

Table 9.12 will help you compare the income flows of fixed and variable immediate-income annuities. This illustration is based on a $100,000 investment for a couple age 70 who want a joint life income providing 100 percent of the same income for the surviving spouse. The variable accounts assume a 9 percent investment rate of return.

These income streams are for life. The chart stops at age 100, but the income keeps going and going and going for as long as either you or your spouse is alive.

Each of the preceding options has advantages and limitations. Don't try to pick just one option. If you do, the odds are you will choose the wrong one. It could be too aggressive or too conservative. In Chapter 1 we talked about risks, such as investment risk and inflation risk. Think in terms of combinations of your options in order to anticipate managing all of your risks.

Let's look at a combination worth considering. Assume you and your spouse are both age 70, with $400,000 in your IRA, faced with creating a distribution plan. Let's create a blend of incomes:

TABLE 9.12

Age	Fixed	3% AIR	4% AIR	5% AIR	6% AIR
70	$8,179	$6,000	$6,636	$7,320	$8,016
71	$8,179	$6,350	$6,955	$7,599	$8,243
72	$8,179	$6,720	$7,289	$7,888	$8,476
73	$8,179	$7,112	$7,640	$8,189	$8,716
74	$8,179	$7,526	$8,007	$8,501	$8,963
75	$8,179	$7,965	$8,393	$8,825	$9,216
76	$8,179	$8,430	$8,797	$9,161	$9,476
77	$8,179	$8,921	$9,220	$9,510	$9,745
78	$8,179	$9,441	$9,663	$9,873	$10,021
79	$8,179	$9,991	$10,128	$10,249	$10,304
80	$8,179	$10,574	$10,615	$10,639	$10,596
81	$8,179	$11,190	$11,126	$11,044	$10,896
82	$8,179	$11,841	$11,660	$11,465	$11,204
83	$8,179	$12,531	$12,220	$11,902	$11,521
84	$8,179	$13,262	$12,808	$12,355	$11,847
85	$8,179	$14,037	$13,426	$12,826	$12,183
90	$8,179	$18,635	$16,980	$15,463	$14,007
95	$8,179	$24,738	$21,477	$18,642	$16,104
100	$8,179	$32,841	$27,164	$22,474	$18,516

- A $100,000 recalculated minimum required distribution invested in stocks, bonds, and mutual funds
- A $100,000 joint life fixed annuity
- A $100,000 joint life 3 percent AIR variable annuity
- A $100,000 joint life 5 percent AIR variable annuity

By combining these four options, we can create the following lifetime of income as seen in Table 9.13.

The table assumes a 9 percent rate of return on the recalculated portion and the two variable annuities. It also illustrates waiting until age 70½ to begin taking income from the IRA. This age

TABLE 9.13

Age	Recalculated	Fixed	3% AIR	5% AIR	Total Income
70	$3,817	$8,179	$6,000	$7,320	$25,316
71	$4,157	$8,179	$6,350	$7,599	$26,285
72	$4,528	$8,179	$6,720	$7,888	$27,315
73	$4,932	$8,179	$7,112	$8,189	$28,412
74	$5,348	$8,179	$7,526	$8,501	$29,554
75	$5,825	$8,179	$7,965	$8,825	$30,794
76	$6,344	$8,179	$8,430	$9,161	$32,114
77	$6,875	$8,179	$8,921	$9,510	$33,485
78	$7,486	$8,179	$9,441	$9,873	$34,979
79	$8,108	$8,179	$9,991	$10,249	$36,527
80	$8,779	$8,179	$10,574	$10,639	$38,171
81	$9,502	$8,179	$11,190	$11,044	$39,915
82	$10,281	$8,179	$11,841	$11,465	$41,766
83	$11,047	$8,179	$12,531	$11,902	$43,659
84	$11,944	$8,179	$13,262	$12,355	$45,740
85	$12,814	$8,179	$14,037	$12,826	$47,856
90	$17,624	$8,179	$18,635	$15,463	$59,901
95	$21,732	$8,179	$24,738	$18,642	$73,291
100	$22,333	$8,179	$32,841	$22,474	$85,827

has been illustrated because, by law, you must begin taking income at least by age 70½. It is perfectly fine to begin your income at 65, or 62, or any age. It is also perfectly fine to assume a rate of return lower than 9 percent, but if you do, don't expect these results.

All four of these options create a lifetime of income. Let's summarize how they work together:

- The recalculated portion is 100 percent liquid at all times, and can be invested in any number of investments, such as stocks, bonds, or mutual funds.

- The fixed portion creates a steady, predictable lifetime of income that will help pay for fixed lifetime expenses such as food.

- The conservative 3 percent AIR portion creates a lifetime of income that provides an excellent long-term hedge against inflation.

- The more aggressive 5 percent AIR portion provides more income during the early years of retirement, when you might want more income for travel and other early retirement expenses.

- The first year's cash flow of $25,316 represents 6.32 percent of the original $400,000 value.

- By the fifth year, the cash flow is $29,554 or 7.38 percent.

- By the tenth year, the cash flow is $36,527 or 9.13 percent and increasing.

- At age 85 the cash flow will be $47,856 or 11.96 percent.

This is a winning combination, especially for your IRA or other qualified plan assets.

Don't wait until retirement to find out where you are heading! You are on a financial journey. You need to know where you are today and where you are headed. You need a plan, and you need to start now! It is a long trip, and it requires planning. Don't tell me you are too busy. If you are a busy baby boomer, seek out a qualified financial advisor to help you get started and provide guidance along the way.

Your second choice is to plot your own course. The tables and worksheets in the next chapter will help you if you choose to do it yourself. The important point is that you need a plan now! Without a plan, you can never look forward to retirement!

LESSONS AND STRATEGIES

1. We will enjoy a longer, healthier retirement than any previous generation.
2. We need to plan carefully how we will generate income from our primary retirement vehicles, because our retirement will most likely be 30 to 40 years long.
3. Early election for Social Security benefits is not recommended. Waiting until you qualify for full Social Security benefits at the normal retirement age of 65+ makes sense.
4. Determine exactly the age you must be to qualify for full benefits.
5. Pay attention to your annual Social Security projected benefit statement. Start saving these statements for future review.
6. If you participate in a defined benefit pension plan, begin planning your retirement income choice as early as age 55. Don't limit your planning options by waiting until retirement. If you purchase life insurance as part of your plan, you will be able to elect the highest pension income option (the life only option) at retirement.
7. Participate in your employer's retirement plan [401(k), 403(b), pension plan, profit sharing plan, etc.].
8. You will need to supplement these sources of retirement income. Consider purchasing immediate-income annuities for part of your retirement income. Think in terms of combinations, blending fixed and variable lifetime incomes.
9. Your IRA will probably be your largest financial asset once you retire. Choose your IRA income options carefully. Again, think in combinations. Consider both fixed and variable annuities for some of your IRA income at retirement.
10. You may need to annuitize some or all of your qualified plan, IRA, and nonqualified assets to create sufficient retirement income. Choose top-quality life insurance companies to provide this lifetime income.

How Much Retirement Income?

We have covered your best options for retirement income, but how much retirement income will you need? Will you need more income than we have discussed so far? Will you need to annuitize a portion (or all) of your savings to create the income you will need? Are you putting enough in savings every year to ensure a reasonable income at retirement?

Where Are You Now?

With any journey, you need to know exactly where you are now in order to plot your course for your final destination. Think about how carefully you plan your summer vacations. If you live in St. Louis, you don't just jump into the car the first day of vacation and head south, especially if your goal is to visit Alaska! You need to map out a course from your current location to your destination. You should also check out your car to make sure it is in good shape for the trip. You'll have to pack carefully; shorts and flip-flops might not be the best way to pack for salmon fishing in Alaska in the month of January! It takes a bit of planning for a successful two- to three-week vacation. Careful planning is key to a successful retirement that will last 20 to 30 years.

In earlier chapters, we met the Smiths and the Joneses. Mr. and

Mrs. Jones are doing OK, but the Smiths could use some help in their retirement planning. In this chapter we will help the Smiths by:

- Examining their net worth today (their current position)
- Determining their retirement income goal (their destination)
- Projecting the capital that will be needed at retirement to meet their retirement income goal (plotting their course)

The first thing we need to do is take careful inventory of the Smiths' assets and their liabilities. As we list their assets, we need to ask key questions, such as:

- Do they have too much in liquid assets, such as checking accounts, passbook savings accounts, credit unions, or money market funds? There is a price for this liquidity in that the returns on these accounts are low. Can some of this money be repositioned into longer-term investments with better investment opportunity?

- How are their investments being taxed? They need to look at last year's tax return, Schedule B, to check this out. Could these assets be invested elsewhere to reduce their taxes each year?

- Are they adding to their investments every month? Perhaps they need to have money withdrawn from their checking account every month to make sure they are saving enough for retirement.

- Are they paying attention to their qualified plan investment choices? Is it a good plan? Are they investing too much or too little in the plan? Have they made careful investment choices?

Next, we need to list and examine their liabilities. Again, we need to ask important questions, such as:

- Do they have too much borrowed on their credit cards? Are they able to pay off this debt every month, or do they have a balance carried over every month? They should get this debt paid off, because the interest cost could be 18 percent or more. (If they want a tax-free, guaranteed investment return of 18 percent, they should put paying off this debt at the top of their investment priorities.)

- Have they examined their mortgage interest cost? If today's mortgage rates are 2 percent lower than their existing mortgage, it is time to refinance. If they plan on staying in their home for 10 years or longer, refinancing for a 1 percent lower current mortgage rate can make sense.

■ Are they paying too much nondeductible interest buying depreciating assets? Do they really need that new car? Or, do they need to save and invest those dollars for retirement?

It takes time to go through this examination process, but it is very revealing!

Assets

To determine the Smiths' net worth, subtract their liabilities from their assets. The balance (net worth) is working for the Smiths' retirement. This is the important first step for their financial journey. Figure 10.1 shows a worksheet I call a financial road map. Let's fill it out step-by-step to help the Smiths plan their journey.

The Smiths have built a "net worth" of $350,000 to date, including:

■ Home equity

■ Savings and investments

---

1. Present net worth $_____

2. Gross household income $_____

3. Retirement income goal
   a. 80% × $_____ (income at retirement) $_____
   b. Less Social Security benefits   –_____
   c. Less defined benefit income (if any)   –_____
        Portion of goal I must create by investing $_____

4. Capital needed for retirement income
   a. Total capital needed $_____
   b. Less projected value of current net worth   –_____
        Additional capital I must create for retirement income $_____

FIGURE 10.1 Financial road map worksheet.

1. Present net worth $ 350,000

2. Gross household income $ 125,000

3. Retirement income goal
   a. 80% × $_____ (income at retirement) $_____
   b. Less Social Security benefits   −_____
   c. Less defined benefit income (if any)   −_____
       Portion of goal I must create by investing $_____

4. Capital needed for retirement income
   a. Total capital needed $_____
   b. Less projected value of current net worth   −_____
       Additional capital I must create for retirement income $_____

FIGURE 10.2   Financial road map worksheet showing net worth.

- Qualified plans
- Personal property

Their two incomes total $125,000 per year. Let's add this information in Figure 10.2 to see where they are today.

Next, we need to help the Smiths project their income at retirement. Let's project that their current income increases at the rate of 3 percent per year. Using Table 10.1, we can guesstimate their income in 20 years, just before they retire.

The Smiths' current income of $125,000 is projected to grow by 3 percent per year. Using this table, we see that their income will be

TABLE 10.1

Future Value of $1,000 Current Salary, Assuming Various Percentage Increase						
Salary Increases	5 Years	10 Years	15 Years	20 Years	25 Years	30 Years
3%	$1,159	$1,344	$1,558	$1,806	$2,094	$2,427
4%	$1,217	$1,480	$1,801	$2,191	$2,666	$3,243
5%	$1,276	$1,629	$2,079	$2,654	$3,386	$4,322
6%	$1,338	$1,791	$2,397	$3,207	$4,292	$5,743

1. Present net worth $ 350,000

2. Gross household income $ 125,000

3. Retirement income goal
   a. 80% × $ 225,750 (income at retirement) $ 180,600
   b. Less Social Security benefits   −_____
   c. Less defined benefit income (if any)   −_____
      Portion of goal I must create by investing $_____

4. Capital needed for retirement income
   a. Total capital needed $_____
   b. Less projected value of current net worth   −_____
      Additional capital I must create for retirement income $_____

FIGURE 10.3   Financial road map worksheet showing retirement income goal.

approximately $225,750 when they retire at age 65 (125 × 1,806 = $225,750). Most likely, they will need at least 80 percent of this preretirement income as retirement income. That equates to a retirement income need of approximately $180,600 at age 65 (80 percent × $225,750). That's more than they are earning now, which is why they need to plan. Let's add their income goal to the financial road map worksheet in Figure 10.3.

Social Security will help in creating a portion of this retirement income. Use Table 10.2 to guesstimate the Smiths' Social Security benefits.

TABLE 10.2

Approximate Benefit	Age 62	Age 65
Low wage earner	$518 per month	$598 per month
Average wage earner	$853 per month	$977 per month
High wage earner	$1,100 per month	$1,279 per month
Maximum wage earner	$1,241 per month	$1,433 per month

The maximum wage earner was able to earn at least the maximum wage base amount during working years.
Source: Office of the Chief Actuary, Social Security Administration, year 2000.

Multiply this monthly number by 12 to guesstimate the annual Social Security benefit.

The Smiths are high wage earners and should qualify for roughly $34,392 in Social Security benefits per year at age 65. They will receive a more accurate forecast from the Social Security Administration a few months before their birthdays each year. Let's round it off to $35,000 and add this information to their financial road map in Figure 10.4.

The Smiths, like most Americans, do not have a defined benefit pension plan. They will have to become serious investors to create this additional $145,600 retirement income to meet their goal. How much capital will they need? Assuming they withdraw 5 percent per year as income, they will need $2,912,000 in investment capital by age 65 ($145,600 divided by 5 percent = $2,912,000). Mind boggling, isn't it? Impossible? No. Will it require planning? Yes!

The future growth of the Smiths' current net worth over the next 20 years will be part of the answer. Using Table 10.3, we can project the value of their current net worth at retirement in 20 years.

Using this table, we see that $1,000 compounding at 8 percent will grow to $4,661 in 20 years. The Smiths' current net worth of

1. Present net worth		$ 350,000
2. Gross household income		$ 125,000
3. Retirement income goal		
a. 80% × $ 225,750 (income at retirement)	$ 180,600	
b. Less Social Security benefits	– 35,000	
c. Less defined benefit income (if any)	– _____	
Portion of goal I must create by investing		$ 145,600
4. Capital needed for retirement income		
a. Total capital needed	$_____	
b. Less projected value of current net worth	– _____	
Additional capital I must create for retirement income		$_____

FIGURE 10.4 Financial road map worksheet showing projected Social Security benefit.

TABLE 10.3

	Lump Sum Investing: $1,000 Compounding Annually					
Return	5 Years	10 Years	15 Years	20 Years	25 Years	30 Years
6%	$1,338	$1,791	$2,397	$3,207	$4,292	$5,743
8%	$1,469	$2,159	$3,172	$4,661	$6,848	$10,063
10%	$1,611	$2,594	$4,177	$6,727	$10,835	$17,449
12%	$1,762	$3,106	$5,474	$9,646	$17,000	$29,960
14%	$1,925	$3,707	$7,138	$13,743	$26,462	$50,950

$350,000 should grow to $1,631,350. That is part of the solution. Let's add this projection to the Smiths' financial road map in Figure 10.5.

Where in heaven's name are the Smith's going to come up with $1,280,650? Does it seem impossible? Using Table 10.4, let's determine how much the Smiths must invest every month for the next 20 years to create $1,280,650. Every $100 per month they invest at 8 percent creates $59,295 in capital. They need 21.60 times this amount! The bottom line is that they need to invest roughly $2,160

1. Present net worth $ 350,000

2. Gross household income $ 125,000

3. Retirement income goal
   a. 80% × $ 225,750 (income at retirement) $ 180,600
   b. Less Social Security benefits   –   35,000
   c. Less defined benefit income (if any)   –_____
      Portion of goal I must create by investing $ 145,600

4. Capital needed for retirement income
   a. Total capital needed $ 2,912,000
   b. Less projected value of current net worth   – 1,631,350
      Additional capital I must create for retirement income $ 1,280,650

FIGURE 10.5   Financial road map worksheet showing projected value of current net worth.

TABLE 10.4

	Monthly Investing: $100 per Month Compounded Annually					
Return	5 Years	10 Years	15 Years	20 Years	25 Years	30 Years
6%	$7,012	$16,470	$29,227	$46,435	$69,646	$100,954
8%	$7,397	$18,417	$34,835	$59,295	$95,737	$150,030
10%	$7,808	$20,655	$41,792	$76,570	$133,789	$227,933
12%	$8,249	$23,234	$50,458	$99,915	$189,764	$352,991
14%	$8,720	$26,209	$61,285	$131,635	$272,728	$555,706

per month at 8 percent to meet their goal. It is better that they realize they have a problem now rather than find out at retirement.

The Smiths' Options

If they can't invest $2,160 per month at 8 percent to reach their goals, the Smiths need to examine their options. They can:

- Reduce their goals. They might consider retiring on 70 percent of their preretirement income. This may or may not be a realistic option. Remember, they have to keep up with their neighbors, the Joneses.

- Work longer. They may not be able to retire at 55 or 60. They may have to work well past age 65 to reach their goals.

- Reposition their current portfolio and future savings hoping for a better return than 8 or 9 percent. Keep in mind that if they get too aggressive, they will be substituting one problem for another.

- Examine their spending habits. Is a new car really that important? Perhaps they are considering the purchase of a new $20,000 car. Even if they have a trade-in and arrange for 0 percent financing, their payments could still exceed $500 per month for three years. What would that new car really cost? Just about $75,000. Let's do the math. If that $500 per month were invested at 8 percent, it would be worth $20,265 in three years. If left to compound for 17 more years, it would be worth $75,000 when the Smiths are ready to retire at age 65. Again, is a new car really that important?

Saving and Spending Habits

We know that the rate of return earned on investments has a major impact on building capital. But just as important are our saving and spending habits. We have far more control over our habits than over the stock market.

Let's look at savings habits first. The savings rate in this country is lower than that in all major industrialized countries and has been decreasing for several years. In 1970, we were saving 8 percent of our disposable income. In 1991, this number was down to 4.7 percent. By 1994, the rate had decreased to 3.8 percent. As of 2001, the savings rate had dropped to slightly over 1 percent. Over time, this will have a major impact on many retirees. A study completed by New York University economist Edward Wolff in 2002 revealed that 40 percent of households preparing for retirement (people ages 47 to 64) don't have enough saved to replace even half of their preretirement income. Experts tell us we will need 75 to 80 percent of our preretirement income to live comfortably in retirement.

What has happened? We have become a nation of people with poor spending habits. Aggressive advertising and creative store displays have made us impulsive spenders. Think about your last trip to a large store. You may have only had four items on your shopping list, but chances are you ended up buying twice the number of items you intended to buy.

Seventy percent of credit card holders carry a balance. Today's average household has close to $8,000 in credit card debt. Let's see how damaging this can be. If you make only the minimum required monthly payments (3 percent of the remaining balance), your minimum payment will be recalculated each month until it is paid off. Assuming you make no more credit card purchases and you are paying 18 percent interest, it will take you 42 years to pay off this debt. You would pay almost $22,000 in interest on this $8,000 loan. Your payments would total close to $30,000. It is no wonder there were close to 1 million personal bankruptcies (an all-time high) in 2002.

Let's see what can happen if you pay off this debt at a faster clip. Paying off this 18 percent credit card rate debt over 10 years would require payments totaling over $17,000.

Perhaps you can find a credit card charging a lower interest rate. Let's assume you are charged only 13 percent. Paying off this $8,000 balance over 10 years will still cost you over $14,000 in payments. Check out your projected cost on the Internet at Bankrate.com to find out the real cost of your credit card debt.

To break this impulse buying habit, you know what you need to do: Get rid of your credit cards. Assuming you are married, figure out how much cash each of you needs each week. Give yourselves a cash allowance. Learn to stretch your cash to cover your needs and not your impulsive wants. Write down your cash expenses for a week or two. You might be in for a big surprise. For example, your first stop in the morning might be at Starbucks on your way to work. How many dollars are you giving Starbucks every day? It might come to $15 a week, which adds up to $750 per year. How many colas do you buy from the soda machine at work? Is it $10 per week? Is it possible to bring a thermos of coffee or a six-pack of cola from home?

Every Sunday, the newspaper has ads enticing us to buy the latest in large flat-screen TVs. But before you spend that $7,000, ask if it will get any more channels than a $200 set. That fancy new TV doesn't cost only $7,000. It will cost you $48,000 if you are age 40. How could that be? If that $7,000 was invested in something that appreciates (instead of a TV that will only depreciate) it might earn 8 percent until retirement in 25 years. So, before you buy that fancy TV, ask yourself: Is it worth the $48,000 it will cost in the long run?

One of the most expensive impulse purchases is a new car. Let's consider the cost of a luxury car versus a moderately priced car. A new BMW 540i can cost roughly $16,000 a year to operate. A moderately priced Toyota Camry LE will cost about $8,500 annually to maintain. Several items contribute to this difference in cost, for example, depreciation, insurance, taxes, and repair bills. But there is much more to consider. Again, if you are age 40 and you invest this savings of $7,500 per year for 25 years at 8 percent, you will have over $548,000 in investments at retirement. The real cost of a new BMW is over $548,000. The BMW is a nice car, but not that nice. The Toyota can take you to just as many places as the BMW. And the cost savings provides you the opportunity to build an additional $548,000 for retirement.

But before you run out and buy that new Toyota Camry LE, please consider a used Toyota. The used vehicle may have more maintenance costs, but it will be far less expensive to insure. The real benefit of buying a used car comes from how you invest the cost difference over time. The cost difference between a new car and a three-year-old car might easily average $3,000 per year. Let's do the numbers: $3,000 per year, invested at 8 percent for 25 years, can create over $219,000. I'm driving an 11-year-old car and I love it! Please, think long and hard before you buy expensive depreciating assets.

It also pays to shop carefully for your car insurance. In 2002, auto insurance premiums increased an average of 9 percent, the biggest increase in over a decade. In the past, many insurers offered attractive packages if you bought both home and auto insurance together, but that is often not the case today. Many companies are increasing homeowner rates in many states by as much as 20 percent to offset storm-related losses. Today, it pays to shop. If you have a great driving record, check out Amica Mutual Insurance, Erie Insurance Exchange, and Geico Direct. Are you driving a big four-wheel-drive vehicle? The insurance premium can vary by as much as $1,000 per year between insurers. The big three in auto insurance are State Farm, Allstate, and Farmers Insurance. It's a good idea to get a quote from at least one of the big three. The next time you are on the Internet, check out insweb.com, which shows rates for 40 auto insurers. It makes good sense to call an independent agent and ask him or her to find the best homeowner and auto insurer. While you are at it, talk to him or her about increasing your deductibles. The premium difference can be substantial. Invest the money you save in a separate account to handle small claims in the future.

It also pays to check your life insurance costs. If you purchased term insurance several years ago, it should be reviewed. Term insurance premiums have dropped dramatically in the last five years. You may be able to either increase your coverage without spending more money or reduce the cost for the same amount of coverage.

Checking Your Progress

If you still have trouble finding the dollars to invest, it's time to check your checkbook. Find out where the money goes. Pull out your check records for the last six months, or better yet, the last year. Create columns on a pad of paper to help you see where the money goes. For example, set up columns for house payments, car payments, credit card payments, utilities, car insurance, life insurance, vacations, clothing, groceries, and so on. There is one more column for checks made out to cash. Many couples find these "cash" transactions (including trips to the ATM) account for up to 40 to 60 percent of their banking transactions. Most of us have absolutely no idea where that money goes. In the future, make just one check out to "cash" every week. That is your allowance account. It's time to get a better handle on where your money goes.

Do you have a column titled "monthly investments"? It is much easier to fund a Roth IRA or a college savings account for your children if the investments are budgeted and invested on a monthly basis. It may be time to change the order of the columns on your pad of paper. The first column should read "monthly investments." Your priority should be to pay yourself first each month. Most financial institutions, such as mutual fund companies, encourage you to set up a check-a-month investment program. The company will withdraw the investment automatically from your checking account each month. Most of them will let you pick the date it comes out of your account, such as the first or the fifteenth of the month. It will take you a month or two to get accustomed to your investments being automatically withdrawn from your checkbook. This is a great new habit to begin as soon as you pay off your credit card debt.

Key Decisions You Need to Make Today

You need to determine where you are on your financial journey! It's time to roll up your sleeves and get to work!

- Carefully complete your financial road map (See Figure 10.1.)

- Find out how much you need to be saving in order to meet your retirement income goal.

- Be conservative in your investment rate assumptions. I suggest no more than 10 percent. An assumption of a lower 8 percent or 9 percent is even better.

- Take advantage of your employer-sponsored retirement plans. Remember, many employers match at least a portion of what you contribute.

- Take advantage of tax-deferred investments, such as Roth IRAs, which can help you and your spouse build capital faster.

■ Accept the fact that you may need to annuitize a portion of your retirement assets to create the lifetime income you will need.

Questions to Ask Yourself

After completing your financial road map worksheet, you need to ask yourself some serious questions about where you are heading on your journey.

■ Are you taking full advantage of your employer-sponsored investment plans, such as a 401(k) plan? Is your employer matching your contributions? This would help tremendously.

■ Are your current and future investments tax efficient? Have you considered tax-deferred annuities to build your capital faster? Are you holding onto your stock positions for long-term growth and favorable capital gains tax treatment?

■ Have you established a budget? Are you an impulse buyer? Are you running up credit card debt?

■ Are you saving more as your income increases?

■ Have you established a monthly investment program that takes money automatically out of your checking account? (What an easy way to add to a mutual fund account or a tax-deferred variable annuity!)

■ Do you qualify for a Roth IRA? The Roth IRA is ideal for single investors with adjusted gross income under $95,000 and married couples with adjusted gross income under $150,000. You and your spouse (if married) can each invest $3,000 per year, which will compound without taxes and create tax-free income at retirement. When you are age 50 and older, you contribute an additional $500 per year. Again, set up your Roth IRA with an automatic bank draft from your checking account. Pay yourself first every month.

■ Are you considering the purchase of an immediate-income annuity at retirement? If you have tax-deferred annuities, are you considering the lifetime income options available at retirement? Annuitization will allow you to maximize the lifetime income on the assets you have with an insurance company. Those assets might be tax-deferred annuities, the cash value in your life insurance policies, or the monies you invest in an immediate annuity.

■ Are you taking advantage of all the above before you consider more aggressive investing to meet your goals? Aggressive investing in hopes of earning 14 percent or more adds a whole new dimension of risk. I hope you earn more than 8 percent. That certainly is possible, but I don't want it to be mandatory for your portfolio to have above average returns for you to retire in dignity.

LESSONS AND STRATEGIES

1. Complete your financial road map.
   - Determine where you are today.
   - Decide where you want to be at retirement.
   - Plan on how you are going to get there.
2. Review your expenses over the last year.
3. Pay off your credit card debt.
4. Pay yourself first every month by setting up a monthly bank draft for investing.
5. The objective is to improve your net worth every year.
6. Review your progress every year.

PART THREE

THE KEYS TO KEEPING WEALTH

Long-Term Care Planning
Mistake 5: Not Having Adequate Insurance

Allow me to introduce you to two different Smiths. Murray Smith is age 74. His wife, Shirley, is age 72. Shirley's mother, Sophie Scheer, is age 108. Liz Doup of the *South Florida Sun-Sentinel* reported their story on Sunday, May 27, 2001. That week the Smiths moved Sophie into an assisted living facility after caring for her in their home for the previous eight years. Mrs. Scheer is quoted in the article, "I want to die in my own bed, but it isn't going to be."

Because the fastest-growing age group in America is age 85 and over, we need to ask ourselves whether we will be responsible for the care of an elderly parent at some point in the future. Care giving can take its toll physically, mentally, and financially.

The next question is, "What plans have you made concerning your own possible long-term care needs?"

Mistakes and Myths

Many people think of long-term care solely in terms of a nursing home. But you need to consider:

- *Home health care.* All of us want to remain in our own home as long as possible. This typically requires some degree of special assistance.

- *Adult day care.* This may be anywhere from a few hours to eight hours a day.

- *Assisted living care.* There are facilities ideal for elderly people who no longer want to live alone. These apartment-like facilities provide the elderly the opportunity to live in a setting with people their own age, most of whom need a minimal amount of care.

- *Nursing home care.* There are three levels of care provided in nursing homes: custodial, intermediate, and skilled.

Most men spend little time in a nursing home. Their wives struggle to keep them at home as long as possible. Only when it becomes physically impossible to care for men at home do their wives place them in a nursing home. Recent statistics show that 52 percent of nursing home patients die within 100 days. That statistic really applies to married men. Most of their long-term care needs occur before they go to a nursing home. Men typically require more home health care and adult day care.

The situation is quite different for women, who are twice as likely as men to need nursing home care. The surviving spouse (typically the wife) has no one to care for her. She will go to a nursing home much sooner and in better health and will live there longer than her husband did. The nursing home is the last resort for both men and women, but the financial drain can begin many years before the nursing home. Only 22 percent of people age 85 and over are in nursing homes. We all know how expensive nursing homes can be ($55,000 to $65,000 per year). But the earlier stages of long-term care needs can also cause a significant financial drain. For example, a recent study by the AARP reveals the following figures:

- Average cost of an in-home visit by a skilled nurse: $109

- Average cost of an in-home visit by an aide: $64

- Monthly cost of an assisted living facility: $2,000 to $2,500

In-home health care can cost $36,000 per year. Thirteen million Americans are currently receiving some form of long-term care. It is not just a problem for the elderly: 40 percent of people needing care are between the ages of 18 and 64.

Figure 11.1 shows how people paid for long-term care services in 2001.

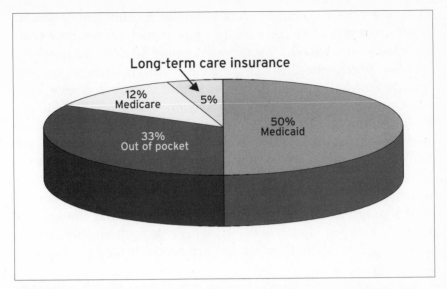

FIGURE 11.1   Paying for long-term care. (Courtesy of American Health Care Association)

One myth is that Medicare takes care of nursing home care costs. Medicare was never intended to provide substantial long-term care coverage. Unfortunately, Medicare covers only 100 days of skilled nursing home or in-home rehabilitative care (after a required three-day hospital stay). Only the first 20 days are fully covered; Medicare provides reduced coverage for the remaining 80 days. This coverage is most often provided to an elderly person recovering from an accident, such as a broken hip. You can see that Medicare covers only 12 percent of the long-term protection needed. Think of Medicare as health insurance. Medicare does not provide benefits for adult day care, extended home health care, or custodial nursing home care, all of which can create a financial and emotional drain on families.

A second myth is that Medicaid will provide for nursing home costs. Medicaid does provide for 50 percent of today's nursing home residents. However, it is impossible for anyone with financial wealth to qualify for Medicaid. Medicaid is a federal program, but it is administered by the states. Each state sets its own guidelines for qualifying for Medicaid. The bottom line is that Medicaid is designed for those elderly patients who have no meaningful assets. Recognize it for what it is: Medicaid is a welfare program designed to provide nursing home care for the indigent. Medicaid is available only after you exhaust your financial assets, including the money you saved for retirement. Some advisors suggest you transfer all of your financial assets to your children so you can qualify for Medicaid. That process would require you give away all of your assets at least three years before asking Medicaid to pay for your nursing home care. Aside from the moral issues involved with this approach, you need to consider other facts. Have you visited nursing homes that accept Medicaid recipients? Many facilities accept both self-paying and Medicaid residents. If so, they maintain a separate area for Medicaid residents. Have you examined the differences between the Medicaid area and the self-pay area? Remember, Medicaid does not provide for home health care, adult day care, or assisted living care needs. It only provides for nursing home care.

A third myth is, "It won't happen to me!" Let's examine the facts as provided by the Health Insurance Association of America in 2002:

- Seven million people over age 65 will need long-term care this year.

- Forty percent of people age 65 or older will spend some time in a nursing home.

- Seventy-two percent of people age 65 or older will need home health care.

- The average length of stay in a nursing home is 2.7 years.

- Ten percent of people will be in a nursing home longer than five years.

- The national average cost of nursing home care exceeds $55,000 a year, which is roughly $150 a day.

Categories of Nursing Home Care

Skilled nursing care is needed when conditions require highly trained professional help. This level of care requires a licensed nurse and rehabilitation services. Let's assume you fall and break a hip. After hip surgery, you may require special therapy and skilled nursing care before returning home. This type of special care is typically needed for less than 60 days.

Intermediate nursing care is not as intense. It is designed to help patients with stable conditions that require daily supervision and monitoring by skilled professionals. This level of care might take place in a facility or at the patient's home.

Custodial care is a lower level of care provided to those who need assistance with the normal activities of daily life. These activities may include bathing, eating, and dressing, for example. This level of care might take place in a facility or in the patient's home.

Many people intend to use their savings and investments for these additional expenses. In fact, in 2000, the "do-it-yourselfers" paid a total of $23.9 billion for these services. This out-of-pocket method of payment paid 33 percent of the costs that year. This method works just fine for elderly couples with a net worth of $10 million or more, but it is a disastrous plan for the majority of us. According to studies reported in *Business and Health* in January of 1997, 70 percent of single individuals and 50 percent of couples with one partner in a nursing home are impoverished within one year. Since that study in 1997, nursing home costs have skyrocketed.

For most of us, our largest financial asset is our qualified plan or IRA. This is an asset we should be preserving for several reasons:

- We will be relying on these dollars to provide a lifetime of retirement income for ourself and our surviving spouse.

- IRA assets receive special treatment at death, creating substantial estate benefits for our heirs.

In Chapter 9 we discussed the importance of building retirement capital with qualified plans and IRAs. At retirement, most investors transfer their qualified plan assets to a rollover IRA. Let's revisit the Smith and Jones families. At retirement, the wealthier Jones family had $1 million in retirement plan and IRA assets. They transferred their qualified plan assets to an IRA for several reasons:

- They wanted more investment choices than their 401(k) plans provided.

- They wanted more retirement income choices than the limited options provided by their 401(k) plans.

- They wanted their children to have more options on taking distributions of these assets when settling the estate.

At the same time, their neighbors, the less successful Smith family, had built up $340,000 in their 401(k) plans. The Smiths could take the easier path and do nothing. They could leave their retirement assets in the 401(k) plan. Does it really make any difference?

The Hidden Value in IRAs

IRAs are the most important financial asset to preserve for your family. Over time, an inherited IRA can be worth 6 to 10 times its initial value. In 1987, a law was passed making it possible for the children or heirs to inherit an IRA from the parents and stretch out the IRA distribution over their life expectancies. But the language of the law was not clear. In January of 2001, the IRS clarified the law.

Let's see how this new, fantastic planning option can benefit the Smith family if they transfer their qualified plan assets to an IRA. Let's assume the Smiths imitate the Joneses and eventually transfer their qualified plan assets into traditional IRAs. Let's also assume they make no withdrawals and the account continues to grow. At age 70½, the account will be worth approximately $500,000. At that point they must begin withdrawing at least the minimum required distributions. Assuming they continue to earn 8 percent, their IRA will be roughly $750,000 at ages 84 to 90, when they pass this account to their children. (See Figure 11.2.)

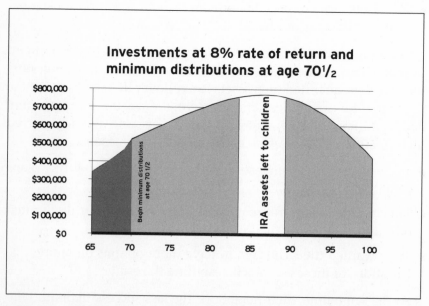

FIGURE 11.2 Performance of a $340,000 IRA account at age 65.

New, simplified IRS regulations issued in January of 2001 make IRA assets extremely valuable for our children. Why? The beneficiaries (typically our children) can elect to stretch their IRA inheritance, receiving it as income over their life expectancy. Let me demonstrate how valuable this can be. Let's see in Figure 11.3 how much income this IRA inheritance can create over the children's lives.

Each child has until December 31 of the year following the inheritance of the IRA to begin a lifetime income stream. The oldest child (Paul) has the option to take a lump sum distribution, pay 35 percent in taxes, and have $162,500 left to spend. Better yet, Paul now has the option to stretch out his $250,000 IRA inheritance as income over 33.1 years (his life expectancy). In year one, Paul must withdraw at least 1/33.1 of the account value. That is roughly 3 percent of $250,000, or $7,500. If the account earns 8 percent, the account is growing by roughly 5 percent. In the second year, Paul's income will be 1/32.1 of the larger account balance. Paul continues to earn investment returns on the balance in the account until it is totally paid out over the 33.1 years. Assuming an 8 percent return over this period, Paul's 33 years of income will total $1,266,000. This is fantastic news!

It is even better news for the youngest child, Peter. Peter can stretch his $250,000 IRA inheritance over 42.5 years. Assuming an 8 percent return, his total income will be $2,151,000. I can just hear

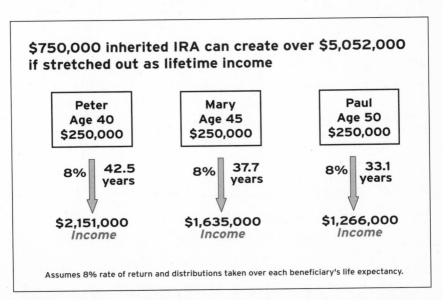

$750,000 inherited IRA can create over $5,052,000 if stretched out as lifetime income

| Peter
Age 40
$250,000 | Mary
Age 45
$250,000 | Paul
Age 50
$250,000 |

8% | 42.5 years   8% | 37.7 years   8% | 33.1 years

$2,151,000 *Income* $1,635,000 *Income* $1,266,000 *Income*

Assumes 8% rate of return and distributions taken over each beneficiary's life expectancy.

FIGURE 11.3   Stretch-out IRA. (Based on IRS single life expectancy tables)

Peter talking to his older brother and sister: "Mom and Dad always did like me better than you! I'm going to get more benefit from their estate than you will!" The fact is that all the children get a larger estate if they take their inheritance as income over time.

Should one of the children die during the payout period, his or her heirs can continue the stream of income for the balance of time remaining. The heirs cannot start a new payout period, but they can continue the payout period begun by the initial beneficiary. This ability to take the IRA inheritance as income over their life expectancies increases the value from $750,000 to over $5 million. This is a great new planning opportunity for the Smiths' children, because they can create over $5 million in income from this $750,000 IRA inheritance and live happily ever after.

But remember: This ability to leverage the inheritance is most often not available to heirs of a qualified plan, such as a 401(k). These plans do not have to provide this key benefit. Only IRA plans and 403(b) plans automatically provide this lifetime income benefit to maximize your estate's value. Don't be lazy like the Smiths! Roll your qualified plans to IRAs, for all the reasons we just discussed.

There are three possible events that could prevent this tremendous lifetime income benefit from becoming a reality for your children or heirs:

1. Estate taxes force the children to liquidate the IRA to pay the taxes. Life insurance can solve the estate tax problem. (Estate planning will be covered in the next chapter.)

2. The children take the money in a lump sum and waste it. Special trust planning can prevent the Smiths' children from wasting their IRA inheritance. (This will also be covered in the next chapter.)

3. The IRA becomes the source of liquidity to pay for long-term care needs.

Using IRA Savings for Long-Term Care Needs

The average cost today for nursing home care exceeds $55,000 per year. Even an assisted living facility costs $30,000 per year. You can redirect some of your current income to handle these expenses. But many retirees find they need to supplement their retirement income by as much as $100 per day, or $3,000 per month, to cover these expenses. Unfortunately, these costs are not standing still. Let's consider inflation. In 10 years, these additional expenses could be over $4,500 per month. Let's assume the Smiths are currently in good health. Let's also assume they will have no need for long-term care for at least 10 years.

Let's assume there is a need for home health care and adult day care in 10 years, when Mr. Smith is age 75. By then, the additional income needed to cover these expenses could be $4,500 per month ($54,000 per year). Let's also assume the combined federal and state income tax rate is 36 percent. The Smiths would need to withdraw an additional $84,375 from their IRA to create the $4,500 additional cash to meet these extra expenses. As these expenses increase each year, they will need to make even larger withdrawals from their IRA. Let's assume these additional withdrawals are necessary for four years. In Figure 11.4 you see the effect on their IRA.

The IRA is cut almost in half as we use taxable withdrawals to take care of Mr. Smith's care needs. Let's look at 10 additional years. Let's assume Mrs. Smith needs additional cash to meet her long-term care needs. Let's also assume the costs have risen to $6,000 per month ($72,000 per year). Again, if the IRA is Mrs. Smith's main financial resource, additional distributions of $112,500 must be

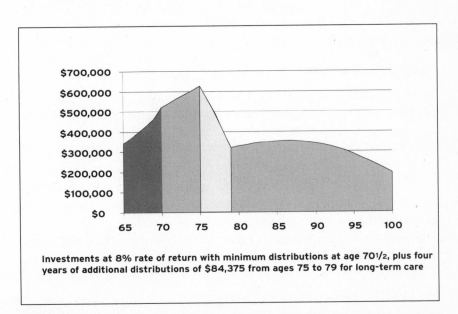

Investments at 8% rate of return with minimum distributions at age 70½, plus four years of additional distributions of $84,375 from ages 75 to 79 for long-term care

FIGURE 11.4 Four-year impact on IRA of additional withdrawals for long-term care needs beginning at age 75. (Based on IRS single life expectancy tables)

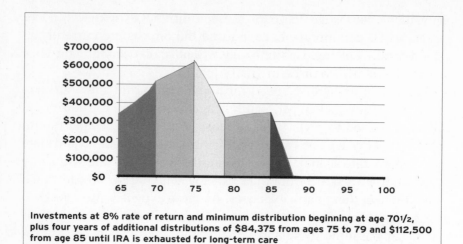

Investments at 8% rate of return and minimum distribution beginning at age 70½, plus four years of additional distributions of $84,375 from ages 75 to 79 and $112,500 from age 85 until IRA is exhausted for long-term care

FIGURE 11.5 Impact on IRA of additional withdrawals for surviving spouse's long-term care needs beginning at age 85. (Based on IRS single life expectancy tables)

made to net the cash needed to cover her health-related expenses. Let's look at Figure 11.5 to see the effects on her IRA.

There may not be enough in the IRA to cover the long-term expenses of the surviving spouse. There will be little if anything left as an inheritance for the children. This is not a pretty picture, but there is a solution!

Long-Term Care Insurance

Long-term care insurance is now an excellent option. A few years ago, this was not a good solution. Most of the long-term care policies offered in the 1980s and early 1990s were poorly designed and were being offered by lower-quality insurance companies. Many of those companies have gotten totally out of the long-term care insurance business by selling off their policies to other insurance companies. Other companies have increased the premium costs by 60 percent or more. It was chaos!

Finally, there are quality companies, such as John Hancock, offering affordable solutions that provide excellent value for today's consumer. Let me give you an example of what to look for in a long-term care policy:

■ Make sure the issuing insurance company is a top-quality insurance company. Don't just look for the lowest cost. Stay with reliable insurance companies. Look at policies offered by John Hancock, UnumProvident, and GE Financial. I would not recommend policies issued by low-quality insurance companies such as Conseco or Penn Treaty Insurance Companies.

- A good policy will provide benefits if you need assistance with any two or more of the following activities of daily living:

  —Bathing

  —Dressing

  —Eating

  —Toileting

  —Continence

  —Transferring (getting from a bed to a chair, etc.)

- Select a 100-day waiting period before benefits begin. It saves you money. You will be responsible for the costs for the first 100 days.

- Choose a comprehensive policy that covers all four areas of long term needs:

  1. Home health care

  2. Adult day care

  3. Assisted living care

  4. Nursing home care

- Most companies offer a choice of benefit duration, such as two years, four years, six years, or for life. Generally, the six-year benefit period is affordable and will cover the long-term expenses for the majority of buyers.

- Most policies provide a daily benefit, such as $50 per day, $75 per day, or $100 per day or more. The $100 per day benefit will provide the additional cash needed as supplemental income to cover most long-term needs, such as adult day care and assisted living.

- Consider a policy that provides increasing benefits over time. Remember, you must physically qualify for this long-term care policy. That means you probably won't be receiving any benefits for quite a while. A policy providing $100 per day today will need to provide much more in 10 or 20 years to offset inflation.

- If you are married, look for additional benefits. One benefit might be a premium discount for buying two policies. Another benefit to consider is a shared care rider. This very affordable option allows the surviving spouse (typically the wife) to extend her benefit period with all unused benefits remaining from the husband's policy. It also allows the first spouse (typically the husband) to use some of the benefits of the second spouse's policy if necessary. For example, let's assume both the husband and the wife purchased a policy providing for an initial benefit of $100 per day for four years. Each policy's $100 per day initial benefit increases by 5 percent per day each year. Let's assume the husband needs care beginning 11 years after purchase. By year 11, the daily benefit of each policy is up to $163 per day. Let's assume the husband dies after receiving two years of his policy's four years of benefits. His spouse is entitled to his two years of unused benefits should she need it. In this example, her benefits are now extended to a total of six years. What if the husband uses all of his original four years of benefits? She can elect to use some or all of her four years of benefits for his care. The shared care rider makes sense for married couples as a way to expand the coverage for either spouse.

- Buy your coverage as soon as you recognize this problem. It will be less expensive today (while you are younger), and the coverage increases each year until the year you need the benefits.

The Cost of Long-Term Care Insurance

You need to consider purchasing this type of coverage before retiring for several reasons:

- It will be less expensive if you start early. The premium is designed to be level for life, so it makes sense to lock in your costs when you are young. Here is an example of what you might pay at different issue ages:

  —One thousand dollars per year if purchased at age 55. (Married? Double this premium cost.)

  —Four thousand seven hundred dollars if you wait until age 75 to purchase a similar policy.

- You may not be able to qualify for the coverage if you wait too long. You are in better health at age 55 than you will be at age 75. Remember, you must be in good health at the time of issue.

- The benefits will increase between the time the policies are issued and the time they are actually needed. A policy providing $100 per day today might provide $163 in 10 years, or $265 per day in 20 years, with no anticipated increase in premium cost. The younger you are when you purchase this coverage, the greater the eventual benefit will be. A policy paying $265 per day in benefits in 20 years could pay out over $580,000 in tax-free benefits over 4 years.

This is affordable coverage. As you get close to retirement, you need to make adjustments in your other insurance coverage. For example, do you need to maintain your disability income insurance? Most disability policies provide benefits only until age 65. Maybe it is time to scale back your disability coverage and perhaps your term life insurance coverage. The primary need for term life insurance is to replace lost income for a dependent spouse and minor children. As you approach retirement, the premium being allocated to disability insurance and term life insurance might be better spent on long-term care insurance.

Also consider your homeowner's insurance. Perhaps you can increase the deductible, which will reduce the premium cost. That premium savings could be redirected to purchase long-term care.

The Benefits of Long-Term Care Insurance

You have many options when purchasing a long-term care policy, so let's narrow it down. You should consider a policy with the following features:

- A $100 per day benefit. This will cover most in-home health care expenses, adult day care fees, and assisted living costs, as well as two-thirds of today's average nursing home care costs.
- Inflation protection that automatically increases the daily benefit by 5 percent per year.
- A 100-day elimination period (you will have to pay for the first 100 days of care).
- Six years of benefits (your choices are 3, 4, 5, or 6 years or for life).
- Providing for all levels of need, including:
  —In-home health care
  —Adult day care
  —Assisted living care
  —Nursing home care, including skilled care, intermediate care, and custodial care

It is important to cover all levels of need. Many of us will spend more time in the first three levels of need than in nursing homes. Nursing home care is just a small part of the problem. There is only a 23 percent probability of staying in a nursing home for over one year, and only a 10 percent chance of being there for more than five years. That's why it is important to plan for in-home care, adult day care, and assisted living care.

Table 11.1 shows an example of what a policy with these benefits might cost.

Let's assume the Smiths purchase this protection at age 65. Their two policies will cost $3,840 per year. Mr. Smith feels he won't need benefits until age 75. Mrs. Smith wants to know what benefits her policy would provide if she needs care in 20 years, when she will be age 85. Table 11.2 tells it all.

Mrs. Smith might pay her premium for 20 years before she needs benefits. By then, she would have spent $38,400 ($1,920 per year for 20 years). That is a lot of money! But the benefits have grown to $265 per day for up to six years. If she needs just 145 days of benefits at that point, she will be getting back her investment in the policy (145 days at $265 per day = more than $38,400).

What does it cost if the Smiths don't purchase long-term care coverage? Their IRA might easily be exhausted if it is used as the primary source for long-term care needs. Consider the risk. If the $750,000 IRA is exhausted, the children lose the opportunity to stretch the IRA to over $5 million in lifetime income! The new, better-quality long-term care policies are affordable insurance, protecting your largest financial asset—your IRA.

As of July 8, 2003, there is a bill in the Senate that would allow individuals a tax deduction for long-term care insurance premiums.

TABLE 11.1

Issue Age	Annual Premium
55	$1,070
60	$1,390
65	$1,920
70	$2,880
75	$4,700

TABLE 11.2

Year	Daily Benefit	Total Benefit Over 6 Years
First Year	$100 per day	$219,000
Year 10	$163 per day	$356,970
Year 20	$265 per day	$580,350

Hopefully Congress will pass the Long Term Care and Retirement Security Act of 2003 in the near future.

LESSONS AND STRATEGIES

1. Medicare is not the answer. Medicare is designed to provide health care, not nursing home care.
2. Medicaid is welfare and is available only if you have no financial assets.
3. If you choose to self-insure these costs, there is a probability you will end up on Medicaid.
4. Most of us will have our largest pool of capital in our IRAs. Because of the lifetime income potential for the children or heirs, IRAs have become the most important assets in an estate.
5. If the IRA is used to pay for long-term care, it will drastically reduce the value of the estate.
6. Consider the purchase of long-term care insurance to protect your IRA.
7. If you are close to retirement, consider reallocating your insurance dollars. You may no longer need disability income insurance or all of your term insurance. The monies spent on these policies can be reallocated to purchase long-term care insurance.

Wealth Transfer Planning

Mistake 6: Not Having a Written Plan for the Distribution of Your Wealth

Groucho Marx, one of this country's most beloved comedians since the 1930s, lost control of both his care and his estate. In the 1970s, Groucho's health had failed to the point that someone had to take over his financial affairs. In a highly publicized trial, his longtime companion, Erin Fleming, battled Groucho's 27-year-old grandson in court for conservatorship. But the fighting continued after Groucho's death. Erin Fleming was sued for illegally siphoning $400,000 from the estate (valued at $2 million at the time). The case was settled in 1988, 11 years after Groucho's death. Fleming was now broke and after years of legal fees there was little left of the estate to distribute.

Remember Charles Kuralt, the CBS newsman who traveled through small communities and reported folksy stories in his wanderings around the countryside? It turns out that a lot of his wanderings were with a girlfriend. He spent over three decades with her, much of the time at his fishing retreat in Montana. Before his death in 1997, he wrote her a promise that she would inherit the Montana property, which was valued at $600,000. This promise came as a big surprise to his wife of 35 years, who knew nothing of the affair until after his funeral. After two years in court, his girlfriend was awarded the Montana property. Who had to pay the estate taxes on this $600,000 property? His wife.

At some point in the future, everything you own will be transferred to someone else. All too often, estates are unwittingly transferred to:

- Ex-spouses (beneficiary designations not updated)
- All children equally (whether they deserve it or not)
- Your estate (which must be determined by a long, drawn-out probate court process)
- The wrong charity (if you do not have the right to change the beneficiary of a charitable trust document)
- The IRS (estate and income taxes at death)

You want to avoid these mistakes with your estate.

Dying Without a Will

Dying without a will is called dying *intestate*. Dying with a will is called dying *testate*. It not only sounds nasty, it is nasty to die without a will.

Let's assume you are married and have children. You might think that your spouse would inherit your estate. Unfortunately, that is not the case. In Missouri, a surviving spouse gets only half of the assets and the surviving children receive the other half. In Illinois, just one state away, the surviving spouse is entitled to only one-third while the children inherit two-thirds. What if the widow is age 70 and in need of these funds while the children are fully raised and on their own? The children receive their court-directed portion whether they are minors or age 55!

What if the children are minors? Let's assume a husband dies, leaving $300,000 for his wife and three minor children. Let's also assume there is no will and the state rules leave only one-third ($100,000) to the surviving wife and the minor children inherit the remaining two-thirds ($200,000). The surviving parent or another adult would be appointed to watch over the children's share. This guardianship arrangement can be both expensive and cumbersome. For example, in Pennsylvania, the surviving parent cannot be the sole guardian. The guardian may need to pay an attorney to request court approval for every major expenditure from the children's assets. Some states are more lenient. In Illinois, for example, only "necessary" expenditures can be paid out of the children's money. The surviving spouse may have to petition the court to use this money for basic needs such as college costs, clothing, and even music lessons. These rules can leave a family financially strapped while the children are growing up. What happens when the children reach legal age? They get a lump sum of money.

What if the estate is worth $3 million? Only $1 million would go to the surviving spouse without estate taxes. The balance going to the children will be subject to estate taxation, which can be as high as 48 percent in 2004.

What happens to a couple that has no children? In many states, the surviving spouse may receive only one-half, with the balance going to the deceased's parents and siblings. Most couples would prefer that it all go to the surviving spouse.

And what happens if there are no surviving family members? The state will get the money. Most individuals would prefer their estate go to friends or to charity.

Dying With a Will

First, you need to visit an attorney and have a personalized will drawn up as a starting point for planning your estate. It will cost somewhere between $75 and $400, depending on how complicated it is. (It could end up becoming very expensive if you do not have a will, because the state has basically drawn one up for you. As we saw earlier, the state's handling of your affairs most likely would not be to your liking.)

Who represents your children's interests if they are minors? Without a will, the courts will appoint someone, often an attorney. This stranger will be hired to represent your children's interests until they become adults. Most of us would prefer to have our surviving spouse handling these parental obligations without court intervention and the related costs. This can be accomplished easily with a simple will.

Perhaps your children are grown and earning a good living with no need for an inheritance. Who represents the surviving spouse, who may need all of the estate? In most states, the adult children will still inherit one-half to two-thirds if you do not have a will.

There are many quirks in the various state laws. I'm sure you can create a better plan than your state law provides. Make it a priority to spend time with an attorney to establish the will of your choice.

No one wants to face up to his or her own mortality. We would like to put off talking to an attorney as long as possible. But consider what can happen. Let's look at Marilyn Monroe's estate. Marilyn's estate was a nightmare. Her parents were deceased and she had no brothers or sisters. Her estate was tied up in probate court for 18 years while potential heirs and creditors fought over it. Probate and attorney fees consumed more than $1 million of the estate. By the time it was all settled, there was little left to distribute. All of the costs and delays could have been avoided had Marilyn written a valid will.

There are other issues to be determined, especially if you have minor children. As a parent, it is important that you have your affairs in order. It is possible that you and your spouse may die together. Who will take care of minor children? Without a will (dying intestate), the court will designate someone to raise the children. It might be a distant relative living out of state. You might prefer your children to be raised by friends who live in your community. Again, dying testate (with a will) can make your wishes come true.

You may need more than a will; you may need one or more trusts to establish the best plan for you and your family. A will establishes who will inherit your assets. A trust can establish when they inherit the assets. Your legal documents need to be revisited periodically when:

- There is a change in your marital status.

- There is a change in the number of children to whom you wish to transfer your wealth.

- You change state residence.

- There is a major change in your financial net worth due to inheritance or investments returns.

- There are major tax law changes, like the 2001 tax law changes, which affect estate tax planning.

Other Legal Documents

While you are at it, you need to talk to your attorney about other important legal documents:

- *Living will and health care power of attorney.* These documents allow you to establish specific instructions in the event of a terminal condition. You may not want to be kept alive by machines past a certain period of time. You can appoint the person to carry out your wishes.

- *General power of attorney.* This is an important document for young adults, as they can appoint a parent with this power. The parent can legally handle banking, motor vehicle, and tax return obligations of the student or child. This document also makes it possible for the parent to take care of the child's affairs should the child become incapacitated, say as a result of an accident.

- *Durable power of attorney.* This important document appoints a specific person to take care of the financial affairs of an individual should he or she become incapacitated. The person named can only take care of financial decisions. The powers cease at the individual's death.

- *Living trust.* This document goes beyond the durable power of attorney document. A trust does not die when you die. It carries out your wishes past your death. The assets registered in a living trust avoid the probate court process. This document is very helpful for elderly singles who are concerned about who will handle their affairs should they become incapacitated later in life and how their estate will be distributed. Few people transfer every asset to a living trust. A trustee can only manage assets specifically named in the trust. Therefore, a living trust is not a complete substitute for a durable power of attorney. A living trust will also benefit married couples who want to make sure that both the husband and the wife can take advantage of their estate tax exclusions, as most living wills have a clause that places a part of the assets into a credit shelter trust at the owner's death.

- *Credit shelter trust.* In the year 2004, both a husband and a wife can transfer $1.5 million to their children or heirs without incurring an estate tax. (The amount of assets that can be sheltered from estate taxes will increase between now and 2010.) But this doesn't happen automatically. It takes careful planning to pass $3 million without estate taxes. A credit shelter trust is an important tool for married couples. More on this trust for married couples in a moment.

Beneficiary Designations

Many of your investment accounts allow you to name the heirs (beneficiaries) so that these assets can avoid the probate process and related costs (attorney fees, court fees, administrator fees, etc.).

This might save your heirs 1 to 4 percent in costs. The probate process often lasts over a year, and probate records are public records available to anyone who wants to see them. It's important to review the beneficiary designations of accounts such as:

- Life insurance policies (both personal and group)
- Accidental death insurance plan at work
- Tax-deferred and immediate annuities
- Employer-sponsored qualified plans, such as 401(k), profit sharing, defined benefit, and 403(b) plans
- IRAs
- Employer stock purchase plans
- Employer-sponsored deferred compensation plans

If these accounts are set up properly, all of these assets can avoid the costs and delays of probate. If you name your estate as the beneficiary, it will force all of these assets into probate, as the courts must determine the meaning of "your estate." If you use a vague beneficiary description such as "all my children equally," you are again creating a probate nightmare. The court must figure out who those children are. There may be children from a first marriage, children from a second marriage, adopted children, stepchildren, illegitimate children, and so on.

Please review all of these beneficiary designations, especially if your marital status or the number of children has changed.

Estate Taxes

It's not difficult to have a net worth of over $1.5 million today. Take a moment to add up the value of the major assets you own, such as:

- Life insurance (including your group insurance)
- Qualified plan assets
- IRAs
- Investment securities
- Home and personal property
- Investment property
- Business ownership

As of January 1, 2004, each of us can pass $1.5 million to heirs other than our spouse without incurring estate taxes. The Economic Growth and Tax Relief Reconciliation Act of 2001 increases the amount that can be transferred without taxes each year, as shown in Table 12.1. The top estate tax rate also decreases through the years. Table 12.1 illustrates the changes in the coming years.

New Estate Tax Exemptions and Rates

This tax law is the most frustrating legislation taxpayers and their advisors have ever had to deal with. Between now and the year 2009, the estate tax exclusion will increase and the top estate tax rate will decrease. This is fairly good news, but things get a little crazy after that. Let's look at the year 2010. If we assume Congress makes no changes in the law between today and 2010, there are some major changes coming in that year:

- The estate tax will be repealed for tax year 2010 but will return in 2011 and later. (More on this confusion in a moment.)

- Currently, heirs inherit our capital assets with a step-up in cost basis. Their cost basis would be the value of the assets as of the day of our death. They could sell the appreciated assets and incur no capital gains tax. Beginning in tax year 2010, there will be limits as to how much of the estate will receive a step-up in cost basis. This means wealthy families with highly appreciated

TABLE 12.1

Year	Estate Tax Exclusion	Top Estate Tax Rate
2002	$1,000,000	50%
2003	$1,000,000	49%
2004	$1,500,000	48%
2005	$1,500,000	47%
2006	$2,000,000	46%
2007	$2,000,000	45%
2008	$2,000,000	45%
2009	$3,500,000	45%
2010	$0	0%
2011	$1,000,000	55%

Courtesy of IRS

assets will incur a new tax problem on inherited assets: They will inherit a capital gains problem. The heirs would have the deceased's cost basis, with two exemptions:

—A total of $4.3 million of basis can be added to assets transferred to a surviving spouse. It is possible that a surviving spouse can inherit a capital gains tax problem. The first $4.3 million of appreciated assets he or she inherits will not have the problem. Everything else will.

—A total of $1.3 million of basis can be passed to heirs other than a surviving spouse. This means the children or heirs can inherit $1.3 million of appreciated assets without inheriting a capital gains problem.

It is possible for the surviving spouse to avoid a capital gains tax problem but transfer the problem down to the children.

Sunset Provision

Again, this tax law is the most frustrating law we've ever had to deal with. There are changes in the income and estate tax rates throughout the years until 2011. Year 2010 makes no sense at all. And, by December 31, 2010, the president and the Senate must reapprove the entire 200 pages of the Economic Growth and Tax Relief Reconciliation Act of 2001 (if it is not rewritten in the meantime). As this law is written, the provisions of the law will expire on December 31, 2010. For these new provisions to continue, at least 60 percent of the Senate must reconfirm the provisions and the president must approve their actions. As the law is written, the estate tax exemption reverts to $1 million and the estate tax rate returns to 55 percent in the year 2011 and beyond. All of this is based on no tax law changes between now and 2010. My guess is that Congress will readdress several of the provisions of this law around the year 2008 or 2009 (possibly earlier) to prevent the chaos of 2010 and later. However, you should make plans based on the existing law, not on what you wish the law was.

Table 12.1 shows that estate tax exclusions are going up through the years until 2010 and estate tax rates are going down from 50 percent to 45 percent. You would think estate tax problems are going away, but they are not. Estate tax planning will be just as important in the years to come as it has been in years past. First of all, most people's estates are increasing. Second, most couples don't

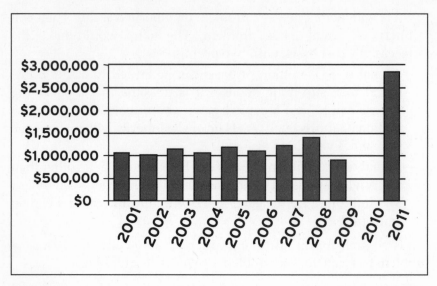

FIGURE 12.1 Estate taxes on a $3 million estate, assuming 8 percent growth of assets.

die in the same year. A surviving spouse could easily live 10 years longer, meaning the estate would grow for 10 more years before the taxes were due at the surviving spouse's death. Let's look at the estate tax on a $3 million estate growing at 8 percent per year. Figure 12.1 reflects these changes for all single, divorced, or widowed estates. It also reflects the estates of married couples who have not established a credit shelter trust.

Again, there is little tax relief in this new law. The figure starts with the estate in 2001, which is before the new 2002 law went into effect. Let's assume the estate grows at 8 percent per year. At best, the increases in exemptions and decreases in tax rates help to slow down the growing tax problem. You can see that the tax stays at roughly $1 million through 2009. In 2010, the estate tax law is supposed to disappear. Unfortunately, the relief shown in 2010 will most likely not happen because of the sunset provision written into this law. We will most likely see new legislation at some point before 2010 to prevent the nightmare of 2011.

Credit Shelter Trusts

As mentioned earlier, there is a special type of trust that is important for married couples with estates in excess of $1.5 million. Remember, everything you own is included in your estate.

There is no estate tax due when transferring assets from one spouse to another. There is an unlimited marital transfer of assets allowed while you are alive and at death. The estate tax problem occurs when we transfer our wealth to someone other than our surviving spouse.

In 2004 and 2005, it is possible to transfer up to 1.5 million to individuals other than a surviving spouse without triggering estate taxes. Using the estate tax table, we find:

Gross tax before credits	$555,800
Less credits in 2004 and 2005	$555,800
Next tax on $1.5 million estate	0

Unfortunately, most husbands pass everything they own to their surviving spouse. This is done through a *sweetheart will:* "Dear Sweetheart, I leave everything to you." This sounds nice, but it is a flawed estate plan. If you pass everything to your spouse, only your spouse's tax credit will be available. Your current credit exemption of $555,800 is forfeited if you leave everything to your surviving spouse.

Let's examine a $3 million estate. Assume the husband dies first, in January of 2004, leaving all of the assets to his surviving widow. She pays no tax, because she enjoys the unlimited marital deduction. Let's assume she dies a year later in 2005. The entire $3 million will be included in her estate. Estate tax rates begin at 45 percent in 2004 and 2005. Table 12.1 shows that the top rate can be as high as 47 percent in 2005. The husband's unused tax credit cannot transfer to his surviving spouse. His tax credit of $555,800 will be wasted if everything is transferred to his widow.

Let's calculate the taxes on her $3 million estate in 2005:

Gross tax on $3 million before credits	$1,270,800
Less credits in 2005	$555,800
Net tax on $3 million estate	$715,000

There are two ways the couple can use his $1.5 million exemption:

1. They can leave $1.5 million of his $3 million directly to the children at his death.

2. They can establish a credit shelter trust to hold $1.5 million of his assets.

Let's first consider giving the children $1.5 million at his death. How will this go over with his spouse? She gets the home, personal property, and some of the investments. How much income will this provide her? If they were worth $50 million, it would not be difficult to give $1.5 million to the children at his death. She could survive on her $48.5 million inheritance.

But, what if the estate was only $1.6 million? Would it make sense to give the children $1.5 million, leaving the wife with only $100,000? We would be using the husband's tax credit, but we would not be providing enough for his surviving spouse.

There is a better solution. If you are married with an estate worth over $1.5 million, you need to work with your attorney. Your attorney can design a credit shelter trust to solve many problems. This type of trust goes by many names:

- A bypass trust
- The B trust of an A and B trust plan
- Part of a living trust
- A testamentary trust
- A family trust

Regardless of what it is called by your attorney, here is how it works. Both the husband and the wife establish a credit shelter trust. For 2004 and 2005, this trust can shelter up to $1.5 million from estate taxes. Let's return to our $3 million example and have the husband die first. Assume this trust is funded with $1.5 million of assets (using his credit) at his death. The trust document says something like this: "The $1.5 million in the trust is to be invested by the trustee for the lifetime of my surviving spouse. My surviving spouse has the lifetime right to all of the income created by the trust and also a right to the $1.5 million of principal in the trust, should she need it for health, education, welfare, and other reasons. Upon her death, the assets remaining in the trust are to be distributed to our children."

The intent of this credit shelter trust is threefold:

1. It provides both income and principal for the surviving spouse.

2. It keeps the assets in the trust outside of the surviving spouse's estate, using the credit of the first spouse to die to shelter $1.5 million from taxes.

3. If the surviving spouse does not need distributions from the trust, the assets in the trust can continue to grow for the eventual benefit of the children or heirs. All of the growth will be estate tax free.

In this example, the assets remaining in the husband's trust are outside of the widow's estate. In 2004 and 2005, we are sheltering $1.5 million from taxes by placing this money in his trust at his death. The other $1.5 million (in the wife's estate) will pass to the children at her death in 2005. Her credit of $555,800 will be used at her death to reduce her estate taxes to zero.

Credit shelter planning is critically important for married couples with estates over $1.5 million. In our $3 million estate example, credit shelter planning will save this family over $700,000 in estate taxes. Trust planning will be just as important in the years to come. Why? First of all, most people's estates are increasing. Let's look at the estate tax on a $3 million estate growing at 8 percent per year, assuming the married couple has established a credit shelter trust. Figure 12.2 illustrates the estate tax relief created by funding a credit shelter trust.

If you are married and have a net worth in excess of $1.5 million, take advantage of your right to reduce your estate taxes by

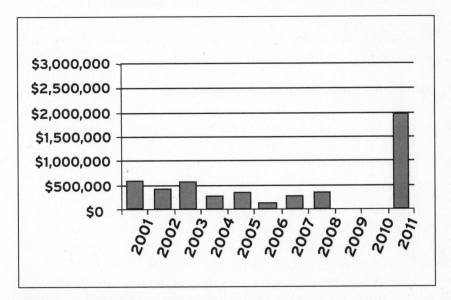

FIGURE 12.2 Estate taxes on a $3 million estate with credit shelter planning, assuming 8 percent growth of assets.

establishing a credit shelter trust. Make this a priority, as it can save your children or heirs needless estate taxes. See your attorney for details.

Sharing Your Wealth with Children and Grandchildren

Most people are familiar with the gifting rules. You can gift $11,000 per year to anyone you choose. If you are married, you and your spouse can jointly gift $22,000 per year to the people chosen. Take advantage of this tremendous estate planning opportunity.

- You pay no gift taxes on this transfer of assets to your children or heirs.

- They do not have to declare these gifts as income.

- These annual gifts (and all of the growth) are outside of your estate.

Over time, these annual gifts are very meaningful. Let's assume you have three children. Let's further assume you and your spouse make $22,000 joint gifts to each child for 10 years. Assuming an 8 percent return, these accounts will be worth almost $956,000 in just 10 years!

Gifting is not about giving away your assets. Paying taxes is giving away assets! Gifting is how you keep your assets in your family, where they belong. If you can afford it, take advantage of this great estate-planning tool.

Special Planning for Special Assets

Many investors have one or a combination of three special assets:

1. Tax-deferred annuities

2. Qualified plans

3. Traditional and Roth IRAs

These are the fastest-growing assets most investors own. Because they compound without taxes, they build the greatest amount of capital for retirement income. For that reason, they can play a major role in creating adequate retirement income. Special planning is necessary to preserve the value of these special assets for the children or heirs.

In the previous chapter we saw the importance of protecting

IRAs for the less fortunate Smith family. Let's see how this great new planning option can benefit the wealthier Jones family. Mr. and Mrs. Jones have retired and moved their qualified plan assets into traditional IRAs. At Mr. Jones's death, his IRA transfers to his widow. Let's assume the value of the IRA is $1 million at her death. At that time, the three Jones children are ages 35, 40, and 45, a bit younger than the Smiths' children.

The new regulations allow the children to divide the $1 million into three separate IRA accounts without triggering taxes. They have until December 31 of the year following their mother's death to establish these new separate accounts. Each child can begin an income stream of inheritance based on life expectancy. Look at Figure 12.3 to see the impact on this portion of their inheritance.

Each child can stretch out his or her IRA inheritance over his or her life expectancy. Each child will continue to earn investment returns on the balance in the account until it is totally paid out. Assuming an 8 percent return over this period, the Jones children can have an income distribution in excess of $8.846 million.

Here is how it works. The youngest child, John, can stretch out his inheritance over 47.3 years. The first year's distribution will be 1/47.3 of the account's value. That is less than 2 percent of the account. If the account is earning 8 percent, the account continues to grow as John takes his required minimum distribution. In year two, the distribution will be 1/46.3 of the account's value. In year

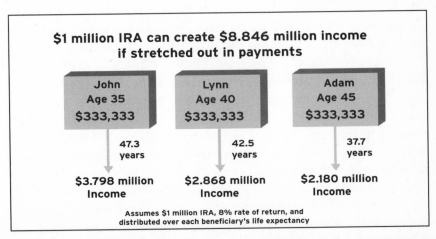

FIGURE 12.3 Benefits of an IRA for the Jones children. (Based on IRS tables of minimum distributions)

three, the distribution will be 1/45.3 of the account and so on for a total of 47.3 years. The account continues to enjoy the tax-advantaged growth of the IRA until the account is exhausted. Assuming an 8 percent return over the 47 years, the payments to John can total $3.798 million. That's not a bad lifetime income from a $333,333 inheritance! Lynn, the middle child, age 40, can stretch out the distribution over 42.5 years. The oldest child, Adam (age 45), can only stretch out his inheritance over 37.7 years because he has a shorter life expectancy. Should Adam die before he has received his 37.7 years of distribution, his children or heirs can continue to leverage the account by continuing the original payout stream begun by Adam. In short, Adam and his heirs can receive approximately $2.180 million in benefits over time.

What a great gift to children and grandchildren: the ability to leverage an inherited IRA into a long-term income stream worth roughly eight times the initial value of the IRA.

A Need for Special Planning

We've seen that the estate tax rate can be as high as 48 percent in 2004. These special assets (tax-deferred annuities, qualified plans, and IRAs) require special planning because they are subject to both estate taxes and income taxes when they are passed to the next generation.

First let's consider the tax-deferred annuity. After paying the estate taxes, if any, the beneficiaries of the annuity have to pay income taxes on the built-up gain in the tax-deferred annuity. This double tax could exceed 50 percent. Don't like this picture? Let's see how Mr. and Mrs. Jones might use their tax-deferred annuity. Remember, they invested $100,000 in their annuity 20 years ago. At age 65, it is worth $466,096. The annuity can be annuitized to maximize their retirement income. They will have to pay taxes on the built-up gain as it is received in payments throughout their retirement. But, if a lifetime income option is chosen, the annuity will have a value of zero for estate tax purposes. Remember, the lifetime income can be provided for one or two lives. The Joneses can elect one of the joint life with income to the surviving spouse options. If they don't need all of this income, they can gift some or all of it to their children. The children can spend it, invest it, or better yet, use this annual gift to purchase a large life insurance policy on their parents' lives. The children won't inherit the annuity, but they will inherit the insurance proceeds, which will be both income and estate tax free.

Now let's consider the qualified plan and traditional IRA assets. These two special assets will be subject to even more income tax, because the entire balance of these accounts is subject to income tax. After paying estate taxes, the children or heirs will have to pay income taxes as they take distributions. If the children or heirs take their inheritance in a lump sum, it will be added to their other sources of taxable income that year. It could easily force them to pay income tax subject to the top income tax rate. This double taxation can be as high as 67 percent. This is not what most people want to happen to the assets they've worked so hard to build.

There is one nice thing you can say about the IRS's plan: It is simple. You don't have to do anything; it's all in place. Do nothing and the IRS can confiscate as much as 67 percent of your IRA or qualified plan. If you don't like the IRS's plan, you have to take action. It is not difficult to change this ugly picture. Let's see the simple steps Mr. And Mrs. Jones took to accomplish this:

- At age 65, they began taking a modest 3 percent income from their IRA. (They decided not to wait until age 70½ to begin taking this small income.)

- They have to pay income tax on the income they receive from their IRA. After paying a portion in income taxes, they have over 2 percent remaining, which they don't need to maintain their standard of living.

- They are gifting this 2 percent after-tax cash flow from their IRA to their children.

- The children are using this annual gift to purchase life insurance on their parents. This 2 percent annual gift will buy more than enough life insurance to pay the estate and income taxes due on the IRA, and thus preserve the value of these double-taxed assets. Life insurance owned by the children (or a special life insurance trust created for the benefit of the children) will create income and estate tax–free dollars to pay these taxes.

Let's look at this from another angle. Assume the Joneses' estate is going to be subject to the top estate tax rate. Part of their estate is $1 million in IRAs. At age 65, they begin withdrawing $30,000 per year (3 percent). After paying roughly $10,000 in income taxes, they have $20,000 left to gift to their children each year. This $20,000 annual gift can purchase a $1 million life insurance policy on the lives of Mr. and Mrs. Jones. The policy is called either a *survivorship* or a *second-to-die* policy. The insurance company pays the death benefit when the survivor (the second spouse to die) dies. That is when all of the taxes are due. Life insurance is a tremendous gift for your children, because it protects the assets you have spent a lifetime to build.

If you are single, widowed, or divorced, this gifting process still makes sense to protect your largest financial assets. The policy will be a different design than the one described earlier, but it will solve the same problem.

Whether you are single or married, you need to do all you can to protect the value of an IRA account for your children or heirs. No other asset can be so beneficial to your heirs. Remember, Mr. And Mrs. Jones have $1 million in their IRA, which can create an income estate of $8.846 million for their children and grandchildren. Three events could prevent the $8.846 million income inheritance from happening for the Jones family:

1. The children could take the lump sum, pay income taxes of 35 percent, and squander the balance. The parents can have their attorney establish a trust for each child to receive the IRA proceeds at their death. These trusts can distribute the proceeds in the account over each child's life expectancy to leverage the value of the inheritance to $8.846 million in income. Most of these trusts will be worded to allow the trustee to accelerate the distribution should it be necessary for the child's health, education, welfare, or other reasons the trustee feels are appropriate.

2. Large estates will have estate taxes due nine months after the surviving spouse dies. IRAs have the liquidity to pay the estate taxes. But, if the IRA must be liquidated to pay the estate taxes, it will force immediate income taxation, taking away the stretch-out opportunity. This problem can be prevented by a combination of credit shelter planning and adequate life insurance designed for estate tax planning.

3. The IRA will be a major source of retirement income for Mr. and Mrs. Jones and might have to be used as the main source of

dollars for emergency needs, such as long-term care. Today, long-term care costs average more than $50,000 per year. Assuming an annual increase of 5 percent, these costs are projected to be more than $130,000 in 20 years. Some of the Joneses' regular retirement income can be diverted to cover some of these costs, but they may need supplemental income to cover the balance of these expenses. Let's assume the Joneses need to create an additional cash flow of $72,000 per year for long-term care. If they rely on their IRA for this need, they would have to withdraw an additional $100,000 from their IRA. Why so much? They have to pay income taxes on the additional IRA distribution. Long-term health care policies for Mr. and Mrs. Jones would provide tax-free dollars to take care of their long-term health care needs and preserve the IRA for their children.

Estate Planning for Everyone

No one wants to do estate planning. After all, no one wants to deal with death and dying. But it is important. You have seen families left with financial nightmares that could have been prevented with a little planning. We have all seen the emotional nightmares families have had to endure, such as deciding when to pull the plug on life support systems, or arguments over how fancy the funeral should be.

Let me share a personal experience with estate planning. My father died while I was in college. It was hard on all of my family, but the greatest comfort to my mother was the peace she found as a result of planning my father did many years before he died. He had left instructions for organ transplants at his death. Because of his planning, two people were recipients of cornea transplants. What a tremendous gift!

Estate planning is for everyone, whether rich or poor. With planning, you can provide long-term benefits for your family. With planning, you can protect your dignity in death. With planning, you can provide for people less fortunate than you. If you have no close family to take care of, discover how you can help others by leaving your estate to charity. Getting started is the hardest part, but once you complete this planning, you will experience incredible peace of mind. You've worked hard to build your assets. Make sure there is a plan to transfer those assets the way you want.

LESSONS AND STRATEGIES

1. Don't accept the government's plan; create your own plan. Your plan will be a far better one.
2. Begin with a will and other simple documents, such as a living will and a durable power of attorney.
3. If you are over age 65, consider a living trust for estate tax planning and to make sure someone has the legal authority to take care of your financial affairs should you become incapacitated.
4. If you are married with an estate over $1.5 million, work with your attorney to establish credit shelter trusts. It can save your family hundreds of thousands in estate taxes.
5. If you are single, widowed, or divorced with an estate over $1.5 million, look into establishing a life insurance gifting program for your children or heirs to protect your estate from estate taxes.
6. If you are married and your estate exceeds $3 million, you must consider both trust planning and life insurance to cover estate taxes.
7. Preserve your IRA. It is the most important asset in your estate, because it can be leveraged by as much as 6- to 10-fold if the children or heirs use the IRA as a lifetime income inheritance.
8. Don't leave assets in a 401(k) or 403(b) plan when you retire. Move these and other qualified plan assets to an IRA, so your children will be able to leverage these assets. Plans other than IRAs and 403(b) plans normally do not provide the lifetime income option for your children or heirs.
9. Consider long-term care insurance to protect your IRA for your spouse and your children.
10. Give gifts to those less fortunate than your family. Consider organ donations and charitable donations as part of your plan.
11. Don't procrastinate! Get help, get started, and create your plan.

Getting Your Financial House in Order

Mistakes 7 and 8: Procrastination and the Failure to Seek Professional Advice

N ow that you are highly motivated, you need to implement a solid plan for you and your family. Here are some common reasons for procrastinating:

- "It's too complicated."
- "I don't have time right now, with the holidays and all. Maybe next month."
- "The market is too volatile right now. Maybe next year."
- "I don't have any money right now. After my next big raise I can consider doing something."
- "Maybe I should try it on my own. I hate paying anyone a commission."
- "I still have some questions. I'd better not do anything right now. I'll probably make a mistake. I'd better wait until I know what I'm doing."

I've heard all of these reasons and many more. You are not unique! You are acting normally, because you don't know the future. Most of us go through the "I don't need it, I don't want it, it's too hard for me" thought process. But the truth is you are denying yourself and your family the peace of mind that comes from having a carefully designed financial plan in place to bring you a sound, secure financial future. However, there is plenty you can do right now. The trick is getting started.

Where Do You Get Started?

It is time to gather and review your assets. Here is a list of the main financial items you need to examine closely and the questions you need to ask yourself.

I. Financial statements (mutual fund statements, bank statements, credit union statements, brokerage statements, insurance and annuity statements, and employee benefit statements):

1. Is there any rhyme or reason to how my money is invested? Am I taking too much risk or being too conservative?

2. What is my definition of risk? Is it loss of principal? Loss of purchasing power over time? A reduction of income stream?

3. Am I properly diversified? Am I taking advantage of asset allocation opportunities and dollar-cost averaging?

4. Am I taking full advantage of my tax-advantaged opportunities, such as my employer-sponsored retirement plan and IRAs?

5. With my individual securities (stocks, bonds, employer stock), do I have a plan for when and why to buy and sell these investments? Do I have more than 10 percent of my wealth in employer stock?

6. Am I keeping too much in "safe" accounts that are fully taxed and not earning enough to offset the long-term risk of inflation? What interest are these accounts paying me?

7. What do I expect as a reasonable rate of return on my portfolio over time?

8. What is my mental time frame?

II. Insurance policies:

1. How much do I have? Do I have enough? Are my policies overpriced? Are they the right type? Who is the owner? (If you or your spouse owns the insurance, the proceeds will be in the survivor's estate, possibly triggering or being subject to estate taxes.)

2. Do I have long-term care insurance? Is it a modern policy

provided by a top-quality company? Does it cover all levels of long-term care needs? (Consider long-term care coverage if you are age 55 or over.)

III. Beneficiary designations:

1. Are the beneficiary designations correct on all of the following accounts?
   - Life insurance (both personal and group insurance)
   - Annuities
   - IRAs
   - Qualified plans
   - Stock purchase plans
   - Deferred compensation plans
2. Are the beneficiary names correct? Are they specific or too vague? (If vague, these assets will end up in probate to determine the beneficiaries.) Have I forgotten anyone?
3. Wills, trusts, and other legal documents:
   - Do I have the proper documents?
   - Are they up to date? (Remember, there was major tax legislation in 2001 that impacts estate tax planning.)

Step 1: Review Your Financial Status

Once you have these financial accounts spread out in front of you, you need to add them up and see where you are. Remember, you are on a financial journey. You need to know exactly where you are today to plot your course.

Add up your financial assets and then deduct your outstanding loans (mortgage, car loans, credit card loans, student loans, etc.). The net result is your current net worth. This is the number you must improve every year. Don't make the mistake of increasing your debt as your investment portfolio increases. Resist the urge to splurge when you see your investments increase in value. You need to examine your net worth periodically to make sure you are making real progress toward your financial destination.

Step 2: Complete Your Financial Road Map

Complete the financial road map worksheet in Figure 13.1 if you didn't do it in Chapter 10.

Use the figures in Chapter 10 to help you complete your road

---

1. Present net worth $_____

2. Gross household income $_____

3. Retirement income goal

    a. 80% × $_____ (income at retirement) $_____

    b. Less social security benefits –_____

    c. Less defined benefit income (if any) –_____

    Portion of goal I must create by investing $_____

4. Capital needed for retirement income $_____

    a. Total capital needed $_____

    b. Less projected value of current net worth –_____

    Additional capital I must create for retirement income $_____

FIGURE 13.1   Financial road map worksheet.

map. If you don't want to complete this yourself, hire a professional to do it for you. One way or the other, it's got to get done.

Now that you have a clear picture of your financial destination (how much capital you need to build for retirement), how will you get there?

The Smiths found they were far short of reaching their goal. The Smiths are not going to have adequate capital at retirement unless they make improvements in their savings rate. You may need to make changes in your current program to meet your goals.

If there is a shortage, you need to make changes to get back on track. Even if you are on track to meet your retirement income goals, you need to examine other personal needs and goals for you and your family.

To make up any shortages, consider:

- A Roth or traditional IRA
- Adding more to your employer-sponsored qualified plan
- Investing a lump sum in a tax-deferred annuity
- Purchasing a variable universal life policy to provide insurance for your family while accumulating tax-protected cash values for your retirement
- Establishing an automatic bank draft to invest every month in a mutual fund, a variable annuity, or a variable life policy

Take advantage of all of these opportunities. Your financial independence depends on it!

Step 3: Determine How Much Investment Risk You Can Take

At first glance, you might say, "As much as I need to take in order to meet my goals." As you complete your financial road map, you might think, "Gee, if I just go for a 14 percent rate of return, I can meet my goals." This can lead to unacceptable investment risk. Let's get a handle on how much market risk you can take, based on your assets. For example:

- As you review your existing portfolio, see how much is invested in high-risk versus moderate- to low-risk investments. If you see it is very conservative, could you reposition a portion of these investments to areas that can be more rewarding?

- How large are your liabilities in relation to your assets? If your ratio of debt to assets is large, you may not be able to take on additional market risk. If you have little debt, you can take on more market volatility.

- How large are your liabilities when compared to your income? Is it difficult to make ends meet every month because of mortgage payments, credit card debt, and other bills? If so, don't take on more investment risk until your debt load is under control.

- How much life insurance do you have in comparison to your salary? If you have insurance that is five times your salary or more, you can take on more market risk, because your family has adequate liquidity for emergencies with life insurance.

- How do you spend your income? Are some of your investments already subject to extremely high risk? Do you tend to spend a large percentage of your income on recreational gambling? This may be all of the high-risk investing you can afford.

There are several other considerations when contemplating additional market risk:

- How long have you been with your current employer? Is your job secure?

- Is your income stable?

- Are you and your spouse on the same wavelength regarding market volatility?

■ Will you be financially responsible for the care of an elderly parent in the near future?

After considering these questions about taking on additional market risk, you need to answer the following question. Let's assume you have $100,000 invested and the market is declining over the next quarter. At what point will you take action? Check only one box.

☐ $95,000 (down 5% for the quarter)

☐ $90,000 (down 10% for the quarter)

☐ $80,000 (down 20% for the quarter)

☐ $70,000 (down 30% for the quarter)

☐ $60,000 (down 40% for the quarter)

☐ $50,000 (down 50% for the quarter)

Next, assume you have $500,000 invested in this declining market. Does it change your answer?

INVESTOR, KNOW THYSELF Whether you make all of your own decisions or you work closely with an advisor, you need to be able to clearly recognize and define your tolerance for risk. Read the following descriptions carefully and choose the one that best fits you. If you are married, make sure your spouse takes the same test separately.

☐ I am extremely conservative. I want to preserve my principal at all cost. I understand I will earn a very modest yield, which will be less than the income available from other investments.

☐ I am moderately conservative. Preserving my investment is very important, but I also want and need to earn a higher yield.

☐ I am somewhat conservative and also somewhat aggressive. I want to strike a balance between preserving my capital and growing my capital. I realize and accept the fact that the value of my portfolio may fluctuate. I realize I will not be maximizing my current yield, as part of my portfolio will be invested for growth of capital.

☐ I am moderately aggressive. I am more concerned about growing my portfolio than earning current income. I want to keep ahead of inflation. Current income from my portfolio is not a priority. Any dividends or interest earned would be reinvested to grow my portfolio.

☐ I am aggressive. I am willing to accept a fair amount of risk and portfolio volatility for the potential to gain significant returns over time.

Let's return to the financial road map worksheet. If you find you are short of your retirement goals, don't automatically take on more investment risk. That leap can make your life miserable, especially if your spouse disagrees with that decision. Consider all of the following factors before taking on additional market risk. As painful as it might be, you may have to:

- Reduce you retirement income goal to 70 to 75 percent of your current income
- Extend your working years
- Examine your spending habits and tighten your belt
- Reduce your debt to free up dollars for investment
- Consider changing jobs to one that provides better retirement benefits
- Accept the fact that you might have to purchase an immediate-income annuity when you retire in order to create an adequate income for life

Step 4: Decide Whether or Not You Need Help

Many of you have the time, energy, and desire to do your own thing. If that is your plan, you need to do your own homework. The Internet can be an important tool to help you help yourself. Here are some of the major Web sites that can help you begin your planning:

- www.quicken.com—Can help you create a plan going forward.
- www.moneycentral.msn.com—MSN Money, again a fill-in-the-blank financial planning tool.
- www.troweprice.com—T. Rowe Price offers a financial plan for a fee.
- money.cnn.com—Go to personal finance and then click on "calculators"; a fill-in-the-blank plan and other useful information.
- www.cbsmarketwatch.com—Click on "personal finance" to run financial projections.
- www.aarp.org—AARP site; click on "online retirement calculator" to see their projections.

- www.analyzenow.com—Click on "computer programs"; both free and inexpensive retirement planning tools are available.

- AOL Personal Finance—A source for general financial information.

Be careful if you intend to use these Web site retirement planners. You will be asked to input several assumptions, such as:

- Projected rate of return—Be conservative! Don't assume 12 percent. An 8 to 10 percent assumption is more realistic.

- Future inflation rate—A 2 percent assumption is probably too low. Input your personal projected rate of inflation. It might be 3 to 5 percent.

- Number of years in retirement—If you are retiring at age 65, you need to assume at least 30 years of retirement.

- Retirement income needs—You will be asked to pick what percentage of preretirement income you think you will need in retirement. Thinking you can live comfortably on 50 percent less money in retirement is not realistic. You need to assume you will need 80 percent or more to enjoy retirement.

Many of these Web site programs have flaws. Look for these shortcomings:

- Most programs rely on average rates of return and average rates of inflation. The software's assumptions may be unrealistic. Examine these assumptions carefully.

- Some programs assume only 20 years of retirement. You could easily outlive these projections.

- Many programs assume your principal will decline in a straight line. We know that investment returns fluctuate from year to year, which means your principal will not decline in a straight line. Remember the Monte Carlo simulations we examined earlier.

- Most programs do not factor in the taxes due on qualified plan and IRA distributions. You need to remember that these distributions are taxable (except for Roth IRA distributions, which are tax free).

- Many programs assume that defined benefit pension payments will automatically increase to offset inflation. Unfortunately, most of these pension plans seldom increase the payments to retirees.

- You might want to run a projection on several of these Web sites. Don't be surprised if their projections are drastically different.

There are other helpful Web sites you should check:

- www.unitedseniorshealth.org—A nonprofit organization, United Seniors Health Council, founded in 1950 and based in Washington, DC. This Web site will provide you with impartial answers on long-term care insurance and other issues of interest.

- www.savingforcollege.com—A great resource for detailed information on the various 529 college savings plans available through those states sponsoring these tax-favored plans. It also lets you calculate the future costs for the college of your choice. You can also go to the college aid calculator to see if your family might qualify for financial aid.

- www.immediateannuity.com—For immediate annuity income quotes from various insurance companies.

- www.insweb.com—For auto insurance quotes from 40 different insurance companies.

- www.insurance.com—From Fidelity Investments for auto insurance quotes from four major insurance companies.

If you elect to make your own investment choices, you will need to select a discount brokerage firm to place your orders to buy and sell your investments or negotiate a discount from a full-service brokerage firm. Make sure you know what your costs will be. There could be substantial hidden fees. For example, at Schwab, you can incur additional maintenance fees if you make fewer than eight trades per year. Those inactive account fees could be $50 per year for an IRA and as high as $180 per year for a regular account.

Make sure the firm you choose is financially sound. E*Trade Group, Inc. lost more than $400 million in the two-year period of 2001 to 2002. Ameritrade Holding Corp. lost $141 million from 2000 to 2002. Make sure you ask for an annual report of the firm to determine if it is financially sound before you do business with it.

Are you getting overwhelmed? If so, you need professional help! The advice and services of an investment professional can save you time and prevent you from making costly mistakes.

Not convinced? I can understand that feeling. The decade of the 1990s was considered the decade of the no-load funds. No one wants to pay a load. That sounds like a heavy burden. But let's look at the facts. Over the 1990s, the 6,742 load funds averaged a return of 11.48 percent. But you had to pay a load. The maximum load was 5.75 percent, but most investors paid less because of quantity discounts. (For example, most front-end load funds reduce the charges from 5.75 percent to 3.5 percent or less on investments of $100,000.) During the 1990s, the average investor paid 3.60 percent. Over that 10-year period, that load would have averaged 0.36 percent per year. That charge reduced the average return from 11.48 percent to 11.12 percent over those 10 years. The real question is: "Was the advice of a professional advisor worth the average cost of 0.36 percent per year over the 1990s?" As a consumer, you had the option to do your own thing by selecting the average no-load fund.

Over the same ten-year period, you had 3,742 no-load funds from which to choose. The average no-load return was 11.06 percent over that 10-year period. That is less than the 11.12 percent load-adjusted return for the average load fund. It is not a question of load or no load. It is a question of advice or no advice.

But the 1990s are just a small part of the total picture. In 2000, only 20 percent of mutual funds were purchased directly from mutual fund companies. That percentage is projected to decline to 18 percent in the next five years.

What is going on here? More investors are turning to advisors to help them select the funds that are best for their risk tolerance and goals, whether they are load or no-load funds. Over the last five years, many programs have been designed that combine both types of funds into an asset-allocated strategy. The traditional load is waived in these programs, so all the funds in these programs become no-load.

The advisor charges a fee for his or her advice on building and adjusting the asset allocation of all of the funds in the advisory program. From time to time, a fund selected in the program needs to be replaced. For example, let's assume the manager of one of the funds has left or retired. What should you do? The new management might be an improvement, or the new management might not be qualified to run the fund. Here is another example. Perhaps a manager strays from the original focus of the fund. The fund may have been selected as part of a portfolio of funds, because the manager was an outstanding value-style manager, excelling at finding stocks overlooked by others that have unrecognized value. Perhaps he or she begins buying growth stocks of late, because the market has recently favored growth stocks. It may be time to fire that fund, as there is no consistent pattern of management style. This is called *management style drift*. The bottom line is: You, the investor, may have no idea how your money is being invested and no idea whether the manager has the resources and expertise to be making these major changes in management style. (Most managers can't excel at both money management styles.)

A good financial advisor should be able to more than justify any real or perceived costs. Some decisions in life are better left to professionals who have the time, the training, the focus, and the resources. If you need legal advice, find the best attorney you can. Then pay him or her for the advice. If you need brain surgery, you don't shop for the cheapest surgeon or try to do it on your own. You find the best brain surgeon you can, and pay for his or her professional services and advice. This is no less true for advice on lowering your taxes, making sure your children have the funds available for a higher education, ensuring the welfare of your family, and creating the peace of mind that you and your spouse have a plan in place that will provide you with an adequate retirement income for life.

Investing is always difficult because it plays on our emotions. When our portfolio is growing, we feel optimistic, confident, and smart. We tend to take greater risks. When it is shrinking, we feel nervous and anxious and begin to doubt our decisions. At times, the stock market looks shaky. Instead of facing investments as an opportunity during those unsettled markets, we shy away from risk. During these times, we can't see the forest for the trees. A qualified advisor, using a disciplined, unemotional approach, can help us stay focused and on course to reach our financial destination. Shift the emotional load to your financial advisor to help you with these financial decisions.

Finding the Advisor Who Is Right for You

If you take the time to interview three prospective advisors, you will most likely find the one that is right for you. Where do you find advisors? There are four main sources:

1. Ask friends and family members for their recommendations.

2. Ask your lawyer or CPA for his or her suggestions.

3. Attend public seminars presented by investment professionals.

4. Look in the yellow pages for national securities firms or certified financial planners.

Interviewing the Candidates You Have Selected

Each interview will probably last an hour. Make this important time commitment. In three short hours, you will be able to choose the person and the firm you can work with for the rest of your life. But make sure the meetings are based on your agenda, not the advisor's agenda. It is a simple two-step process:

1. Determine what you need.

2. Find out whether or not the advisor can help you fulfill your needs.

The personal needs checklist in Table 13.1 will help you establish your personal priorities. The advisor you choose (and the firm he or she works with) needs to have strengths in the areas where you need help. Knowing your personal needs will help you in the interview process. Carefully complete the financial road map worksheet

TABLE 13.1

Personal Need	Need	Don't Need	Not Sure
Review both income and expenses			
Examine and clarify risk tolerance			
Review current investment portfolio			
Review qualified plans and IRAs			
Create an investment strategy			
Review your current life insurance			
Create a current net worth statement			
College planning for children/grandchildren			
Long-term care planning			
Income tax planning			
Retirement income planning			
Estate tax planning			
Review of wills, trusts, and other documents			
Ongoing advice			
Other			
Other			

and the personal needs checklist before the interviews. This will prepare you to direct the interviews with your needs in mind. Remember, it's your agenda. Make sure you get answers to your questions first in the interview, before you discuss other issues.

YOUR PRIORITY OF PERSONAL NEEDS

1. _____

2. _____

3. _____

4. _____

YOUR INTERVIEW QUESTIONS FOR PROSPECTIVE ADVISORS

1. How many years have you been in the business?   _____

2. How many of those years were with your current firm? _____

3. Special training/designations? (e.g., CPA, CFP, CLU) _____

4. What licenses do you have?

   Series 6? (limited product offerings)   _____

   Series 7? (much broader product selection) _____

   Life Insurance?   _____
   (required for life and annuity recommendations)

   Registered investment advisor?   _____
   (required in some states)

   Other licenses?   _____

   Other areas of expertise?   _____

5. Special titles? (VP, associate VP, etc.)   _____

6. What are the requirements to qualify for that title? (amount of production, longevity in the business, does everyone have the title) _____

7. Size of your firm? (local, regional, or national firm) _____

8. Where are stock and bond trades executed? (New York Stock Exchange or other major exchange)   _____

9. Do you place your orders directly or through a separate company? _____

10. Other comments about the way your firm conducts business

_____

_____

If you are only placing a once in a lifetime stock trade, none of this is necessary. If you are looking for a long-term advisor to help you and your family, you need to find out who you are dealing with.

CLIENT SERVICE QUESTIONS

1. What special services do you provide your customers? (investment portfolio reviews, mutual fund reviews, life insurance reviews, annuity reviews, legal document reviews)

_____

2. How do you communicate with your customers?

Newsletters _____

Phone calls _____

Reviews _____ Frequency _____ (quarterly, annually)

Client education seminars _____

Frequency _____ Topics _____

3. In general, what is your personal philosophy about investing?

_____

4. What should we expect from you in return for the commissions and fees we will be asked to pay? _____

5. If I need assistance, whom will I be speaking to? (you, your sales assistant, a call center in another city) _____

6. How would your clients describe you? Why did they choose you? _____

7. Other comments you would like to make about yourself or your firm _____

_____

Again, if this is not going to be a long-term relationship, account service is not important. Review your needs checklist. If you need ongoing help, the service you get is important.

Selecting an advisor after these initial interviews will be easier if you have a clear picture of the values that are most important to you. Perhaps the following list can help you decide, especially if it is a close race between two candidates. Rank your values from 1 to 6.

What Do You Value Most in an Advisor?

____ Trustworthiness and integrity

____ Knowledge and competency

____ Understanding of your needs

____ Availability for consultations

____ Responsiveness to requests

____ Commissions and fees

Most investors choose the order of priorities as shown, with trustworthiness and integrity being the number one priority. Your priorities might be different. That's perfectly okay. Just know what your priorities are. Take a few minutes to rank your priorities. It will help you immensely in selecting your advisor.

One Last Check

You should check with the industry regulators to see if there have been any complaints filed against a given advisor. You can call the NASD at 800-289-9999 or check out www.nasdr.com. This is the national regulator for the investment industry. You can also check with your state investment regulators and insurance regulators to see if any disciplinary actions have been taken against an advisor.

Once you have chosen an advisor, be prepared to answer a lot of questions. Your advisor needs to get to know you and your family in order to give you his or her best advice. Be prepared to answer questions about:

I. Your career:
   1. When would you like to retire?
   2. Do you feel secure in your employment?
   3. What will you do the first day of retirement?
   4. How do you intend to spend your time once you retire?

II. Your family:
1. What is everyone's health?
2. Which children or grandchildren will most likely go to college?
3. Have you estimated the costs for their education?
4. Have you established a savings or investment plan to build assets for your children's college educations?
5. Are there special needs for handicapped children that need to be considered?
6. If your children are married, what is the quality of these marriages?
7. Are your children mature enough to handle large gifts and an inheritance?

III. Your investment portfolio:
1. What is the current makeup of your investments?
2. How did you accumulate what you have?
3. How many years did it take to accumulate your current portfolio?
4. How will you know when it is time to sell any or all of the assets in your portfolio?
5. Are you too concentrated in one stock, such as your employer's stock?
6. How did you choose the mutual funds you own?
7. How much do you keep in liquid assets? Which liquid assets did you choose?

IV. Your life insurance portfolio:
1. Do you have enough life insurance, especially if you have a young family depending on your income? (Hint: $1 million invested for income for a widow and children might create only 5 percent after inflation. That's an income of $50,000 per year. Is that enough?)
2. Is there enough insurance on your spouse?
3. Do you and your spouse have group life insurance provided by your employers?
4. If so, how much group insurance?

    5. Are the owners and beneficiaries correct? (If your net worth is larger than the estate tax exemption ($1.5 million in 2004), you need to begin planning to reduce estate taxes.)

    6. What type of life insurance do you have?

    7. If you are age 60 or older, have you considered long-term care?

V. Retirement planning:

    1. Are you participating in an employer-sponsored qualified retirement plan? (If so, be prepared to offer details.)

    2. Have you established Roth or traditional IRAs? (Again, provide details.)

    3. Do you have variable universal life insurance?

    4. Do you have tax-deferred annuities?

    5. Do you know how much you should receive in Social Security benefits?

    6. Does your employer provide a defined benefit pension plan? Do you know how much retirement income it will provide?

    7. How much income do you anticipate needing in the early years of your retirement?

    8. Will it be necessary for you to help in the financial support of your parents at some point in their lives?

    9. How much income do you anticipate needing in the later years of retirement, considering medical costs and inflation?

    10. What do you feel inflation will average over the rest of your life?

VI. Estate planning:

    1. Do you have a will?

    2. Have you established additional legal documents or trusts?

    3. Who owns your life insurance? Is your life insurance part of your estate or owned outside of your estate (by the heirs or a life insurance trust)?

    4. Are your children or beneficiaries aware of their rights to inherit your IRA and stretch out the receipt of the IRA proceeds as income over their life expectancy? Will your children react prudently? Should special planning

be considered to make sure the children leverage this IRA estate benefit?

VII. Is there any investment asset you would never feel comfortable in owning?
   1. Mutual funds?
   2. Individual stocks?
   3. Bonds?
   4. Commodities?
   5. Options?
   6. Other? _____

VIII. Risk tolerance planning:
   1. Let's assume your investments dropped 10 percent in value over the next quarter. How would you react?
      - Sell (panic)
      - Freeze (too afraid to react)
      - Buy more (consider it a buying opportunity)
      - Call for advice
   2. Let's assume your investments dropped 20 percent over the next three months. How would you react?
      - Sell (panic)
      - Freeze (too afraid to react)
      - Buy more (consider it a buying opportunity)
      - Call for advice
   3. Let's assume you have $100,000 invested and the market is declining over the next quarter. At what point will you take action? Check only one box.
      - ☐ $95,000 (down 5 percent for the quarter)
      - ☐ $90,000 (down 10 percent for the quarter)
      - ☐ $80,000 (down 20 percent for the quarter)
      - ☐ $70,000 (down 30 percent for the quarter)
      - ☐ $60,000 (down 40 percent for the quarter)
      - ☐ $50,000 (down 50 percent for the quarter)

IX. Would you be comfortable investing a portion of your money in a higher-risk investment in hopes of an above average rate of return? What portion?

1. Ten percent
2. Twenty percent
3. Thirty percent
4. More _____ percent

X. Financially speaking, what would you most like to change about the rest of your life? What is your number one financial priority?

_____

_____

So What's Really the Answer?

The answer is up to you. It always has been, and it always will be. But now you are prepared to make those important decisions that will have a major impact on your financial journey. Now you are prepared to avoid the eight biggest mistakes investors make with their money.

Above all, take care of yourself and your family. By now, you know where you need to begin. Let's get started.

LESSONS AND STRATEGIES

1. Gather your assets.
2. Determine your current net worth.
3. Complete your financial road map worksheet.
4. Determine where you need to be at retirement.
5. Project the retirement value of your existing investments.
6. Project the future value of your current contributions to qualified plans, IRAs, and other ongoing investments.
7. Decide what changes you need to make in your saving and investment habits to meet your destination.
8. Determine where you need help by using the personal needs checklist.
9. Set priorities.
10. Consider professional advice.
11. Interview potential advisors.
12. Ask key interview questions to see if potential advisors have the resources to help you.

13. Know what characteristics you value the most in an advisor. Then choose your advisor accordingly.
14. Be willing to answer questions about you and your family to help your advisor make proper recommendations.
15. Get started now!